D1107985

EMERSON
on the Soul

EMERSON
on the Soul

Jonathan Bishop

HARVARD UNIVERSITY PRESS
Cambridge, Massachusetts
1964

Distributed in Great Britain by Oxford University Press, London

Library of Congress Catalog Card Number: 64-25052

Printed in the United States of America

TO THE MEMORY OF

STEPHEN EMERSON WHICHER

ACKNOWLEDGMENTS

I should like to express special thanks to Mr. William A. Jackson and the Ralph Waldo Emerson Association for permission to quote from Emerson's unpublished journals; to Miss Carolyn Jakeman of the Houghton Library for assistance in consulting them and in arranging for a photograph of some pages; to the Department of English, University of California at Los Angeles, for a research grant; to Houghton Mifflin Company for permission to refer to their edition of the journals; to Columbia University Press for permission to quote from the letters. The Grant-in-Aid Fund of the Department of English at Cornell University has paid for the preparation of my manuscript.

Debts of a more general character are harder to identify and acknowledge. Readers familiar with the intellectual style of the Department of English, Amherst College, will recognize traces of my experience there as an instructor in the strategy as well as in some of the separate arguments of this book. I owe more immediate thanks to scholarly encouragement from William H. Gilman and the late Stephen E. Whicher. My friends Warner Berthoff of Bryn Mawr and Taylor Stoehr of Cornell have given me careful critical readings from which I hope the book has benefited.

Ithaca, May 1964   J. B.

CONTENTS

Note on Texts   xi
Introduction   1

PART I · THE SOUL

Definitions   19
The Original Relation   25
The Active Imagination   33
The Senses   37
Science   45
History   59
The Moral Sentiment   66
Compensation   72
The Whole Soul   77
The Vital Mind   81
The Instinctive Conscience   86
Self-Reliance   92

PART II · THE SOUL'S EMPHASIS

The Literary Test   101
Words   109
Rhythm   112
Metaphor   119
Tone   128
Audience   143

PART III · THE SOUL'S EMPHASIS IS ALWAYS RIGHT

The Emersonian Career: First Crisis   165
The Limits of Temperament   176
Second Crisis   187
The Later Doctrine of the Soul   203
Emerson as Prophet   215

Notes   231
Index   245

NOTE ON TEXTS

Quotations from the works are all from *The Complete Works of Ralph Waldo Emerson*, ed. Edward Waldo Emerson, Centenary Edition, 12 vols. (Boston: Houghton Mifflin Co., 1903–1904), abbreviated in the parenthetical references as W, with the appropriate volume and page number. Other abbreviations are:

L   *The Letters of Ralph Waldo Emerson*, ed. Ralph L. Rusk, 6 vols. (New York: Columbia University Press, 1939).

C-E.L.   *The Correspondence of Thomas Carlyle and Ralph Waldo Emerson, 1834–1872*, ed. Charles Eliot Norton, 3rd ed., 2 vols. (Boston: James R. Osgood and Co., 1883).

E-L   *The Early Lectures of Ralph Waldo Emerson*, ed. Stephen E. Whicher and Robert E. Spiller (Cambridge: Harvard University Press, 1959–).

J   *The Journals of Ralph Waldo Emerson*, ed. Edward Waldo Emerson and Waldo Emerson Forbes, 10 vols., Centenary Edition (Boston: Houghton Mifflin Co., 1909–1914).

The new edition of Emerson's journals has not yet progressed far enough to include any of the passages I have quoted in this study. I was therefore not able to make use of the more accurate text it will provide future students. At the same time, I wished to reproduce the words of the manuscript as closely as it could be done in normal type. This can be a matter of some importance when one tries to follow changes of language from a journal entry to a lecture or essay version. For this reason, and for the sake of consistency, I have quoted directly from the manuscript for each journal quotation, omitting Emerson's own cancellations and following his corrections; for the sake of convenience I have attached a reference to the place in the 1909–1914 edition where it can be found.

EMERSON
on the Soul

INTRODUCTION

THE OLD Arnoldian truism continues true. To criticize is to know the world, to see the object as it really is. And in human affairs, of which art is one kind, the "object" is always an action. The critic of literature, therefore, is someone seeking to discover in works of imagination the major actions of that imagination within them. What, he must ask himself, is going on? He will try to recognize the context, modes, quality, and import of each primary action represented, and among these especially the actions occurring within the language that addresses him.

If we approach the work of Emerson with such a definition of criticism in mind, we may at first be inhibited by difficulties that do not appear when the works of art we study are whole, independent, and expressly fictional. The job of disentangling the "object," the essential actions, can seem unusually hard. What, exactly, is "Emerson"? Where, in the broken sequences of essays, the scattered poems, the large numbers of letters and journals, the overlapping continuities of published and manuscript material, is it possible to identify a central core of imaginative activity that will throw into intelligible relief the multitudinous details of doctrine and rhetoric?

The answers supplied by the critical tradition are as various as the evidence is manifold.[1] Emerson has been at various times a heroic influence, a philosophic or literary achievement, a background against which to set the achievements of other writers. Most consistently, he has been a representative of certain human possibilities. But the question arises anew for each generation, for each reader: what possibilities? A confident discovery, a fair judgment, has never been easy to make. The range of affirmation that can be found in Emerson's work is unusually wide. Energies and interests ordinarily opposed are present in an odd though compelling harmony; yet at the same time much seems omitted. It is difficult to distinguish, either in principle or among particulars, the exciting truth from the trivial illusion, the authentic insight from its near self-parody.

And in the midst of one's ambivalence, one's alternations of respect and dismissal, trust and boredom, there lurks intermittently a doubt that one's apparent discoveries of an imaginative reality may after all be only reflections of some bias and conventionalism, not true features of an action observed. Emerson tests his critics as few writers do. His sensitivity to the natural acts of life exposes whatever is dead and artificial in his reader's responses. His serenity, his independence, his grace and agility are perpetually escaping the categories of the professionalized intelligence. His wit and conscience threaten the cleverness by which the social self conceals its own moral cowardice. Like Lawrence, Emerson has a way of exposing the unconscious limits and refusals of the very critics who suppose themselves to have identified for correct admiration the essence of his achievement.

The prevailing definitions of that essence have changed more than once over the years. The first generation of Emersonians, taking up the definition surviving from the age that knew Emerson chiefly as an exemplary person, tended to regard the works as a kind of transparent medium through which to make contact with a distinguished spirit. It was the prophet of high thought and feeling, the guide of the earnest young, the ideal American scholar and gentleman, who survived for them as significant. The various essays and poems were therefore read for the voice of conscience and freedom, of "the friend and aider of those who would live in the spirit," in Arnold's familiar phrase. Anecdotes from the biography could for such readers become evidence that a Plutarchian hero had once walked American earth. Such a way of reading, commencing with Arnold and Chapman, extends nearly to modern times in the criticism of the Humanist group. It survives now chiefly in its negative complement, a distrust of the Emersonian *morale* as insufficient, incorrect, or obsolete. This distrustful attitude lives a kind of ghostly existence in the minds of many who do not know the work at first hand, or know it only as filtered through hostile judgment. In published criticism this negative version of the old moral Emerson persists in the shape of the prejudice against him that friendly critics often assume in their readers.[2]

The next important shift of critical definition came as a consequence of the academic rediscovery of intellectual history. The best work in "American studies," from Parrington to Matthiessen to the present, has helped to make current a view of Emerson as essentially the promulgator of certain ideas. For the nature and interdependence of these, the works then became evidence. This work has given us a vision of American intellectual history in which Emerson finds a crucial place. Yet there can be danger in such a definition for a figure of Emerson's peculiar quality and stature. The approach from intellectual history can involve an unconscious condescension, a diminishing of the object observed. To attend especially to Emerson's "ideas" in their proper historical sequence is to find him either a minor manifestation of a world-wide system of influences more sharply expressed in earlier authors or merely a transmitter of these ideas to men better able to exploit and correct their implications. The very expansion of our knowledge of the development of Calvinist and Unitarian thinkers, of German philosophy, and of Platonism can serve to reduce the apparent significance of Emerson's contribution to the notions he rephrased for his generation. The ideas themselves, moreover, abstracted from his rendering of them, invite easy rebuttals or qualifications. These criticisms may then be found by implication in the major works of Hawthorne and Melville or supplied from the historian's own sense of what has happened to improve the definition of reality since Emerson's time. The decline of Emerson the thinker, so paradoxically bound up with our increased knowledge of the content and sources of his thought, has helped to reduce the claims of Emerson as influence and as artist. The labor of intellectual history can make Emerson seem paraphrasable at the expense of making him uninteresting.

A later academic generation of Emersonians, trained in the history of ideas but with an interest in the substance of philosophy as well as its story, has taken a sharper look at Emerson's thinking and discovered in it an analogy to, and in some sense a source for, the set of intellectual discoveries concerning the nature of knowledge that we sum up roughly as "symbolism." Inspired by Cassirer, Susanne Langer, and the achievements of modern critical philosophy, students have found Emerson's work a suggestive inquiry into the epistemological relation between the mind and nature, the knower and the known, the eye and the object it perceives. The essential Emerson then becomes man thinking, seeing, knowing. According to Charles Feidelson, not only Emerson but all the artists of the American Renaissance can be seen as preoccupied with "the figure of man seeing, the mind engaged in a crucial act of knowledge. . . . These men were committed to a common theory and practice of perception."[3] This statement would presumably receive assent from Sherman Paul and Robert Pollock, though the stress would differ from one member of what can be called a common school to another. Feidelson is rather fashionably concerned with Emerson as an originator of an intellectual method whose full literary importance is better studied in Hawthorne and Melville or the moderns, while Paul is interested in the strategy of "correspondence" by which the transcendentalists solved the philosophic problems of knowledge and perception.[4] Pollock wants ultimately to place Emerson's contributions to epistemology in a Catholic frame of reference.[5] But all show the benefit of contemporary semantic and philosophic sophistication, and their cumulative impact has been the rediscovery of a point of view from which Emerson's work may be taken seriously by a modern mind. This represents a real advance in comprehension over the older historical view, in which Emersonian ideas tend to become dead counters, to be known about but not thought through. If Emerson is really telling us about the way the mind organizes its experience in symbolic systems, we can read him in the hope of finding instruction on a matter that concerns all "scholars."

But an objection can be made to this point of view as a way of defining the "essence" of Emerson. In the first place, it tends to overintellectualize the content of his message. Emerson's master term, after all, is not the "Mind" but the "Soul." The action of the intellect, though of tremendous importance, was no more than a part of the whole activity his works celebrate, comment on, exemplify, and recommend. The action of the conscience, or "moral sentiment," was at least equally important—and underlying both faculties, Emerson believed, was a still more primitive and essential agency, for which he had various names, natural and supernatural. Epistemological or semantic analysis will only explicate that part of the whole act of experience that can appear in an intellectual shape. A critic who makes too much of what he can discover by pursuing such an analysis therefore runs the risk of confusing a portion of Emerson's intended meaning with the whole. So far as this happens, he can diminish Emerson's claims upon our attention in a way that parallels the reduction the work can suffer when studied by the historian of ideas. One approach shows us the man's thought, the other his thinking; of the two, the second is clearly to be preferred. But both can end by defining an Emerson who is too exclusively a man of mind.

The semantic point of view is also one from which it is not necessary to keep in mind the concrete facts of *literary* achievement. So far as Emerson is an artist in words, he still tends to be left out of the picture. That Emerson is essentially an artist, and his work chiefly interesting as literature, has not so far been the principal argument of any whole book of criticism, though references, often very shrewd ones, linking the method of his thought to the specifics of expression may be found. Yet most readers will be tantalizingly aware that the qualities of the Emersonian style are somehow close to the center of imaginative action for which they are searching. Emerson was a moral influence and may at some future time be one again; his work contains a system of ideas, and he may be read as demonstrating an intellectual method; but he is also, and in a way crucial to one's understanding of him in these other capacities, a man of words. It is *through* his tone, his metaphors, and his prose rhythms—the "literary" manifestations of his genius—that aspects of his message are conveyed which cannot be understood in any other way. Neglect the literary quality of the work, and one may miss the true meaning of its meaning.[6]

Some of the dangers implicit in all intellectualistic approaches are avoided by what may be called the biographical approach. The implied definition of the essential Emerson in such an approach would still be man thinking, though thinking not in a historical or philosophic void, but as an individual, a man with motives and an education, subject to specific emotional and intellectual influences, and possessed of purposes that changed over a lifetime. The several specialized studies of Emerson's reading, aesthetics, theory of history, and debts to particular writers can be seen as supporting such an identification of the central issue.[7] So too may the long scholarly effort involved in the publication and republication of the private papers. The single book that probably best represents the idea of Emerson as a mind with an individual history is the justly influential *Freedom and Fate,* by Stephen Whicher.[8] Somewhat shaped by the semantic approach mentioned above, it supports the insights so derived by exposing the pattern of Emerson's intellectual life. It has been Whicher's special service to make the connection between Emerson's life and the movement of his thought indisputable for the present generation. Yet in the midst of one's appreciation for the achievement of this book, and the other works whose assumptions are comparable, one can still feel that the point of view adopted involves a certain neglect of the literary particulars.

It can be chastening to realize that the most suggestive critical remarks, those which seem to do the best justice to the core of Emerson's vision, have often been by-blows—impressionistic summaries by men who have responded to the Emersonian appeal directly and deeply without taking on the burden of trying to explain it in respectable academic prose. There is something at the heart of Emerson's message profoundly recalcitrant to the formulations of the discursive intelligence. The point intended by a maker of aphorisms may indeed be better caught in a second aphorism drawn from a complementary originality in the reader. The ability to formulate sentences that ring true about Emerson's achievement was the special gift of several of the first Emersonian commentators. It is this gift that makes John Jay Chapman's essay, for instance, still an indispensable piece of criticism. Some modern instances might be found in Sherman Paul's introduction to his book on Thoreau,[9] where he says more of value about Emerson the imaginer and provoker of an original relation to the universe than in the whole of his formal study of the man; or in the sensitive introduction to the paperback, *Emerson—A Modern Anthology,* by Alfred Kazin and Daniel Aaron; or best of all in the oblique and disturbingly excellent survey of American literature by Warner Berthoff.[10]

Remembering such good remarks can prompt a renewed allegiance to the Arnoldian ideal. A simple test for a satisfactory reading would be to ask whether it answers important questions about the meanings of the major work. We would wish to be as sure as we can of the action the chief essays and poems seek to define in the half-disguise of words. I think too that we are more apt to feel we are making progress in the right direction if we come out with a better understanding of the early Emerson, the sensibility at work in the revolutionary essays and in the journals of the middle years. There has been in recent scholarship a tendency to focus more attention on the later work. There are reasons enough for such a bias: the mere need for new matter to comment on, overfamiliarity with the Emerson of anthologies, perhaps a latent lack of sympathy with Transcendental doctrine. Yet the "mature" Emerson is still most interesting and comprehensible when we see him as having grown from an earlier position that remains more searching, more original, and more problematic than that of the later thought. Something similar might be said of the Emerson of the unpublished lectures and journals. The most considerable work being done on Emerson through the next few years will be the publication in full and accurate form of the manuscript papers. The sheer weight of such an enterprise can have the inadvertent effect of diverting one's attention from the Emerson who continues to live in texts that have been in print for decades. But this "new" Emerson is not really so new; if changes of emphasis are necessary, they are less profound than novelty might lead us to think. The key is still to be looked for in the familiar texts. No one who grasps a part of Emerson's meaning there should find himself seriously altering his view through a study of the antecedent or secondary material, although a survey of this, published, to-be-published, and not-worth-publishing, can increase his respect for the quality of Emerson's public expression.

When we turn back to the major work we discover, I believe, that the major action Emerson meant to present is broader than the acts of conscience and intellect that criticism has accustomed us to notice. He seems to be talking about something more obvious, crucial, inclusive, and illusive. We must call it the act of experiencing as such. As a prophet, Emerson is apparently seeking to identify the sources of valuable experience, to name and liberate the springs of admirable action. He opens his attention to these in all realms of life: physical, practical, aesthetic, intellectual, moral, mystical. He tries to establish the conditions for initiative in each dimension of experience, to connect these possibilities one with the other, to recommend each separately and together as potential energies for his reader. Finally, as an artist, he seeks to commit the best sense of this manifold message to the local particulars of his discourse. The hope latent in this strategy is that an imaginative response to literary activity will provoke a more direct intuition of his discoveries. The prophetic Emerson may be paraphrased after a fashion by the "understanding": the artist requires a more lively, delicate, and empirical sympathy. And only as this develops in us can we find ourselves prepared to comprehend the prophecy.

In so entrusting the essence of his meanings to the qualities of his language, Emerson is unusual in his or any age. Emerson is a prophet *because* he is an artist (unlike, say, Carlyle, who is a prophet in spite of not being an artist). To be sure, this makes him an artist of something not commonly made the focus of imaginative discovery, since it is less a "something" than the very mode of operation of imaginative discovery itself. He is trying to tell us about the act of experiencing so that we may experience more, and better. As Keats's poems are both about the poetic imagination and practical demonstrations of its powers and limits, so Emerson's work consists essentially of doctrines and demonstrations intended to show the ways we can best experience our experiences. The good reader of Keats ends by knowing what is meant by the term "imagination." The reader of Emerson has similarly to try to understand the presumed subject of the act of experiencing, which he calls the "Soul." This in turn means not only trying to understand why and how Emerson "divided" this Soul into separate faculties, but also identifying the psychic meaning of each faculty through the literary activity that manifests it. Emerson is presenting us, I believe, with a fundamental *schema* for experience. He differs from other prophets who have done as much not only in the proportions and relations he establishes among the elements of the manifold Soul, but in the degree and manner in which he sinks his message in his language.

To the explication of this central action of experiencing as Emerson understands and conveys it, this book is devoted. I have risked being deliberately systematic in setting forth the different aspects of the Soul, and later in discriminating the corresponding dimensions of literary accomplishment. It seemed better to acknowledge, even exaggerate, the systematic methods of the "understanding." Books of criticism are necessarily committed to these methods, even when they seek to uncover within the object of discourse modes of action that precede systematization. With this excuse, I have invented some fairly ostentatious Technical Terms and have gone so far at one point as to present a chart. I hope the very queerness of these classificatory devices will make it easier for my reader to see through and forgive them.

Books of criticism, even those whose pretensions are necessarily ancillary, also imply a position on larger cultural issues, whether or not these appear overtly. To describe and explain is always also to advocate. And to talk on behalf of Emerson is to engage oneself in a war of values, in which judgments about the importance of certain literary figures in the American past are a way of talking about human preferences for the future. My last chapter, therefore, ventures some comments on the relevance of Emerson's example and achievement to the possibilities of experience in our time. Here I need only say that these speculations derive from an assumption that Emerson is a true ancestor: that *Nature* is our primal book, and that the tradition of prophecy and art descending from it leads not only through Emerson's later work and through Alcott and Thoreau to Dickinson and Frost, but most strongly through the vital center of Melville, Whitman, William James, Henry Adams, and Wallace Stevens; it thus constitutes, though not our only tradition, still our greatest, our one indispensable tradition. In an age in which the seminal claims of Hawthorne and Twain have had somewhat more than their due, this fact might be better understood than it is. If it were, we should be able to make better sense of the very untraditional welter we are in now. Emerson is still our good old cause.[11]

Let me complete this necessarily rather abstract introduction by demonstrating in miniature the sort of thing I shall do in detail. There is a certain risk in incorporating long quotations in books of criticism, but let me ask the reader to read this one and to determine which of the sentences in the following passage from *Nature* is the best and which the worst. Laying my own cards on the table, I should be willing to exaggerate and say there is one of each: one of the best remarks in Emerson and one of the silliest.

To speak truly, few adult persons can see nature. Most persons do not see the sun. At least they have a very superficial seeing. The sun illuminates only the eye of the man, but shines into the eye and the heart of the child. The lover of nature is he whose inward and outward senses are still truly adjusted to each other; who has retained the spirit of infancy even into the era of manhood. His intercourse with heaven and earth becomes part of his daily food. In the presence of nature a wild delight runs through the man, in spite of real sorrows. Nature says,—he is my creature, and maugre all his impertinent griefs, he shall be glad with me. Not the sun or the summer alone, but every hour and season yields its tribute of delight; for every hour and change corresponds to and authorizes a different state of mind, from breathless noon to grimmest midnight. Nature is a setting that fits equally well a comic or a mourning piece. In good health, the air is a cordial of incredible virtue. Crossing a bare common, in snow puddles, at twilight, under a clouded sky, without having in my thoughts any occurrence of special good fortune, I have enjoyed a perfect exhilaration. I am glad to the brink of fear. In the woods, too, a man casts off his years, as the snake his slough, and at what period soever of life is always a child. In the woods is perpetual youth. Within these plantations of God, a decorum and sanctity reign, a perennial festival is dressed, and the guest sees not how he should tire of them in a thousand years. In the woods, we return to reason and faith. There I feel that nothing can befall me in life,—no disgrace, no calamity (leaving me my eyes), which nature cannot repair. Standing on the bare ground,—my head bathed by the blithe air and uplifted into infinite space,—all mean egotism vanishes. I become a transparent eyeball; I am nothing; I see all; the currents of the Universal Being circulate through me; I am part or parcel of God. The name of the nearest friend sounds then foreign and accidental: to be brothers, to be acquaintances, master or servant, is then a trifle and a disturbance. I am the lover of uncontained and immortal beauty. In the wilderness, I find something more dear and connate than in the streets or villages. In the tranquil landscape, and especially in the distant line of the horizon, man beholds somewhat as beautiful as his own nature. (W.I.8-10)

Perhaps one's first impression as he reads along here is the undistinguished mildness of most of it. But the good and bad remarks do stand out. The bad one, presumably, is the "transparent eyeball" sentence, perhaps the best known sentence of Emerson's among readers who wish to make fun of him. I shall want to look at it again in a moment, but first let us examine the good one. This, as I take it, is, "Crossing a bare common, in snow puddles, at twilight, under a clouded sky, without having in my thoughts any occurrence of special good fortune, I have enjoyed a perfect exhilaration," and its coda, "I am glad to the brink of fear." Suppose one agrees that this is the noticeably good place in the paragraph.[12] Can its excellence be accounted for? The subject matter, in the broad sense, would not explain it; the whole paragraph is about the response of man to experience, and almost all the individual sentences attempt to express or recommend the joy of contact with nature. Such redundancy is a usual principle of order, indeed, in an Emersonian paragraph; the separate sentences are often more or less synonymous ways of saying "the same thing." Another sentence near by is an example: "Not the sun or the summer alone, but every hour and season yields its tribute of delight; for every hour and change corresponds to and authorizes a different state of the mind, from breathless noon to grimmest midnight." Here is the same point being made quite without distinction—except a little, a tiny amount, in the abstract comprehensiveness of the turn through "corresponds to and authorizes." "Breathless noon," "grimmest midnight," and "yields its tribute" are the stock properties of college rhetoric.

But, in a sharper sense, the motif is important. The good sentence repeats the touch of an actual experience or combination of experiences—the verb "have enjoyed" leaves it open whether the event has occurred more than once. The bareness of the common, the clouds, the puddles of melting snow, quickly identify a concrete image of winter thaw or early spring weather in a New England village. The wry trick the sentence plays depends in part on one's knowledge that those experiences are the least likely to seem occasions of joy at the time. New England weather is at its ugliest, the villages at their meanest, on such chill wet days, and walkers crossing the common are anxious to get home to change their shoes. Here of course is part of Emerson's point; the voice obliges you to take another look at the potential beauty of mean situations.[13]

This brings us to the speaker. It is worth comparing him to the Victorian rhapsode of the other sentence, with the seasons and hours spread out like cards before him. The man in the good sentence exists as an "I." He is calm and unhurried and makes no special requests of his imagined interlocutor, whom he addresses quietly: "we agree," says the tone, "that these are not matters to discuss in a loud voice, using terms we both suspect; we must see such things obliquely." He is modest, polite, reserved; listen to that "any occurrence of special good fortune." It is an educated voice, a little humorous. The modesty continues throughout: "enjoyed," "exhilaration," "glad," are all slightly lower in intensity than what one expects. The word "glad," for instance, acts as it does partly because it is *not* "joyful," and "perfect" means "perfected, that of the whole man," but is allowed to mean more because it might as well mean, to start with, "excellent of its kind, the same sort of exhilaration you get from a winter walk"—which this experience, after all, is.

The imaginative action for which one is searching, then, is at first a physical response to a natural environment and then the self-demonstration of a certain person, a speaker. The subject of action in this experience is alone, and the experience is casual; he is perhaps on his way home after doing an errand on the Milldam. How often has Emerson had this particular enjoyment? He is a connoisseur of such moments. "It is necessary to use these pleasures with great temperance" (W.I.11), he says with prim irony a page later.

Even the rhythm stresses the ordinariness of the occasion. He is walking home, "crossing a bare common, in snow puddles, at twilight, under a clouded sky." The sentence is deliberately not going anywhere unexpected; the details of the natural context are there, each equidistant from the other, each an unemphasized portion of reality. The movement of the sentence imitates the unhurried stride of a walker. Hence the small shock when an announcement is casually made that the "original relation to the universe" desiderated in the opening paragraph of *Nature* has in fact occurred: "without having in my thoughts any occurrence of special good fortune, I have enjoyed a perfect exhilaration." The very casualness of the order forestalls the question, how did this joy occur? What is its cause? The rhythm implies, one cannot say; one can only accurately and modestly take notice and remark that something has happened. A situation has become an event; but the exact course of the metamorphosis, the relation between the scene and the person in it, is inexpressible. "Let us inquire to what end is nature?" Emerson asked to begin his essay; here, unexpectedly, the question is answered. The "end," the purpose, is joy, the release of natural energy to enjoy the environment.

This large joy emerges half-paradoxically out of a clash between gladness and fear. These emotions are not quite polar opposites, since the antithesis of gladness is sorrow and the reverse of fear is security. But ordinarily one would not expect to entertain a state of feeling combining the two. At exceptional times, though, the element of physical alertness both feelings share may come to the fore. When we are afraid, our senses are sharpened, and our body becomes ready to fight or flee. We become more distinctly conscious of our environment as we prepare ourselves to meet something in it that may endanger us. Fear alerts us to reality. When we are glad, on the other hand, we are unusually satisfied with the way things are. We experience our circumstances as pleasurable and feel our own value as an enjoyer of these. A gladness that reaches the brink of fear would then presumably be a satisfaction borrowing some of the special intensity of frightened anticipation, an enjoyment in which complacency is replaced by a certain anxiety as to whether the world will continue pleasing. The exhilaration seems comparable to that of the mountain climber, say, whose pleasurable consciousness of his own physical powers and of the beauty and strangeness of the scene depends very much on the constant danger of life involved in the exercise of those powers. The right move is intensely satisfying because the wrong move is so easy and so fatal.

At such moments we feel our condition; we are vividly aware simultaneously of our environment and of our own life acting within it. We know reality—even the reality of snow puddles—and we know ourselves. Such experiences of physical contact with the world are at the root of what the romantic has always meant by "joy," from Wordsworth to Lawrence. Joy is the emotional and intellectual precipitate of a quick relation to things as they are. Through joy one recovers one's faith that there is a world to be inhabited, a world one can touch at all points together. It is characteristic of Emerson that he should report an experience of this kind which he encountered in the midst of his daily affairs; he did not need, the implication runs, to seek out in extravagant situations opportunities to possess nature and himself.

So much one can say, I think, of the sentence just as it appears. But it also has a literary history. In Emerson's journal for December 8, 1834, is the following entry: "I rejoice in Time. I do not cross the common without a wild poetic delight notwithstanding the prose of my demeanour. Thank God I live in the country! Well said Bell that no hour no state of the atmosphere but corresponded to some state of the mind; brightest day, grimmest night" (J.III.386). It is interesting to observe that it is the paragraph's relatively banal sentence that comes closest to its final form in this, the first literary version; the editorial change from "brightest day, grimmest night" to "breathless noon" and "grimmest midnight" is not a significant step. Little else is present in the words—just enough to make us sure, on reading this entry, that it is a beginning, a germ. One can notice, for example, how the "prose of my demeanour" has become, in the final version, a matter of tone, not a stated entity.

In the next spring is another relevant entry: "The wild delight runs through the man in spite of real sorrows Nature says he is my creature & spite of all his impertinent griefs he shall be glad with me. Almost I fear to think how glad I am" (J.III.459-460). This note bears the date March 26, [1835]; it too contributes a full sentence to the final paragraph and adds as well the essential notion of a paradox of feeling, a combination of fear and gladness. We cannot know how Emerson thought to make just the connections he did, but the result is surely a pivot for the whole paragraph in *Nature*. The achievement can represent the essay as a whole, an essay that is in its turn the plain foundation for everything Emerson publicly said thereafter.

It can be disconcerting, however, to observe the difference in quality between this good moment and its context. The very next remark in the finished paragraph of *Nature* is, "In the woods, too, a man casts off his years, as the snake his slough, and at what period soever of life is always a child." That "too" gives the case away: "There are other advantages to afternoon walks, dear nature-loving reader, which I can think of readily," says the tone. The two sentences are, on one unfortunate level of the author's mind, of equal value.

Still worse is the parody of these excellences in the notorious eyeball sentence. "Standing on the bare ground,—my head bathed by the blithe air and uplifted into infinite space,—all mean egotism vanishes. I become a transparent eyeball; I am nothing; I see all; the currents of the Universal Being circulate through me; I am part or parcel of God." Christopher Cranch unerringly picked this image out to caricature; his drawing (it is reproduced in Sherman Paul's *Emerson's Angle of Vision*) shows the one concrete picture these words irresistibly muster up, a preacherly eyeball staring into the heavens.[14] The *doctrine* about the Soul's relation to Nature, so far as it is paraphrasable, is the same as that of the "bare common" sentence. But the speaker, the I, is innocently absurd at best; the rhythm is a coarse parody of the watchful casualness of the other sentence; and the language is vapid.

A reader's job, then, is plain: to distinguish the excellent moments for himself and, having distinguished, to appreciate the art of the saying he hears and, through the art, the truth said. It is thus that we learn what Emerson has to tell us regarding the Soul.

PART I

The Soul

DEFINITIONS

THE EPIGRAPH of the late Stephen Whicher's fine anthology of *Selections* from Emerson is a sentence from "The American Scholar": "The one thing in the world, of value, is the active soul." The motto is well chosen. For the Soul in Entire Action is the central drama of all Emerson's work. Whatever else may be the immediate topic, this is his real subject. Every sentence, every paragraph, every essay, poem, lecture, or journal note attracts our best attention to the degree that it manifests and promulgates the victory of the Soul. We cannot understand what Emerson is getting at until we have made the connection between the particular piece of wit we appreciate and an ideal of complete human activity.

Such a summary statement is not hard to make and has been made[1]—more often, perhaps, in classrooms than in published studies, which are apt to strike into the problem of Emerson at some less obvious, less important point. But what does this conception of the active Soul mean? How are we to explain it? By an explanation of any idea or action we ought to understand such a representation of it as will render it possible for our own minds, a formulation that will bring forward anew its living truth. It may be presumed that Emerson hoped he was saying truths himself. We are not then approaching him on the right path until our critical progress makes his beliefs and demonstrations more obviously *so*. Otherwise we will find to our chagrin that we have only been learning that someone once said something under the illusion that it made sense.

Suppose, though, we do not slide away, but face the problem. How can we understand what Emerson meant when he so variously argued over a lifetime that the only thing of value was the active Soul? One had best start with the word "soul" itself. Any sentence worked out to concentrate in little the whole of Emerson's doctrine about human possibilities would need the word for a grammatical subject. But its contemporary connotations arc all wrong—religiosity, gentility, hypocrisy—"soul" has a whole set of unhappy associations. Yet in the midst of prejudice a second thought can remind us that we have lost something by the modern degradation of this word. There is nothing that will really replace its useful chord of meanings.

For Emerson the word had not lost to the attritions of irony its noble Christian denotation, or the overtones accumulated by a long generation of romantic poetry and philosophy. The historian of the ideas to which Emerson owed his spiritual vocabulary can trace this inheritance. None of the definitions cast up in a modern dictionary is entirely irrelevant. We can learn there that "soul" means that by virtue of which a living creature is alive, or the essentializing quality of any object, idea, or institution. This is the root meaning. It can mean also the self, or that portion of a man distinct from the body and its urges, especially that portion of the portion that relates to God. This can be either the mind or the conscience. Finally, it is this further portion, considered as something immortal, which survives the death of the body. All these meanings influence each other, and all are involved in Emerson's specialization of the term. If one dips at random into the body of Emersonian prose, taking note of the sentences that contain the word, it is easy to arrive at a rough list of modern synonyms for parts of its meaning: life, energy, sensibility, creativity, courage, emotional reality, love, sentiment, confidence, conscience, essence, authenticity, integrity, identity, intellect, genius, the spirit of an age.[2] In general (that is, in most contexts to some degree) it means the principle of initiative in life, morals, and mind—the imaginable subject of admirable action. It is interesting that we have no such word ourselves, a fact that says something about our cultural condition. Modern terms for desirable subjectivities—my list of synonyms above includes some of them—are perhaps more exact but too specialized, and their meanings seem to have no necessary connection with each other. The one popular general word, "psyche," means the space in which experience occurs, not the responsible initiator of that experience. Apparently we do not believe there is such a thing.

Here and there, through the lectures especially (he feels his formal philosophic obligations far less in the essays), one can find Emerson attempting to schematize the relation of the different submeanings gathered under the term. He will say, for instance, that God enters the sphere of terrestial life as Reason, the agent that perceives absolute truth and good; and Reason descends into unphilosophic affairs as Common Sense, which may in turn be contrasted to the Private Will. Or Instinct and the Understanding (elsewhere the opposite of Reason) combine as Reason to face Nature. The Soul as a whole would then be so much of instinct as would go through the mind to nature or through conscience to moral action. These attempts at abstract formulation, however, are secondhand, occasionally inconsistent with each other, and not terribly important. Emerson could be as baffled by Coleridge as any of that seminal thinker's latter-day adherents. The important aspect of the term to keep in mind is its persistent ambiguous inclusiveness.

Within the circle drawn by its power of reference there seem to be three main realms: intellectual perception, moral individuality, and organic instinct. The Coleridgean "understanding" seems to work for Emerson as a name for consciousness isolated both from impulse and from evaluated feeling. A modern term with approximately the same pejorative weight would be "rationality." Similarly, the spirit of individuality, isolated, becomes "personality," the mundane defensive self—never, for Emerson, an agent of good action on its own. "Instinct" isolated is physical power, about which Emerson had divided feelings, but of which he usually disapproved for the same kind of reason. His appreciation for the proper congruence of all three faculties when they work together as Soul, and his complementary disapproval of any one of them setting up for itself, leads him to a generalized distrust of technical intellect, of traditional social influence, and of the body. It helps to support a corresponding trust in democracy (which is based on the common sense of men in general) and science (which assumes a common nature for common reason to know).

Emerson is interested, then, in the motions of life as actions originating in some actor, or in a faculty of some actor. The ambiguity of the term "soul" allows him to subsume under the term a great variety of such motions and to make each a potential model of any one of the others or of the whole. Thus when animal

force, or conscience, or intellect, or even some natural principle
like magnetism appears as the cause for an event in the world, he
can use that event as a relevant illustration of a major pattern of
experience for which Soul is the master term. This freedom of
illustration is at the root of his interest in heroes; an extraordinary man, even though immoral, is at least a striking instance
of subjective power in action. Such men are not acted upon but
act. So they exhibit at least part of the Soul and stand as metaphors for the full resources of the unheroic who identify with
them.

At the same time, the general notion of the Soul gives Emerson
a criterion by which to judge the inadequacy of ways of life in
which the full powers implied by the term are not used. Judgments can be made against the inhibition of "lower" as well as
"higher" faculties. The Soul incorporates energy as well as
character. The large ambiguity of Emerson's key term implies a
putative whole experience which would engage all the faculties of
the subject together. His theory of the Soul can do implicit
justice to initiatives with which his inherited unconscious habits
kept him out of official sympathy.

The rigors of New England culture hindered Emerson from
doing personal justice to every action his term would theoretically
give him a chance to praise. Analogous influences can inhibit a
modern reader from understanding all that Emerson was able to
admire explicitly. The general ideal is close enough to appreciate
without difficulty; "the whole man" is one of our cant phrases. But
a modern reader would have more difficulty than Emerson in believing, for one thing, that the prototypical experience of the whole
man begins with communion with nature. The very notion seems
as antique as the pastoral genre in which it was traditionally expressed. And pastoral, in life as in letters, seems not merely old-
fashioned, but debilitating, immature, a matter for vacations, not
a foundation for grown-up experience. Maturity, it is easy to
assume, starts with an abandonment of the old infantile pretension to an intimate relation with nature in favor of commitment
to the social mode. Yet Emerson believed that the laudable
motions of good experience included as their ground-note a conscious sense of union between the subject of action and aspects of

external nature. Why? The simple question requires a plain
answer, before one can trust oneself to feel in touch with the
meaning of his idea of the Soul. This, the very foundation of
Emerson's theory of the Soul, is a hard place to get over.

Another hard part of this putative Emersonian Whole is the
moral dimension, what Emerson calls the "moral sentiment." He
meant by this phrase something that for him was an essential
constituent of an entire subjectivity. Therefore the term must
mean, not an outward norm (the automatic definition a modern
reader would give it) or even an "inner check" (the internaliza-
tion of such an outward norm), but an initiating inward force.
The conventional wisdom of Emerson's age made it easy to
accept the natural inwardness of the conscience; the conventional
wisdom of ours makes it next to impossible. A modern reader
would be inclined to start by assuming that moral experience is
learned from without, not generated from an inborn faculty. But
to Emerson the "moral law" is quite a separate matter from the
conventions of the social world. It is a part of the Soul, something native and outmoving, which runs parallel to instinct and
mind. Called upon to define the word Soul formally, he would
doubtless have spoken first of this ethical initiative. The difficulty
is crucial to a sympathetic understanding of Emerson's message.
Here I merely want to take notice of the issue; there will be
more to say about it later.

The Soul's action for Emerson, then, starts in an instinctive
relation to nature and includes (in a way to puzzle about) virtue;
it ends as mind. The metamorphosis of circumstances into consciousness is the consummation of the Soul's great act. The trajectory of that act is sketched in a hundred remarks. For Emerson,
events, things, and institutions are all finally dissolved in intellect,
which finds itself by its own act the re-creator of all it sees. "In
some contemplative hour" experience "detaches itself from the
life like a ripe fruit, to become a thought of the mind. Instantly
it is raised, transfigured; the corruptible has put on incorruption"
(W.I.96). Or again: "I notice that all poetry comes or all
becomes poetry when we look from within & are using all as if
the mind made it" (J.VIII.321).

"Using all as if the mind made it"—there is a kind of danger

in the relief such succinct formulations of intellectual action can
stimulate. For if the more primary relation to nature is forgotten, and the moral element in the action of the Soul neglected,
its intellectual dimension may become too obvious. We can find
it even too easy to accept Emerson's definition of the Soul on this
side. It would be right to think that Emerson meant intellectual
action as the verge or limit of all actions of the Soul. He did not,
though, think that the acts of the mind were all he had the
privilege of celebrating. "Thinkers," as he knew well, tend to
overestimate the independence of the mind (when they are not
denigrating it) and are easily tempted by arguments that apparently sanction their caste bias. They like to feel free of the
world, of their own personal and physical faculties, and rush into
the real freedom of rational action as if it were absolute. But, in
Emerson's terms, this is to interpret the acts of the reason as
instances of understanding merely, or mind separate from the
other agencies of life. Still, probably no inquiry into Emerson's
idea of the Soul (including this one) could avoid overemphasiz-
ing the intellectual dimension of his doctrine, either directly by
partial paraphrasing or indirectly by assuming that his work is
wholly explainable in philosophic terms.

There is another reason for the tendency to intellectualize
Emerson's message. Emerson is dead; only "Emerson" lives.
And this second figure lives only in words. One knows what he
says by reading those words: "he" is my inference, and inferences
are made by the mind. Here indeed is an ultimate meaning for
the word Soul. It must mean the mind of the reader understanding what is before it, following some verbal action upon the page.
This literary action is all that an author can be sure he will share
with his reader. It will be as a mind that the reader's Soul performs. A reader's other faculties are not entirely asleep—how
could they be? Life continues around him and within him; he
cannot help experiencing admirations and repugnances. But when
these faculties act for him as he comprehends the text before his
eyes, they act in subordination to the mind. There is much in
Emerson that comments upon this terminal condition of all
literary action: to announce it, even to exploit it, is one of his
purposes. But its very obviousness can fortify a tendency to over-

intellectualize the idea of the Soul. Emerson preaches against bookishness—but we ourselves read his preachment in a book.

THE ORIGINAL RELATION

Emerson's celebration of the action of the whole Soul, then, means a celebration of a consort of faculties: instinct, conscience, and intellect. Let us take up instinct first; it was primary for Emerson, and it is certainly the most important to us if we are to understand him correctly. How are we to comprehend what he is talking about when he speaks of the joy of a sympathetic contact with the natural world? What action is involved? And why would this joy (the "bare common" passage was an instance) be fundamental to the other proper actions of the Soul, not merely for a nineteenth-century romantic, but for anybody?

Let me try an experiment. As I write these words the plangent strains of a guitar rise through the August air to the window of the room in which I sit. I break off, glad of the interruption. It is not a recording; some Cambridge enthusiast is plucking actual strings, singing fragments of song. He stops, and voices of children supervene, interrupted by tingles and thrums from the instrument. Here for me are physical sensations, active, present, intensely agreeable. Here is a fragment of nature. I am not in the woods, to be sure; I am sitting before a desk, in the midst of a city. But the kind of sympathetic response that a walker in the woods could have in a less qualified but perhaps less concentrated form is actual, here and now, for me. Hearing the music rise through these split bamboo blinds, my spirits rise with it. The flexions and harmonies of sound unite the inward motions of my body with the agreeable qualities of an external reality. I am a bare subject, a sensibility, identified for the moment with this event that fills my ear. And this experience is the physical and psychic foundation of all that is now present to my consciousness; I find these words in a mood of pleasurable awareness generated by a sudden and irreducible sense of being alive. I am not separate from my scene, but, for a moment, one with it.

In such experiences of the present moment, when by pleasure we unite what Coleridge would have called the prime agent of human perception with the features of the scene that satisfy, we can be startled by that aspect of the Soul which engages, says Emerson, in a conscious collaboration with nature. When these experiences are especially pleasing, we cultivate them gratefully, disregarding whatever else we may be doing to attend, for they illustrate our life, and we necessarily put them first.[3] Yet even neutral instances will exemplify the principle, though under a less affecting guise. The guitar interrupted my argument and supplied an inadvertent support to it; let me venture a second experiment of the same kind, and ask my reader to attend to the features of his own scene.

On what do your eyes focus now, if you let your attention relax? Upon some movement within your environment, probably, since nothing that does not move will catch the unguarded attention: perhaps the smoke rising from a cigarette, or a figure slowly crossing a quadrangle outside the window, or a pigeon flying past. Some such noticings are inevitable as long as we are awake within an active scene. It is our "attention," our animal senses, which do this work—not our minds or will. And this work (if so it may be called) is spontaneous. It involves an instantaneous act of empathy, or self-projection: what we see we "go with," identifying each instance of motion as a motion of our own sensibility. Momentarily we *are* each thing we see; that is *how* we see it. Obviously this animal action, this serial identification with each object perceived, does not involve our personalities. I know perfectly well that I as a person am quite separate from the person I see through the window. Similarly, it does not involve our minds. For my mind tells me immediately, or almost immediately, that when I see my fingers move over the keyboard they are my fingers, not me; they are "objects," namable and separate entities quite distinct from my mind, which knows their name and applies it. Such organic acts of perception as I am speaking of, then, must occur on a more "primitive" level of being than selves and minds. And on that level the characteristic mode of action is identification, not distinction and separation.

Let us return now to Emerson. A good instance of the sort of experience for which I have just tried to suggest analogues may be found in a journal entry for April 11, 1834. This was a creative time in Emerson's life; every day's experience counted toward the maturing *Nature*. Let us try to believe that what he speaks of happened, that Emerson too was once as alive as I or you. He visits Mt. Auburn Cemetery to stroll, as he used to do when a student at Harvard:

11 April. Went yesterday to Cambridge & spent most of the day at Mount Auburn, got my luncheon at Fresh Pond, & went back again to the woods. After much wandering & seeing many things, four snakes gliding up & down a hollow for no purpose that I could see—not to eat, not for love, but only gliding; then a whole bed of Hepatica triloba, cousins of the Anemone all blue & beautiful but constrained by niggard Nature to wear their last years faded jacket of leaves; Then a black capped titmouse who came upon a tree & when I would know his name, sang *chick a dee dee* than a far off tree full of clamorous birds, I know not what, but you might hear them half a mile. I forsook the tombs & found a sunny hollow where the east wind could not blow & lay down against the side of a tree to most happy beholdings. At least I opened my eyes & let what would pass through them into the Soul. I saw no more my relation how near & petty to Cambridge or Boston, I heeded no more what minute or hour our Massachusetts clocks might indicate—I saw only the noble earth on which I was born, with the great Star which warms & enlightens it. I saw the clouds that hang their significant drapery over us—it was Day. That was all Heaven said. The pines glittered with their innumerable green needles in the light & seemed to challenge me to read their riddle. The drab-oak leaves of the last year turned their little somersets & lay still again. And the wind bustled high overhead in the forest top. This gay & grand architecture from the vault to the moss & lichen on which I lay who shall explain to me the laws of its proportions & adornments? (J.III.270-271)

This is not a literary experience, though we learn about it from literature. It is only in words because it has to be for us to know it.[4] Emerson writes quite casually and never does make public use of just these words, though the other words referring to the pleasures of nature in *Nature* presumably reflect this excursion and others like it in the same period of his life. The agencies involved are purely organic. Emerson is not "thinking" or "feeling." We are close to the bottom of the spiral of which the *knowledge* of nature is a higher turn, a stage here left implicit in the "laws" referred to at the end of the passage.

What does he recall of his afternoon? Chiefly things in motion, especially living things. These are his "happy beholdings." He saw and heard birds, clouds, leaves; above all he saw (and we, by imagination, see through his words) four snakes gliding, "not to eat, not for love," but only alive for the sake of life. To the Soul that so projects itself into what it sees, nothing is *meant* by the objects focused on that is so important as the bare fact that they exist. "It was Day. That was all Heaven said." Realities of whatever kind establish themselves first and foremost as projected protagonists of our organic identity. We know the sun, the tree, the tune, are there because our attention fastens upon them. We exist with them.

Now, if the subject of such experience is out of doors, the events perceived by this instinctive process of sympathetic identification will be aspects of the most thoroughly given, the most completely exterior, reality of all: the reality of nature. As he responds to actions that take place beyond his conscious control, he will become all the more deeply aware of the mode of being within himself that is equally given, equally an aspect of the natural order. And if these natural actions are the motions of living beings, animal or vegetable, they will reflect to their observer a renewed consciousness of himself, not merely as a natural event but as a living one, a being alive within an organic scene.

We need names for the different aspects of the Soul. Let us use an old-fashioned name for this one. The "faculty" that enjoys such an awareness as I have just described is a subjective agency too elementary to be called mind, too anonymous to be called self. We probably share it with all organic beings sufficiently complex to experience a world of objects separate from themselves. For Emerson, this faculty is the fundamental agency of the Soul. So let us call it, when we are discussing it in artificial isolation from other "faculties," the organic faculty.

All human experiences must necessarily include the action of this organic faculty, since all experiences presuppose an experiencer who learns reality by projecting his being into the different objects of his attention. The presence of this bodily sense is rarely a matter for consciousness, except where the identification in question is unusually pleasurable—or fearful. Pleasure ("joy" in poetic terminology) seems to be a sign that the organic substratum within an experience has become a conscious part of what the experiencer enjoys; it has become "vivid" to him. We might say, in Freudian language, that such pleasure testifies to the body's delight in its own existence as the center of a universe of events with which it can unite its own erotic being. The range of such pleasures would extend from mild enjoyments like listening to the sound of a guitar, through Emerson's appreciation of the natural events of a spring day at Mt. Auburn, to heights of sexual or mystical ecstasy in which the experiencer feels his identity merged with the totality of all that is. In such cases the organic faculty is the prominent subject of action; and this is, first and foremost, what Emerson meant by the Soul.

We can say, then, that Emerson felt the Soul as Life on such and such occasions. Nature was *where* he was free to feel the sense of organic being most completely—hence his walks. Hence too the many poems descriptive of these walks. "Mayday," a compilation of casually composed couplets assembled to celebrate various excursions, is the chief example of the type. There is also a curious little package of notes copied from passages in the journals that report experiences in nature, collected during the late thirties and early forties as if for a lecture. They were not used as such.

He does occasionally observe publicly that his modest excursions did not always involve the desired identification and recreation of the Soul. The negative reports, though, can be as interesting as the positive.

I went into the woods. I found myself not wholly present there. If I looked at a pine tree or an aster, *that* did not seem to be nature. Nature was still elsewhere: this or this was but outskirts & far off reflection & echo of the triumph that had passed by & was now at its glancing splendor & heyday,—perchance in the neighboring fields, or, if I stood in the field, then in the adjacent woods. Always the present object gave me this sense of the stillness that follows a pageant that has just gone by. (J.V.455-456)

These were the low moods. In the ordinary course of life, particularly a scholar's life, life itself is not felt; then the woods are as ordinary as anything at home can be. They rise to "nature" by contagion from within, and the honorific word becomes an objective name for an inward exhilaration. My soul truly "sees"

nature when my organic motions unite pleasurably with those
without; then I am glad, "glad to the brink of fear."

Daily experience of external nature can therefore be continually valuable because its visible motions hint at a fullness of
life that inhibition and routine may prevent one from feeling
within. One walks in the Walden woods to see reflected such
vitality as one does enjoy: this is "joy." But it is also possible
to see in the interrelated variety of the living scene a vast image
of an ideal total vitality from which moods or temperament may
shut one out. It is then one's *ideal* organic identity that is reflected in the surrounding multitude of natural things, as well as
so much of this ideal Soul as may be actual within oneself and
therefore implicit in the individual degrees of attention given to
specific trees, clouds, and birds. The sounds and sights upon
which it is possible to focus, good in themselves, are also partial
instances of a greater apprehension of the environing whole.

Emerson had often to resign himself to the narrowness of the
channels through which he could make an organic contact with
reality. Offered not less than everything, he knew well, as he says
in "Days," that his sensibility could accept directly only a few
"herbs and apples." In that poem he feels scorned for his inability to make better use of his opportunities for experience.
More frequently he is grateful that in spite of his deficiencies,
natural and inherited, he remains free to appreciate the continual
suggestion of a larger power of sympathy. The further ranges
of experience were for him the realms of the "gods," his poetic
term for the unemployed resources of his own being. Though he
could not live in these realms himself, he could at good moments
hear the gods "chant the bliss of their abodes / To man imprisoned in his own" (W.IX.230). To expose himself constantly
to the messages of life conveyed by the natural scene was thus
to test experimentally his own capacity for life. It was also to
stay in touch with his best consciousness that other capacities
existed, though never to be positively enjoyed in the course of
his own limited existence. Nature remained distinctly and perpetually "the supplement to man," which "His hidden sense interpret can" and thus "What friend to friend cannot convey /
Shall the dumb bird instructed say" (W.IX.368).

Clearly the sense of being involved in such experiences is not really to be named, especially by such crude terms as "aspect," "organic," and "faculty," since life acts below the level where terms of any kind have users, readers, and meanings; below the level, indeed, where metaphors like "below" take effect. The critic who wishes to show how any romantic writer endeavors to evoke this dimension of experience in himself and his readers is brought immediately to the same verge of inexpressibility that Emerson or Whitman or Wordsworth or Lawrence faced in the first place. The boundary cannot really be passed, short of re-doing their work with equivalent genius. Of all the inadequate abstractions that name the unnamable common prerequisite of all distinguishable acts, including that of naming itself, "life" is the traditional best of the available secular terms, and one might as well settle for repeating that the Soul at such moments as the experience in Mt. Auburn is entirely the simple sensation of life.

This fundamental life is what Emerson means by "virtue" when he says in "Self-Reliance,"

All things real are so by so much virtue as they contain. Commerce, hus-bandry, hunting, whaling, war, eloquence, personal weight, are somewhat, and engage my respect as examples of presence and impure action. I see the same law working in nature for conservation and growth. Power is, in nature, the essential measure of right. Nature suffers nothing to remain in her kingdoms which cannot keep itself. The genesis and maturation of a planet, its poise and orbit, the bended tree recovering itself from the strong wind, the vital resources of every animal and vegetable, are demon-strations of the self-sufficing and therefore self-relying soul. (W.II.70-71)

A man can look out for evidences of life in the motions of his environment. By an easy extension, which does not affect the nature of one's action, one can look out as well upon "the times," the surrounding activities of the culture in which one lives, and find the vital energy one shares projected into the striking ener-gies of the age, in "the brain of the lunatic; in the wild hope of a mountain boy, called by city boys very ignorant, because they do not know what his hope has certainly appraised him shall be; in the love-glance of a girl; in the hair-splitting conscientiousness of some eccentric person who has found some new scruple to embarrass himself and his neighbors." In such an Emersonian series one is close to the Whitmanesque catalogue of cultural

actions that are visible or imaginable because they severally por-
tray a vitality shared with the imaginer. Only such images of
practical and moral initiative that indeed reflect the force of the
Soul seem genuinely real to it. "I think that only is real which
men love and rejoice in; not what they tolerate, but what they
choose; what they embrace and avow, and not the things which
chill, benumb, and terrify them" (W.I.264).

The immediate difference between Whitman's and Emerson's
appreciations of such "indicators" of the Soul's vitality would,
of course, be the New Englander's characteristic preference for
evidences of vital action that were consistent with the "higher"
faculties of the Soul.[5] Emerson prefers to contemplate the liberal,
the dissenter, and the hoper because their actions manifest mind
and character as well as vital energy. The conservative, on the
other hand, though he too acts with the force of nature, seems
to Emerson to bring only the brutal component of that force to
bear, "relying not on the intellect but the instinct" alone; this
accounts for the fact that "individuals" of that clan "have no
attraction for us" (W.I.268)—which diminishes their claim to
represent the Soul, at least in Emerson's earlier thinking. Though
Emerson came in time to value more highly the practical, political, and social instances of simple organic power, he was always
cut off, for obvious reasons of temperament, from developing
some parts of the full potential latent in his evocation of this
mode of action.

Once we see that the Soul is, at bottom, the sense of being,
we are in a position to understand why Emerson continually
speaks of the Soul as single, the same for all men and all the
objects, physical and mental, that a man can fix his attention on.
For to the rudimentary bodily consciousness there cannot be
more than one life, the one it lives itself. No matter how many
individual entities we perceive by projective sympathy (and we
perceive all entities in this fashion, to start with), we comprehend the existence of each by realizing its unity with our own.
At any one moment, there is always one life experienced, and
no more, though the intellect may then step back to name and
discriminate the different entities. In calling the Soul single and
consubstantial with all the substances of the universe, Emerson
is not being perverse or Platonic; he is simply trying to report a

fact about its characteristic mode of action on this level in everybody.

THE ACTIVE IMAGINATION

FOR EMERSON the action of the artist is a special development of the aboriginal organic contact all men have with the world. "A painter told me that nobody could draw a tree without in some sort becoming a tree; or draw a child by studying the outlines of its form merely"—as the abstractive intellect might tend to assume—"but by watching for a time his motions and plays, the painter enters into his nature and can then draw him at will in every attitude" (W.II.16). No reader in our craft-conscious day would accept a possible implication of the last clause that to identify with the motions of an object of attention would alone suffice to make one an artist. But granted a possession of the craft, with its kit of graphic formulas, Emerson's statement can still be interesting as an account of how acquaintance ripens through sympathy toward re-creation. Certainly beauty, as the essay devoted to the topic affirms at length, can be read as a name for the remotest efflorescence of the organic faculty. Objects are "beautiful" because they appear to possess the ideal characteristics of life: unity, coherence, motion. The perception of beauty thus increases the perceiver's value for life, of which beauty is the proof, or most refined manifestation. A secondary sign of beauty's source in organic power, according to Emerson, is the ability of that power, when it shows itself vigorously in acts of mind and authority, to interest and satisfy our aesthetic curiosity. Organic sympathy, he thought, may even cast a kind of unexpected glamor over ugliness, if the ugly thing coexists with vital power.

A favorite Emersonian metaphor for the consummation of beauty, and hence of the organic impulse, is the circle. Circularity is a prevalent image everywhere in his work and receives its own essay devoted to exploring some of its applications to intellectual and moral affairs. But it is a question whether anything said within that essay accomplishes more in the way of definition and suggestion than the beginning of the first sentence: "The eye is the first circle; the horizon which it forms is the second." We scarcely need even its completion in the observation that "throughout nature this primary figure is repeated without end" (W.II.301). All organisms act to bring themselves and their surroundings into a condition of harmony, and a circle is the best visual and intellectual symbol for this ideal. Instances of beauty are examples of such a consummation available in specific minia- ture to the Soul in a fragmented world. The presence of beauti- ful objects therefore stands for the possibility, which the Soul feels as desire, that all experience will fulfill itself as beauty when rounded gracefully about the perceiving subject.

Some of the natural adjuncts of the circle metaphor turn out to be imaginatively useful. Usually the sweep of the horizon is attractive evidence of the freedom of the eye and the mind that models itself upon the vital action of the eye, but occasion- ally a pejorative potential is drawn upon. Then we read of the philistine Englishman whose "horizon of brass the diameter of his umbrella shuts down around his senses" (W.V.254). The circle can also be a kind of prison, or isolation cell, in which life is locked up, unable to move, unaware of anything but the fixity of its own unhappy limits. Our circle of life is as large as the vitality we enjoy.

The largest circle of all should include the whole universe. With the eye of "idealism" the Emerson of *Nature* can see "the whole circle of persons and things, of actions and events, of country and religion . . . as one vast picture which God paints on the instant eternity for the contemplation of the soul" (W.I.60). The largest circle visible to the bodily eye is the landscape, or outward nature seen as a handsome picture. Enjoy- ment of the organic freedom to see aesthetically converts stale facts to "splendid ornaments . . . rich conveniences," and the "plastic power of the human eye" can, by integrating the "pri- mary forms" of nature into a "globe so that the landscape is round and symmetrical," allow us to take pleasure in their mere existence.

The circle is Emerson's chief image, then, for a completed,

integral, vital experience—that is, in our unideal world, for an aesthetic act of seeing. Aesthetic seeing becomes a type or model of perfected experience. As such it can seem superior to other modes of the Soul's action (such as science), because aesthetic vision necessarily includes a vital sense of concrete sensuous particulars. The enjoyment of landscape is perhaps least complacently an example of vital perception when the report of it engages wit, into which the sense of life flows forth as verbal activity. The famous instance is the paragraph in *Nature* about the "charming landscape" Emerson says he "saw this morning," which is "undoubtably made up of some twenty or thirty farms" but may be reclaimed from the philistine by the aesthetic eye. The most memorable sentence does not appeal to the visual sense alone. "There is a property," he concludes, "in the horizon which no man has but he whose eye can integrate all the parts, that is, the poet" (W.I.8). Part of the meaning of "integrate" here has been anticipated earlier in the paragraph, where the cognate phrase "integrity of impression" was used, implying that "integrate" should echo the Latin *integer* sufficiently to connote a vital authenticity of character as well as unity of composition. The poet puts together the scene before him to make a work of art and, in so doing, re-creates the "integrity" of nature and therefore, ideally at least, of the Soul that comprehends nature.

An aesthetic view of nature is of value, then, as a sign of unrealized vital potentialities, indicating resources not yet sufficiently exercised, powers that mere social "possession" may fatally inhibit. "Every glance we give to the landscape predicts a better understanding by assuring us that we are not right now." The final phrase here shoots out meanings like a roman candle: stress the "are," and it means "just now we do not exist"; stress the "right," and the sentence says, "we are not at the moment in a state of health," or else, "we got the answer wrong this time"; and finally, if all the major words are felt together, they tell us that we are not identical with the "right now," the present moment. The organism is out of touch with its environment.

At the same time, Emerson's intellectual and moral and creative need to move a fact inward, to read it for its interior sense, to rework it, is often tugging at the simpler satisfactions of landscape. The Soul wants more sense of its own action than a passive

appreciation of exterior life will permit. Emerson is capable of
rejecting the aesthetic point of view with some asperity: "The
shows of day . . . if too eagerly hunted, become shows merely,
and mock us with their unreality. Go out of the house to see the
moon, and 'tis mere tinsel; it will not please as when its light
shines upon your necessary journey" (W.I.19). Seen out of
the corner of the eye, the "shows" can preserve their vital magic;
faced directly, they are fixed and trivialized; they cease to be
authentically beautiful. The life, and hence the "reality," goes
out of them along with the sense of motion.

The potentially dangerous passivity of aesthetic seeing can be
restored by vital activity when one responds to constituents of
the scene through the useful actions summed up by the term
"commodity"; or when one's mind begins to engage with the
potential meaningfulness of the thing perceived; or especially
in the work of artistic creation. The artist casts the energies of
the organic Soul in new forms that are beautiful because their
structure repeats and therefore represents that found in natural
entities. Emerson's view of art as an organic activity is developed
in theoretical form in several essays, and references to individual
artists repeat the conviction elsewhere. His own poetry, which
at its best he hoped exemplified the workings of organic inspiration, frequently makes the organic nature of the creative act a
part of its overt subject:

> The hand that rounded Peter's dome
> And groined the aisles of Christian Rome
> Wrought in a sad sincerity;
> Himself from God he could not free;
> He builded better than he knew;—
> The conscious stone to beauty grew. (W.IX.7)

The doctrine these famous lines and others like them enunciate
is familiar for every romantic. They are distinguished, however,
by the direct literary presence of the very organic power they
praise in the authentically inspired master verbs. Works of
architecture become, by active metaphor, living beings shaped by
the hand of a divine creator.

An aesthetic experience too weak or diffuse to move in the
direction of such positive creation excludes action, and action is
the essential attribute of the Soul's life. Nature is not, finally,

something to contemplate in appreciative impotence but, as stated in "Fate," "what you may do" (W.VI.15), either directly in your own person or by sympathetic appreciation. An object looked at passively can be made to yield its full reality only when an active imagination can be found to "go with" it and "say what it is in the act of doing" (W.II.180). When the Soul cannot reimagine the life of the objects it perceives, the circle of contemplative aesthetic communion will become a prison.

THE SENSES

O F ALL the more specialized modes of organic intercourse with nature, the action of the eye is for Emerson pre-eminent. "Seeing" is always a major verb, perhaps more so in Emerson than in the other nineteenth-century heroes of perception—though even in Whitman, in some ways his opposite among the mid-century American romantics, the action of the eye carries a great part of the explicit transcendental burden. An anthology of references to this sense in Emerson's writing would fill pages with specimen statements whose implications would extend to every corner of the Emersonian universe.[6] Everywhere too appears the natural link between visual action and achievements of the higher faculties. If it "is vinegar to the eyes to deal with men of loose and imperfect perception" (W.II.228), the ability to see exactly "unlocks a new faculty of the soul" with every object "rightly seen" (W.I.35). A philosopher "must not guess but observe, without intermission, without end" (J.III.551); and Emerson says of himself, with a typical combination of modesty and assurance, that he is "so purely a spectator that I have absolute confidence that all pure spectators will agree with me, whenever I make a careful report" (J.X.191). The eye is especially, of course, a link between the pure organic faculty and the intellect, between being and words, perceiving and perception.

To observe is to create: the poet "sees the stars, because he makes them" (J.VIII.321). If we see nothing, it must be because our eye has lost its power to embody in its perceptive activity the desire of the Soul to live within its world: "The ruin or the blank that we see . . . is in our own eye" (W.I.73). Our life, our sense of satisfactorily and actively inhabiting our world, is felt in proportion to the number of things that fully attract our attention. The aggressive, penetrating, pursuing power of organic curiosity turns out for Emerson to be most expressible in terms of seeing—perhaps, paradoxically, because merely looking seems on the face of it so helpless and innocent. Thus for an epigraph to the essay "The Poet," the first and probably most important essay of the *Second Series,* Emerson imagines a "Moody child and wildly wise" who "Pursued the game with joyful eyes, / Which chose, like meteors, their way, / And rived the dark with private ray: / They overleapt the horizon's edge, / Searched with Apollo's privilege" (W.III.1) through all of nature. This power of the eye is extended to human affairs elsewhere. If "men do not obey us," it is "because they see the mud at the bottom of our eye" (W.VI.181), and when one's self-command goes, the field of vision constricts: "Cowardice shuts the eyes . . . so that we cannot see the horse that is running away with us; worse, shuts the eyes of the mind and chills the heart" (W.VII.258).

Emerson's characteristic stress on the initial stage of any action involves immense value in the first glance. The "habitual first look" a man casts on any object decides his "whole possibility" (W.XII. 66) and—more absolutely still and so more dubiously—"The genius is a genius by the first look he casts on any object" (W.IV.150). Emerson's reliance upon the eye exposes his weakness as well as his strength. More than one reader must have felt obscurely troubled by the necessary but jarring exception he makes in *Nature* to the strength the experience of nature gives: he can, he says, endure any calamity provided it leaves him his eyes. And we have seen how the notorious and inadvertently comic sentence about the transparent eyeball has given hostile readers in his own time and later a chance to jeer.

The most private sources in Emerson for this special reliance on seeing are hard to trace. The obvious pun of "eye" and "I" suggests a close connection between the faculty of sight and confidence in one's personal as well as one's organic identity. Then too the eye is the megalomaniac among the senses; it takes possession of the universe from a distance and seems itself to be the center from which all existence radiates. It is hard to believe that anyone else *sees*. In these respects sight is the opposite of touch. Sight implies detachment, intellectuality, voluntary control; touch is passive, involuntary, comparatively undiscriminating. There are plainly strong emotional overtones in a preference for one of the senses over the others. To center one's life in the eye and its actions is to reject the intimacy of physical and emotional contact with the world. Sometimes Emerson can claim that to see is virtually to perform every other action of life, for all can be translated into vision; more often a note of regret at so limiting a physical specialization is struck. There is more than a hint of personal meaning in the memorable phrase Emerson used to describe his fellow New Englanders, "educated eyes in uneducated bodies" (W.X.138). And the history of Emerson's troubles with his eyes as a young man in divinity school might tell us much about the special meaning of seeing for him if we knew more about it.[7]

The chief secondary image in the essays for the power of the seeing eye is the sun or the stars. Eye, sun, and stars are linked in many sentences. The stars are the remotest things one can see, and their extreme distance from the eye is an important part of their metaphorical usefulness: they are "like" the eye, yet also at the extreme verge of nature. "The stars awaken a certain reverence, because though always present, they are inaccessible; but all natural objects make a kindred impression, when the mind is open to their influence" (W.I.7). Re-examine remarks like this in terms of their emotional meaning and they are, of course, pathetic: "all natural objects" must include human beings; if they are permanently inaccessible, the vital self is placed in dreadful isolation. Remoteness *is* intimacy, though, if one thinks of the mind itself as a sky, or space, in which "the natures of Justice, Truth, Love, Freedom, arise and shine" (W.I.27). The final intention of Emerson's images of space, sun, and stars is to identify everything with the perceiving subject. The effect is that this lofty wish is modified with tinges of lonely feeling, which color the optimistic assertions with secret self-contradiction, and therefore with a troubled distinction. It often happens that the appeal of a sentence seems to depend in part upon such evoked but incompletely expressed emotional concerns, whose echoes complete as well as qualify the optimistic burden of their meaning. We can see the stars, but only see them.

Though metaphors drawn from seeing are prominent on the surface of the Emersonian rhetoric, the eye is not the only noticeable sense in which the organic substratum appears. We have seen how simple identification of life with life comes before it, theoretically as well as in order of importance, and behind (or below) both modes of organic apprehension must be placed the many instances of a still more primitive kind of organic address to the world, that of eating and drinking. "In how many churches, by how many prophets, tell me, is man made sensible that he is an infinite Soul; that the earth and heavens are passing into his mind; that he is drinking forever the soul of God?" (W.I.136). This is one of many sentences where the relation between the Soul and nature is referred to in a metaphor of drinking. Developed with its inevitable adjuncts, the latent image would be that of a baby nursing at its mother's breast. Once or twice this image is pretty explicit, but most frequently it remains in the background, indicating its presence by an occasional epithet or verb, lending, by the frequency of its unemphatic appearance, a special quality to the perceptual, intellectual, and spiritual events for which it serves as a principal metaphor. "Nature, uncontainable, flowing, forelooking" (W.II.169), is matched by the "glad and conspiring reception" (W.I.194) of this spirit which "takes up the world into" itself. The light of nature "flows into the mind evermore, and we forget its presence. The poet, the orator, bred in the woods, [are] nourished by their fair and appeasing changes" (W.I.31). We hear that "I am a pensioner; not a cause but a surprised spectator of this ethereal water . . . I desire and look up and put myself in the attitude of reception, but from some alien energy the visions come" (W.II.268). The poem "Bacchus" calls for a "wine of wine" that shall bear inward all the speaker's experience of the world. And it is perhaps not altogether a convention of rhetoric that makes him often speak of man as "embosomed" in nature.

I think when we notice such imagery, not only in Emerson, of course, but in other writers, we are being indirectly referred to a mode of experiencing reality that at least at first glance seems rather different from the more adult modes of perception and identification. The relation of an infant to its mother might be summarized aphoristically by the formula, "I eat reality." This is a still more basic organic relation than that which might be conveyed by "I am what I see." It is the least sophisticated of all the ways in which a living being can get into connection with the world. The later stage of absorption by identification may be a development of this basic action in terms of the other senses. I perceive an object outside myself when I identify myself with it; when I unite with it, sympathetically, I bring it in, as it were, and incorporate it into myself. In either case the universe becomes a receptive subject, first by direct ingestion and later by sympathetic incorporation.

We can use individual instances where the assimilative image appears in Emerson as a hint toward the vital meaning of issues to which we would otherwise have to give a merely philosophical attention. A good instance is a dream reported in the journal; perhaps it is especially apropos because it is a dream. Emerson was very sensitive to dreams and understood well that they expressed feelings, motives, and problems not otherwise available to the consciousness. "I dreamed that I floated at will in the great Ether, and saw this world floating also not far off, but diminished to the size of an apple. This an angel took it in his hand & brought it to me and said 'This thou must eat.' And I ate the world" (J.V.485). The dream is a kind of Swedenborgian fancy, whose associations move out in several relevant directions. It is a reversal, for one thing, of the story of Genesis, for here the angel commands the hero to eat of the fruit of the tree of knowledge, instead of punishing him for it. Traditionally it was a crime to know; but after the Renaissance it also became glorious. Emerson was accustomed to associate apples with Newton, who had explained the movements of the earth and the planets by reseeing it and them as apples. Then it is also precisely at the breast of the mother (itself comparable to an apple) that the whole world, or everything *not* the self, can indeed be eaten. To the infant, the whole universe is edible. In such a dream, cultural images of original sin and original intellect recapitulate still more original organic experiences.

There are two passages in *Representative Men* that repeat

some of the themes of this dream. In "Montaigne" the story, complete with its Newtonian associations, is rehearsed in a darker tone:

providence . . . has shown the heaven and earth to every child and filled him with a desire for the whole; a desire raging, infinite; a hunger, as of space to be filled with planets; a cry of famine, as of devils for souls. Then for the satisfaction,—to each man is administered a single drop, a bead of dew of vital power, *per day,*—a cup as large as space, and one drop of the water of life in it. Each man woke in the morning with an appetite that could eat the solar system like a cake; a spirit for action and passion without bounds; he could lay his hand on the morning star, he could try conclusions with gravitation or chemistry; but, on the first motion to prove his strength,—hands, feet, senses, gave way and would not serve him. (W.IV.184)

Here is the violence and megalomaniac egotism of the infant, who can only demand and demand, without being able to impose his will upon the universe though he feels able to devour it whole.

But the universe can also prove too much for its angry inhabitant. The eye is often larger than the stomach. In "Plato" Emerson describes the master idealist as attempting to eat the world and failing: "the mouthful proves too large. *Boa constrictor* has good will to eat it, but he is fooled. He falls abroad in the attempt; and biting, gets strangled: the bitten world holds the biter fast by his own teeth. There he perishes: unconquered nature lives on and forgets him" (W.IV.77). This is the revenge of the universe, to choke the greedy eater—who is himself pictured, not grandly as Adam or Newton, but as the snake or the devil in disguise. If you tried to swallow an apple in one bite, you would choke. But babies and boa constrictors have in common the same method of consuming food—they gulp it whole.

Some have found Emerson's high philosophic message too bland, too delicate a mixture of love, idealism, intellect, and therefore too removed from the energies that support and destroy actual civilization. In such imagery lurks the underground alternative, running beneath the high themes it metaphorizes. Here is a connection with nature not above the realm of personality, but below it, for babies and animals have no personality; here is the life of the unsophisticated organism, striving, greedy, unpersuadable. And the mode of experience to which these images advert has a vital if obscure relation to the action of their spiritual complements, the civilized facilities of the Soul. A man's metaphors mean what they say.

The implication would be that infantile organic subjectivity has verbal and structural continuities with the impersonal adult mind and conscience. Both occur separately from the ordinary social ego. Both are therefore alike for everyone. When acts of the mind are re-examined, certain structural elements in them can look oddly like the organic acts out of which they develop and of which, phylogenetically, they must be a specialized ramification. Like Newton or Emerson, we are alive before we think. The transition from the bodily to the spiritual apprehension is gradual, mounting, to use Emerson's own metaphor, in a spiral line and in such a way that loftier acts of mind duplicate their physical prototype. Rhythm and metaphor are signs that the continuities are preserved and that the helix curves back upon itself smoothly. There is, then, a general truth about experience hidden within Emerson's addiction to metaphors of eating and absorption for the description of mental activity. We feel we know more about moments of perception, and have more reason to believe in their truth, when we encounter them as a kind of incremental repetition in the adult soul of the initial motions made by an animal in contact with its enfolding and succoring environment.

In the presence of such metaphors of nourishment, we have one more of Emerson's strategies (sublimely unconscious as it evidently is) for attaining the widest possible conjunction of his own with everybody's experience. He sets out to speak on behalf of the Soul as subject, Nature as object. All acts in which a lively sensibility is present are susceptible to redefinition in terms of such a model. Hence Emerson's didactic potential: whatever he says is always potentially relevant to his reader's ongoing experience. His sentences may all be a comment on what his reader is doing right then and there. If this Soul-and-Nature model can in turn be seen as rooted in primitive bodily experiences, its appeal and resonance become that much the stronger and surer. The range of reference is expanded. It is everybody's first fate to have been an infant and to go on existing as a body. It is a liberating shock for the mind to have its superiorities reconciled with such antecedent spontaneities, a mark of its balance and "naturalness." Thus the mind, freed from the social self, is reconnected with all the processes of that nature which, in its most characteristic action, the mind *knows*.

Such a pitch of references back to elementary relations with the world renders especially poignant those Emersonian remarks in which a glad acceptance of the "enveloping Now" (W.I.163) is followed by a consciousness of separation, and he can say, "I feel perhaps the pain of an alien world; a world not yet subdued by the thought" (W.I.168). To be sure, he is reassured in happier moments once more "by the moist, warm, glittering, budding, melodious hour, that takes down the narrow walls of my soul, and extends its life and pulsation to the very horizon" (W.I.168). Yet the very recognition at such high times that "I am not alone and unacknowledged" (W.I.10) can suggest a fear that he may be.

The effort to bridge the distance that opens up with the awakening of the higher faculties of the Soul, to return to an ideal homogeneity of experience, is best expressed in metaphors of touch. Idealists, in a scornful moment, are characterized by Emerson as people who "could not make their hands meet around their objects" (W.VI.238). A man afraid of something strange in his experience is advised to face the origin of the terror, to "see the whelping of this lion—which lies no great way back"; he who is brave will then perfectly understand it, for "he will have made his hands meet on the other side" (W.I.104). Here once again is a metaphoric development of something primitive, for to *apprehend* with the hand that is not the hand of the mind is indeed to feel "by knowledge the privilege to BE" (W.I.39), as anyone who has ever seen a young child explore a kitchen cupboard can recall. A child's first acquaintance with the boundaries of the Soul and the world comes through his sense of touch. We learn that other entities exist by touching them, and through touch we cancel the new separation. The hand accompanies the eye, gropingly learning to make out a universe of things among which a detached self moves independently, yet always "in touch."

When Nature escapes the groping hand, she is often for Emerson a teasing, denying woman. In like manner, "there is throughout nature something mocking, something that leads us on and on, but arrives nowhere: keeps no faith with us" and gives us in the end "not satisfaction, but suggestions" (W.III. 189-190). One sometimes feels that Emerson imitates these flirtatious manners in his own prose, the tone of which can be like that of a woman who promises without satisfying. Imitating the qualities of the Other who has frustrated you can be a strategy for controlling frustration. "The cool disengaged art of natural objects makes them enviable to us," he says a little earlier in the same section of the second essay on nature, to the "chafed and irritable creatures with red faces" that we are (W.III.183). A frustrated lover and an angry child could both fill the image here. The first tends to displace the second; as Emerson eroticizes the relationship between the Soul and nature, frustration is softened. "These sunset clouds, these delicately emerging stars, with their private and ineffable glances, signify . . . and proffer" (W.III.173). To speak thus turns feelings of abandonment and separation into the pleasures of flirtation.

Dissatisfaction with breaks in the organic continuity of experience can fade into the half-pleasurable pangs of a lover or even somersault into awed acceptance: the stars are "beguiling— soothsaying, flattering, persuading," and "though their promise was never yet made good in human experience," they "are not to be contradicted, not to be insulted, nay, not even to be disbelieved by us" (J.V.558). Humor qualifies piety here, though resentment has not disappeared entirely.

SCIENCE

IF IT were possible or desirable to follow a strict outline, we would now have arrived at the place to discuss practical experience, or work. If aesthetic sensations are the culmination of organic experience on the passive side, the active side, that which grows most directly from the striving of a man to arrange the environment to suit his needs, is reflected in work for those who cannot be artists or thinkers. Emerson is as much the laureate of direct physical work in and with nature as anybody of his time could be who was so thoroughly the gentleman and scholar. Praise of the practical activities subsumed under the general term "commodity" may be found in many places besides the section of *Nature* so titled. But as he says there, the mere mentioning of this realm of the Soul's action is as much as is necessary. On the whole it was Thoreau who, by personal exploration of the spiritual consequences of work, derived from this species of organic-social action the special profit that authorized a fuller speech.

For a man of Emerson's temper practical work was a duty, a relief, or a tedious interruption of his own native concerns. Preaching its joys abstractly, in the manner of Carlyle, would have gone against his grain. This continued to be so even when, in later years, he came to put more stress on the value as evidence for the Soul of what men of action and affairs accomplished. His best contribution to the question of work was expressed less in his vicarious admiration for sailors, farmers, and railway promoters than in the stress he placed on the vital "act of invention," the "intellectual step," implicit in every practical procedure; "that act or step is the spiritual act; all the rest is mere repetition of the same a thousand times" (W.I.192). Such a comment allies Emerson more closely to Ruskin than to his friend Carlyle, whose strenuous advocacies were less sensitive to the organic obligation to "re-attach the deeds of everyday to the holy and mysterious recesses of life" (W.I.248). Labor that reduces its operative to a machine repeatedly performing some partial act in ignorance of its function disgraces the Soul. Only that work which preserves the worker's subjective antecedence to what he does, only work that comes "naturally," can stand as an instance of organic power developed into social action. But in occasionally saying such things, though he says them well, Emerson's message blends with the current of his age. We look to other critical Victorians to spell out the ramifications of this idea.

We do better to turn directly to what Emerson has to say about the mind. To follow the actions of the Soul as body is to find oneself dealing sooner or later with statements overtly expressive of the Soul as mind. We noticed at the end of our discussion of the organic faculty that, as the Soul began to engage its "higher" faculties, it became increasingly aware of a gap between itself and the world. For an infant, reality is something that can be absorbed directly; later, by sympathetic identification, one can still incorporate reality into oneself. The dimension of experience in which contact with the world occurs in this fashion continues in all organisms as long as they are alive. But with the development of the other faculties, aspects of the universe begin to appear alien from the living subject. As one acquires a self within a social context, one realizes that this self inhabits a world composed of other selves, as much centers of action as one's own. And as the mind develops, together with language, one begins to be conscious of a universe filled with objects different in kind from the faculty that discovers them.

When a two-year-old calls out "light!" and points to a burning bulb, he testifies that he has begun to act within the dimension of intellect: the bulb is no longer merely something to notice by unconscious identification, but also an object distinct from himself for which he now knows a public name. The possession of this name unites him with other users of the same language, who by sharing it can join with him to contemplate the large number of objects for which the name can be used. The child's objective universe now includes all the lightbulbs he can see, lit and unlit, and trash fires, headlights, and stove burners as well. His world is larger than it was. But its discriminated contents are separated from his sense of himself as a living being: the things he can name are merely things, not simply instances of his own vitality. Organically, the lightbulb was his life projected; now, so far as it is a namable object, it is simply a "light."

To think, then, is to detach oneself from the world and the world from oneself: a man of intellect, as Emerson says of Goethe, inevitably "lays a ray of light under every fact, and between himself and his dearest property" (W.IV.284-285). This first necessity of mental action gives Emerson a good deal of concern and provokes a certain doubleness of feeling. To say that "intellect always puts an interval between the subject and the object" is to imply approval for the gain in impersonal clarity. Yet to follow the sentence, as he does in this particular journal entry, with "affection must blend the two" qualifies this attitude;

and to go on to say, as he immediately does, "For weal or for woe I clear myself from the thing I contemplate: I grieve, but am not a grief. I love, but am not a love" (J.VI.242) strengthens one's sense of a loss that Emerson feels paralleling the gain.

When I contemplate I do not, says Emerson, identify myself with either grief or love; I am not obliterated in the emotions I may feel. I survive them, and stand apart, when I reimagine them as grief or love. From the emotional side, this is a loss; from the point of view of the intelligence, it is a prerequisite. One cannot think at all, Emerson is prepared to say, as long as one is the victim of feeling. "A man is intellectual in proportion as he can make an object of every sensation, perception and intention; so long as he has no engagement in any thought or feeling which can hinder him from looking at it as somewhat foreign" (W.XII.38-39). The *objectivity* of insight becomes its characterizing quality, and therefore something to value strongly though not necessarily absolutely.

Consider another standard expression of this idea: "The first effort of thought tends to relax this despotism of the senses which binds us to nature as if we were part of it, and shows us nature aloof, and, as it were, afloat" (W.I.49). "Aloof" reveals a thread of dissatisfaction; nature is like a cold stranger who has hurt one's feelings. But "afloat" (a favorite image) is a pleasing image; nature becomes in its totality a ship upon the ocean of the mind, and its distance and inaccessibility are elements in the charm, as the sight of a ship on the horizon pleases because of its resemblance to a toy. The dilemma whose two parts are embodied in the self-conscious metaphors of this sentence reappears a line or two later, when Emerson makes a point of reminding his reader of the changes the world undergoes when seen from unusual points of view, such as from a balloon or even a carriage, in which it is the observer who becomes at once aloof and afloat. By such alterations of position, what is visible becomes a picture: the "men, the women . . . are unrealized at once, or, at least, wholly detached from all relations to the observer, and seen as apparent, not substantial beings."

Such quasi-aesthetic comparisons throw light on an intellectual necessity. Either the object or oneself *moves* when we think of it: "Making a fact the subject of thought raises it" (W.II.326).

When this motion is attributed to the mind instead of the object of the mind's contemplation, one ends with an argument for self-reliance: "He in whom the love of truth predominates will keep himself aloof from all moorings, and afloat. He will abstain from dogmatism, and recognize all the opposite negations between which, as walls, his being is swung. He submits to the inconvenience of suspense and imperfect opinion, but he is a candidate for truth . . . and respects the highest law of his being" (W.II. 342).

The "he" that is described in these sentences from "Intellect" is of course the scholar, the abstract social role corresponding to the faculty of mind in the Soul. "The American Scholar" is the classic essay in which to see Emerson arguing for the freedom of mind to do its work in the world. The essay becomes more interesting when we remember that, by describing the office of the scholar so affirmatively, he was also talking about his own struggle to create a social role for himself that would replace the old ministerial identity whose forms he had burst through. "Scholar" connotes the kind of commitments we would now call "intellectual"; the essay gives a definition of the man of mind Emerson himself hoped to be. Henry Nash Smith has pointed out that the essay is implicitly organized in opposition to another kind of new American identity, that of the reformer or transcendental activist, a role exemplified at the time Emerson was writing by Theodore Parker.[8] The man of intellect, says Emerson in effect, is socially justified as such; his contemplative achievement is equal in dignity to the practical efforts of the moral athlete. To be a "candidate for truth" was for Emerson to "respect the highest law of his being." To follow this law was a good for the Soul, even if there were no practical results.

Once the mind is free to act without guilt or excessive consciousness of what it loses simply by being mind, what it does is Know. Emerson has much to say throughout his work about the act of knowledge, but probably science is the best single topic in which to see the major outline of Emerson's description of what happens when the Soul acts as mind. It is one of Emerson's oddest and yet most persuasive achievements, of even more value for our time than for his, to have boldly seen scientific activity not merely as a proud instance of the understanding at work, but as a legitimate action of the Soul. In this acknowledgment he is, of course, very much on the opposite side from the defenders of the organic Soul who influenced him, such as Coleridge, and those who have influenced us, such as Lawrence. He does not champion science naively. Considering the innocently materialist and inductive habits of mind one usually associates with nineteenth-century science, Emerson's sensitivity to the subjective element in the scientific imagination is strikingly prescient. From the amalgam of classic and popular sources and eccentric scientific philosophizing which, from all accounts, constituted the suggestive portion of Emerson's reading in natural philosophy, he was somehow able to single out just those aspects of the scientific quest on which recent philosophers of science have put the most stress. He caught in science the intellectual note of discovery, and, of the anecdotes he came across, he made images of natural mental action.[9]

To start with, science meant to him a systematic revolution in definition, a recovery by exact statement of a truth about alien nature. Emerson could find in his experience and reading many nonscientific examples of the mind in action. But science, if only because it is now even more the striking example of the intellect at work than it was in his day, never fails to make the demonstration his argument requires. He is especially sensitive to the intellectual resonance of individual scientific discoveries, some of which he borrows over and over for the sake of the principles they exhibit. "The magnet was thrown into Europe, and all philosophy has taken a direction from it" (J.VII.39). Magnetism supplied him with the concept of polarity, which effectively emblematized his favorite theory of compensation and repeats itself in all contexts so frequently as to become almost glibly allegorical. The authentic appeal of magnetism as an image is easy to trace: it is an insubstantial but immense power, present universally but invisibly, acting abruptly, apparently an essential part of the inmost structure of things, yet capable of manifesting itself in simple bits of stone and metal, easily demonstrable by the adept in parlor experiments, and, though as ancient as the universe, only beginning to be understood in Emerson's day. All these qualities could seem equally true of the mind. The promise that magnetism might show connections with other ranges of natural knowledge, from mesmerism to light, increased the appeal of the parallel between the mode of action of this natural principle and that of the mind able to appreciate it, by suggesting future discoveries that would enlarge the reciprocal illumination. In the flyleaf of a journal volume, Emerson pasted a scrap from a newspaper announcing Faraday's discovery that all metals arrange themselves with reference to an applied magnetic force. The metaphoric import for the universal authority of the Soul is obvious.

The special way in which magnetism was useful to Emerson as a leading image, a metaphor of active intellect already in intellectual form, is illustrated again by his handling of another scrap of science: "Chladni's experiment seems to me central. He strewed sand on glass, & then struck the glass with tuneful accords, & the sand assumed symmetrical figures. With discords the sand was thrown about amorphously" (J.VII.79). This phenomenon, says Emerson, makes Orpheus no fable; if the tuning fork can literally render reality harmonious by organizing grains of sand into a visual pattern that corresponds to the pattern heard by the ear as harmony, and if a horseshoe magnet can bring about a like arrangement silently with iron filings on a sheet of paper, then the mind can rediscover in the behavior of two of its instruments images of the very power to which the instruments owe their existence and meaningfulness.

For Emerson, then, a scientific implement or experiment is an image, but so is it for the scientist himself. A scientist is not merely providing images for the poet or the philosophic critic; it is his own use of the image that is most thoroughly "poetic" as well as "scientific." For his strategy is precisely to find and use the right symbolic structure for the portion of nature he wishes to know and thence, by translating from one vocabulary to another, to comprehend broader and broader areas of intellectual experience.

Emerson's responsiveness to this central scientific strategy makes him sympathize readily with the motives informing the scientist as he acts:

What leads him to science? Why does he track in the midnight heaven a pure spark, a luminous patch wandering from age to age, but because he acquires thereby a majestic sense of power: learning that in his own constitution he can set the shining maze in order, and finding and carrying their law in his mind, can, as it were, see his simple idea realized up yonder in giddy distances and frightful periods of duration. If Newton come and first of men perceive that not alone certain bodies fall to the ground at a certain rate, but that all bodies in the Universe, the universe of bodies, fall always, and at one rate; that every atom in nature draws to every other atom,—he extends the power of his mind not only over every cubic atom of his native planet, but he reports the condition of millions of worlds which his eye never saw. (W.X.130)

These words, we can realize, are exactly true. The pun on "con-stitution" in the phrase "learning that in his own constitution he can set the shining maze in order" neatly expresses what the scientist does in fact do to "know" nature: he puts together his metaphor and thereby constructs the world his metaphor allows him to see. Some of the connotations of Emerson's Newtonian examples enrich the value of his definition as a way of talking about scientific action generally. Newton had a special meaning for Emerson's generation, which the name has lost since. For the eighteenth century, "Newton" nicknames the mind that once and for all defined all motion in space and time, all of nature that could be conceived. He was therefore the arch- or protoscientist; and as such Newton seemed an archenemy of the imagination in the eyes of a generation that had learned from German philosophy and English poetry to blame their alienation from organic nature and from themselves on the intellectual world view Newton stood for. It was part of Emerson's special gift, though, to complicate this conventional counterattack of the romantics. He could redefine the Newton of the Lockists as paradoxically transcendental: as in startling fact a prime representative of just that style of active intellect that especially and crucially concerned the man of imagination. Thus Emerson went beyond Blake, the chief proponent of the simpler romantic view of Newton. For if a poet's professional interest is in the action of language, particularly in its elementary aspect as metaphor, by which words are found for things, then the mind of all minds who stands for the act of finding a language for the whole of nature can become once more a central hero.

Astronomy could for similar reasons become the most suggestive of the sciences to an early Victorian nonscientist. Not only is the subject matter of astronomy the Whole in its visible aspect and comprehensible relations, but the methods of the science exhibit sharply the epistemic gulfs between eye and object, instrument and conclusion, model and reality, in the grossly evident form of physical distance. The necessary philosophic distinctions are thereby rendered easier to distinguish and appreciate imaginatively. Emerson of course is not the first to find astronomy provocative in this way. From its Renaissance beginnings, the history of astronomy has had the most considerable repercussions of any science until Darwin helped to make biology the key source for significant cultural metaphors. But astronomy fits the transcendental side of Emerson's cast of mind peculiarly well and constantly supplies his chief images of scientific or mental extraordinariness, the heroism of the awakened mind. The interests of Reason are not for him in contradiction to the eighteenth-century world view, but an incorporation of it.

Astronomy for Emerson, as for Addison or Paley, supplied examples of an order discovered by a mind. But Emerson had the special advantage of a new insight that could vitally reinterpret such traditional inheritances as the argument from design. For him design was not a proof of the existence of an anthropomorphic divinity, but evidence of the human mind in its natural action of finding patterns in any scene it comprehends. The God whose works and ordinance Kepler, Galileo, and Newton articulated was not an exterior starry artisan, but simply intellect in exceptionally obvious action. This God can therefore be understood as an inward experience of the discoverers, recoverable in outline by any latter-day student who works through their original arguments to make them his own.

If astronomy is a central science for Emerson, the central scientific action is classification—another typically Augustan specialty. He was limited here by the popularizers he read, who were making much of classification in the eighteen-twenties when Emerson did most of his reading in the field. Once Lyell and Darwin had appeared, it could be seen that the classificatory scientists could not progress in geology or in biology, where a more sophisticated developmental model was necessary to explain the facts. But Emerson could understand the act of classification better than those who, like his friend Agassiz, continued to think it the essence of scientific method well past the time when

it had become the stigma of the old-fashioned naturalist. What
Emerson says of classification is true of a more adroit brand of
science than he was probably thinking of when he referred to
the triumphs of the method. As frequently happens, his generalizations are more sensitive to the intellectual issues involved
than the particulars to which, when he felt the rhetorical need to
be specific, he had to attach them. What attracted him in classification was the universal importance of the mental activity
involved, its demonstration that "a perception is always a generalization" (W.XII.40). He who translates facts into the
language of law is one of the spiritual aristocrats who carry
"centuries of observations in a single formula" (W.I.56) and
exhibit the power of that mental instinct which "goes on tying
things together, diminishing anomalies, discovering roots running
under ground whereby contrary and remote things cohere and
flower out of one stem" (W.I.85).

The famous illumination enjoyed at the Jardin des Plantes
during his first visit to Paris is the representative incident for
Emerson's interest in the classificatory act. The experience is
dealt with at some length in the first lecture Emerson delivered
upon his return home, "The Uses of Natural History," which,
together with the others of the same series on similar topics,
constituted a kind of first public draft of *Nature*. This lecture
makes plain that the essence of the intellectual attraction the
French museum had for him was the simultaneous consciousness
its plan developed in the visitor both of the natural objects and
of the order the human mind had put these objects in—an order
discovered to be intrinsically natural, though just as evidently
imposed by the mind. The garden had been ingeniously made by
men; yet it exposed to the eye the true plan of nature as a whole.
It was a living metaphor that was literally true.

The linguistic implications of this experience are evident in
the language Emerson used in his lecture: "Moving along these
pleasant walks, you come to the botanical cabinet, an inclosed
garden plot, where grows a grammar of botany—where the
plants rise, each in its class, its order, and its genus (as nearly as
their habits in reference to soils will permit,) arranged by the
hand of Jussieu himself. If you have read Decandolle with en-

gravings, or with a *hortus siccus,* conceive how much more exciting and intelligible is this natural alphabet, this green and yellow
and crimson dictionary, on which the sun shines, and the winds
blow" (E-L.I.8). The garden confirmed the intuition that to
the intellect nature will turn out to be orderly and comprehensible. It is worth remembering that, at the time Emerson was
delivering this lecture, he was busy renewing his own private
acquaintance with the plants of Concord, with the help of hand-
books.

Classification has its negative side as well. A circle turned
substantial and confining is a wall. This image, about whose
organic meaning I have already written, will also apply to all
intellectual situations in which a single set of terms, a single classification, has begun to constrict the experience of a mind that
originally expressed its native freedom by establishing it. "The
influence of the senses has in most men overpowered the mind to
that degree that the walls of time and space have come to look
real and insurmountable; and to speak with levity of these limits
is, in the world, the sign of insanity" (W.II.272). The reserve
of humor in the tone here is backed by Kantian doctrine, which
makes time and space modes of mental apprehension. Yet if one
substitutes other objective conceptions for "time" and "space,"
the assertion that follows continues to be meaningful: "time and
space are but inverse measures of the force of the soul." Prisons
are to escape from, and the prisoner will find that, as he summons
the courage to approach the intellectual "walls" inclosing him,
they dwindle to nothing or, rather, to ideas of his own creating;
even in their most obtuse obviousness, they "measure" the Soul,
that is, refer back to the force the Soul is prepared to exert on
its own behalf. "A little waving hand," as he says elsewhere,
"built this huge wall" (W.II.302-303)—in any imaginable universe as well as in Orphean legend or mechanical fact.

When one considers an intellectual classification, or wall, with
awakened eyes, it can become merely a system, a necessary mode
of taking hold of reality. One should accept with relief rather
than terror the discovery that each enclosing wall is made by
the prisoner, that the circumference really is a function of its
center—which ought to have been clear from the beginning. One

needs all one's "recipiency," "percipiency," "saliency," if one is to remain ready to dissolve the satisfactory or unsatisfactory scheme, the picture of the world that has hung long enough.

One reason the moment of *first* discovery or illumination is so important to Emerson is that it is only then that the mind actively experiences a double perception of reality and of the system by which it is known. These are the times of high intellect, when one "sees through the design," "presides over it," and so "must will that which must be" (W.VI.27). The interrelation of will and fate, mind and nature, are simultaneously present to the attention. Once a classification has been accepted as the basis for derivative investigations, a single or technical vision suffices. But the disciples imagine that the order their master discovered is *the same as* the state of affairs it holds in suspension: "the walls of the system blend to their eye in the remote horizon with the walls of the universe; the luminaries of heaven seem to them hung on the arch their master built" (W.II.80). When this moment arrives, it is time to disengage once more. The poetic or scientific consummation of every metaphor, every pattern, should be a new opportunity for a radical doubt that immediately commences a search for alternative terms. If this doubt does not start up, the mind is condemned to an ever-increasing subjection to the implications of the old thought. "A man thinks. He not only thinks, but he lives on thoughts; he is the prisoner of thoughts; ideas, which in words he rejects, tyrannize over him, and dictate or modify every word of his mouth, every act of his hand. There are no walls like the invisible ones of an idea" (E-L.I.218). Scientific classification, then, like every metaphoric act, is only liberating in the doing or redoing. The moment the mind is passive before its own past acts, it becomes its opposite, an object of manipulation, the victim of a mental action it no longer initiates. The Soul is no longer present.

Here is an opportunity to refine again on the definition of the Soul as mind. If the word "classification" works for Emerson as a kind of eighteenth-century shorthand for those intellectual systems through which one organizes one's knowledge of the universe, the Oversoul is Emerson's peculiar nickname for any potential wielder of such a system. It is oneself in the act of knowing some state of affairs by way of a system; when we classify, we *are* the Oversoul. Heroically, the Oversoul is "the most advanced man in his most advanced moment" (J.X.454), he who is on the frontier between the last classification, the last painting, the last book, and that undefined nature which, as a multiple pun neatly says, "represents the best meaning of the wisest man" (W.I.214). *Represent* here means "stand for," "act out," and "give back" all at once; this nature fairly does for "the mind of the mind" (W.X.93), the mind when it truly acts, making itself a verb rather than a noun and therefore drawing a true "parallel to the movement of the world" (W.VI.18).

For the Soul as mind, according to Emerson, repeats on the higher spiral of intellectual action its own special version of that same union with the universe we saw occurring on the level of the organic faculty. The most primitive agency of the Soul enjoys nature by identifying with it. The intellect, as intellect, does not unite with the objects it becomes conscious of. On the contrary, it separates itself decisively from them. In the act of knowing an objective world, the mind achieves its own identity as something entirely separate from that world. As Ernst Schrodinger, a modern philosopher of science educated in the same idealist tradition to which Emerson belonged, puts it, "We exclude the Subject of Cognizance from the domain of nature that we endeavour to understand. We step with our own person back into the part of an onlooker who does not belong to the world, which by this very procedure becomes an objective world."[10] This epistemological split between the subject of perception and the object perceived is very much a part of what Emerson has to say about the way the mind works; it is felt by him, organically, as a loss, an alienation from nature, but intellectually as a gain.

The element within the act of knowledge that serves to unite these separated entities is the metaphor—language, classification, instrument, system—through which the mind becomes conscious of its object. One cannot *know* except by way of some symbolic system; and that system will simultaneously display, on every occasion of its use, its identity with the facts it reports and with the mind that invented it. As the garden in Paris proved to Emerson, all systems of knowledge are coincident, when we are using them, with the aspect of nature they allow us to understand. At the same time they are evidently products of the faculty that understands. We say that nature obeys certain "laws"; these laws are at once the way in which nature really works and man-made fictions. One cannot, philosophically, disentangle their double valency. Moments of intellectual discovery, scientific or otherwise, occur when someone invents a metaphor for the world that turns out to be the true name of the world. Nature, as Kepler (following Plato) explained in awe and pride, geometrizes—the universe without works in necessary coincidence with the mind within. The essential difference between the coincidence as it appears on the level of organic experience and as it appears on the level of intellect is that, in the latter dimension, unity is found *within* the metaphor that unites an otherwise disparate Soul and Nature. The necessary identification of the two poles now takes place inside the "language" through which one comes to know the other.

While we are speaking of the similarities between the actions of the Soul as organic faculty and the Soul as intellect, we might notice another common attribute. Like the organic faculty, the mind is single. To quote again from Schrodinger: "Mind is by its very nature a *singulare tantum*. I should say: the over-all number of minds is just one." And again, "consciousness is never experienced in the plural, only in the singular . . . none of us [has] ever experienced more than one consciousness."[11] Schrodinger is not saying here that there is only one *self* in the world. That would be psychotic. He, like Emerson, means by "mind" the intellect apart from the social identity: that which is conscious of an objective universe through some system of metaphor. And of this faculty it is no more than common sense to say that it cannot be experienced except as single. The world a metaphor reports is an objective world because all those who use the metaphor, all those who appreciate the message it conveys, must be occupying the same point of view and therefore exerting the same consciousness. When we say "Oh, I get it," we perform the same action as anyone else who "gets" it. To learn a science is to learn how to interpret its system of metaphors in the same fashion as all other scientists who use the system. Hence it is possible to talk in ordinary language of Science in general as the abstract perceiver of all that is known about objective nature: "Science says that . . ." The metaphor is what we share, and all we share; we unite to make use of it.

The old organic union between subject and object, then, disappears when we enter the domain of intellect, only to reappear in the double reference of the metaphor the presence of which constitutes that realm. And the old organic singleness of sensibility likewise recurs as that single point of view from which the metaphor is usable. Belief in these continuities allows Emerson to claim that instinct and intellect are fundamentally congruous; that the Soul ideally means both in action together. We distinguish them, critically, to account for what is different in their performance or contexts of action, and to render plausible Emerson's account of their combined action; but for him (and for us, when we are truly reasoning) they are really (that is, ideally) one agency.

HISTORY

IF SCIENCE is for Emerson the clearest context of intellectual action in which to show the dependence of that action upon the mediating presence of a language that refers doubly to the subject and to the object, history turns out to be the best arena in which to emphasize the singleness of the mind. Emerson is more originally and searchingly perceptive about what happens when the mind *does* history than he has been given credit for. His theory of history is conveniently concentrated in a single essay, and that essay an early one, which quite suitably opens the significant *First Series*. The essay begins aggressively with a key statement, "There is one mind common to all individual men" (W.II.3). We have just tried to see in what sense this remark could be a truism for science. Let us see how it makes sense for history.

Every man is an inlet to the same and to all of the same. He that is once admitted to the right of reason is made a freeman of the whole estate. What Plato has thought, he may think; what a saint has felt, he may feel;

what in any time has befallen any man, he can understand. Who has access to that universal mind is a party to all that is or can be done, for this is the only and sovereign agent. (W.II.3)

The last sentence especially seems to need interpretation when we think of history. For granted that there is one mind, in what way can it be "the only and sovereign agent" in the affairs of men? History, one might have presumed, consists precisely in the discrimination of separate and distinguishable agents for each separate and distinguishable act. By habit and tradition, one turns to history to escape the exclusive action of the mind; in the multiplicity and confusion of human affairs, if anywhere, its philosophic hegemony (assuming that is granted in the non-temporal, nonsocial sciences) should appear irrelevant.

The clue to Emerson's strategy for restoring the apparent contradictions between his assertions here and the nature of historical truth as he and his modern reader would both know it lies in the intellectual pun all uses of the term "history" preserve. The pun appears clearly in the first sentence of his second paragraph, the one directly following the opening paragraph quoted above. (As so often, the initial sentence of a new paragraph summarizes or interprets the matter of the paragraph preceding it.) Here it is: "Of the works of this mind history is the record" (W.II.3). He means by "history" here both the actions done in the past by various actors and that which is known about them, both the deeds of the historical figures and the deed of the historian who discovers and expresses them. History is simultaneously the manner in which we induce or imagine the past and the past as it is thereby induced and imagined.

So everything Emerson says about history must be read as involving a double reference: the past in which the events contemplated occurred, and the present in which the contemplator himself stands to see them. The pun on the word "history" unites the Soul and Nature, in fact; here is one more way in which to see how the terms employed by the intellect unite fact and mind.

Emerson's theory of history may therefore be read in two ways. If we see him as describing the nature of the past, we will find him a disciple of Cousin, as a recent dissertation has shown.[12] Emerson will then be saying that objectively history consists of a long process in which the common Soul (in this context something like the Zeitgeist) slowly arrives at its full development through the several eons of human time. The various historical epochs are stages in the progressive externalization of this Soul, each embodying an essential element of it. Since (according to Cousin) the mind of each individual contains the same impulse as the entirety of history, psychology and history being reciprocal mirrors of one another, one may find one's own latent traits exhibited in terms of outward public events. The actions of individuals in the past may be understood by individuals in the present because they are essentially identical.

If one reads Emerson's statements about history as statements regarding the nature of the past, one arrives at such a set of opinions about the way human culture has developed. As an objective theory of what happened, this may not seem very satisfactory. It is naive and secondhand even in Cousin, and does not become much more convincing when repeated by a provincial nineteenth-century American. Such views may seem a specimen of the kind of rationalistic evolutionary mythologizing that Victorian amateur historians passed on to each other with a complacency that now seems hard to understand.

But if we read these same sentences for their "subjective" meaning, a less contentious message emerges. If Emerson is talking about what happens within the mind of the historian, he is making a useful comment on the way the intellect works in this particular context. As a transcendentalist, interested in the grammar of the Soul as intellect, Emerson has something to say, even if we distrust him as a cultural historian. For it is certainly true that every vision of the past is seen from some point of view in the present. As Croce, a later and more clear-headed thinker on these matters, puts it, the historian "recreates in himself the thoughts and experience of historical figures . . . all history is present history."[13] And when the historian writes these "re-creations" down, the mind in which they have been re-created becomes a common mind, sharable by all his readers; it becomes, in fact, the same single intellect we have been talking about in connection with science.

Here too is a possible explanation for Emerson's assertion that "the thought is always prior to the fact" (W.II.3) in history. For only within the thought of the historian and his

reader does the fact exist at all. If the historian had not discovered it, and written it down, the fact as we know it would
never have come into being. Since the typical fact of history is a
fact about some definite person's action, that action, so far as it
exists as an object of understanding, so far as it is known to
have happened in history, must become a thought in the mind of
the historian, and thence in the mind of the reader.

As with science, there is never room for more than one mind
at a time. The exercise of the mind in history (in the second,
subjective, sense of the word) thus frees us *intellectually* from
enslavement to circumstance—indeed, from "history" (in the
objective sense of the word).[14] Objective history, so far as it is
known, can be read as a kind of projection or myth of the action
the mind performs to know it. Hence Emerson could afford to be
fairly casual about the literal truth-value of the particular myth
he found in Cousin, since what he was interested in was not the
nature of the past as such, but the way in which *all* views of the
past reflect the mode of acting of the eye that sees them. What
he found mythologized in Cousin's theory of what happened
would be true subjectively of other, perhaps truer, theories about
cultural development.

It is also possible to pick up and reinterpret Cousin's idea of a
parallel between the agents of past events and the individual
traits of the historian. We saw that in science an impersonal
common mind perceives an objective reality with the help of
metaphors. "Classification" is Emerson's term for the discovery
and use of such metaphors. What is the analogue of a system of
classification, a language of explanation, in the study of human
affairs? Evidently it is the private experience of the historian in
his own present world, especially whatever is most important
and constant in his experience. When the historian seeks to know
a truth about the past, he consciously and unconsciously uses his
own character as a metaphor to explain the motives and actions
of the people whose deeds he studies. He "classifies" everybody
and everything in terms of himself. By epistemological necessity
the mind must "explain from individual experience" (W.II.4)—
in each case different individual experience—the matters it contemplates. To the historian himself, there is no difference between mind and metaphor, impersonal intellect and individual

personality: he feels himself to act as one being. His reader, though, can distinguish the two: what the reader understands as true about the past in the book of history he reads becomes an object of the attention of the impersonal mind, now operating in him. The private or class or national assumptions of the historian are to the reader separable from this mind. They become for him merely the instrument by which the reader comes to know what he learns. He may complain that the instrument is inefficient, that the reality of the past is "distorted" by the bias of the author. The reader is similarly unconscious, perhaps, that he too uses his own personality and cultural circumstances to comprehend the truths he consciously disentangles from the bias of his author. But there is no escaping the presence of the human factor as the basic image in terms of which we understand human fact. There is always "a relation between the hours of our life and the centuries of time" (W.II.4). Historical fact cannot even exist as an objective reality without the interposition of a personal element: "The fact narrated must correspond to something in me to be credible or intelligible" (W.II.5).

All such historical metaphors are reversible. My own experience interprets for me the motives of Caesar or Columbus when I put myself imaginatively in his place. But my understanding of these alien persons will in turn allow me, as a secondary gain, an insight into elements of my own character that I could not permit to come to light within the circle dominated by my private vanities. "I can see my own vices without heat in the distant persons of Solomon, Alcibiades, and Cataline" (W.II.5). Thus history can be morally as well as intellectually educative: the Soul grows, or may grow, ethically as well as intellectually in the act of doing it.

But the separate stages in this possible advance of mind should not be conflated, for the sake of the dignity of the Soul. It is possible, I think, to correct some of Emerson's own formulations once we understand his chief point. Thus when he says, "All that Shakespeare says of the king, yonder slip of a boy that reads in the corner feels to be true of himself" (W.II.6), we are free to say, no. If the boy mixes himself up with the king, he learns nothing about either, but only indulges a ready-made fantasy of himself in Shakespeare's language. This is no way to read literature, or history either. What the boy ought to be doing, if he means to find out who the king really is, is realizing that what Shakespeare says of the king is true *of the king*. This can only occur if the boy draws upon his own experience to summon up the reality that Shakespeare invites him to see. Once he has seen the king, by comparing the king to himself, he is free to see himself, by comparing this self to the king. A modern reader would probably prefer to say that it is not so much, or so desirably, individual characters that one learns about as it is whole situations, complete with the systems of value operating within them. Thus Gibbon used eighteenth-century Europe to interpret Rome by comparing them both in their similarities and in their differences; and thus the freshman reader of *Hamlet* may learn to compare the whole universe depicted in that play with his own, in order to increase his knowledge of both.

Through history the mind knows the past. *What* it knows is always agency, that is, life. Here is another connection between the intellectual and the organic. Yet in history, as in any other imaginative context, the connection is the reverse of that found in actuality. In nonsymbolic experience, organic experience, life comes first and thought second. But in the realm of imagination, "life" turns out to be the creation of thought working through language. History is thus intrinsically idealist in metaphysical tendency as soon as the activity of the historian is counted in. For when, to use Emerson's illustration, the student of Egyptian history strives to work out in his head how the pyramids were built, he re-creates the way in which their builders must have worked by reference to his own capacities in like circumstances. He imagines what they did. Their deed, like their very existence, is a supposition of his, made public so far as he puts his reasonings into words, but still a consequence of his own mental action. Once, he says, there really was such and such a set of men, who did as follows; but his convictions of the reality of these men and their work depend entirely upon the strength of his own reasoning. The student does not build the pyramids; he understands how they were built and so converts the pyramids themselves as they now survive into illustrations of his own ideas. Thus "his thought lives along the whole line of temples and sphinxes and catacombs, passes through them all with satisfaction, and they live again to the mind, or are *now*" (W.II.11). The phrase "to the mind" might well be underlined; the life visualized by the historical imagination is strictly an *imaginative,* an intellectual, life. By intellectual action a lost organic existence, as real once as ours is now, is recalled, even reborn—but only in the mind's own terms.

Science and history, then, are to Emerson two great realms of intellect within which may be found the related ideas that there is a single mind, that this mind creates the objective reality it contemplates, and that it does so by making metaphors. But every intellectual action will, upon analysis from the right point of view, disclose the same structure. "Science" and "history" are names for subject matter, not for method, and Emerson's comment on these does not exhaust what he has to say in exemplification, celebration, and criticism of the intellect. We need not formally review this vast dimension of Emerson's contribution to the analysis of Man Thinking, since in the most literal sense every comment on the other facets of the Soul relates in one way at least to the fortunes of the mind. Besides, the manifold specifics of intellectual action will more than sufficiently appear when we come to examine Emerson's literary achievement. Literary action is (in more than one sense) the crux of the Emersonian endeavor. Literature supplies the best instances of mind at work, as well as terms by which to examine that faculty's more specialized pursuits.

The conclusion to which Emerson's results on both science and history would lead is that, without metaphor, no state of affairs is knowable at all. Once one counts in the intellectual subject of action, and the language that subject uses, one finds oneself with a model of mental behavior that is intrinsically "literary." Literature supplies the language one uses to describe the parts of the model. And hence the Poet, the user of words, can be seen as in the best position not merely to identify the structure of intellectual action in science and history but to redemonstrate this structure over and over in ordinary language. He, and only he, can really "tell" us what we are doing when we exercise our intellect.

But we need to complete our preliminary survey of the faculties of the Soul before discussing the literary reflection of any one of them.

THE MORAL SENTIMENT

IN CERTAIN contexts the intellect is as far as the spectrum of the Soul reaches. The ultimate action for Emerson personally is comprehension, insight, awareness of mind. And in the thought of Emerson's middle years one comes to hear more and more of intellectual action as the natural consummation of the experiential process. When one approaches his work from a literary point of view, as every reader must now do, it is easy to respond most readily to the passages that praise the works of the mind, to take Emerson somewhat too exclusively as the hero of that faculty, as the prototypical American scholar. If he is still considered one of our representative men, it is by virtue of his achievement in this, as he delicately and originally demonstrates the grammar of the intellectual life.

But in his earlier and most energetic years, Emerson would have refused to accept without qualification the authority we grant him as celebrant of intellectual action. If the aesthetic point of view seemed to him insufficient because it lacked the sense of active participation essential to full organic experience, so much the more did intellect by itself fail to include a crucial element of the full Soul. Intellect alone works, he says, "cold and intransitive in things" (W.I.125). It needs to be complemented by moral engagements. The Soul's highest manifestation, Emerson believed, was the sense of virtue, the "moral sentiment." The power of the heart to discover within itself the highest good was a cornerstone of his faith. The best heroism was always for him the rediscovery of the moral law, and the attempt to put its requirements into practice in spite of the conventional customs of the world. He believed, firmly and at a depth below the reach of criticism, that this law was intrinsic to the Soul, that it was

universally possible to all human beings, who might discover its
injunctions by consulting the uncontaminated instincts of their
conscience, that it was different not just in degree but in kind from
exterior social regulations of all sorts, and that the individual
enjoyed the Soul fully only when his actions included this moral
element as a defining principle.

These beliefs are, obviously, not peculiar to Emerson. In sub-
scribing to them, he was quite consciously linking himself with a
very old and broad tradition; in one form or another, belief in
the inwardness of the moral law might almost be called *the*
theory of moral action from the Greeks on. He had absorbed
this tradition while a student at Harvard, chiefly through Dugald
Stewart, the Scottish realist.[15] Though he came to question many
other aspects of the culture in which he had been trained, he
always preserved his old belief in an intrinsic moral sense.

But this tradition is a particularly difficult one to get in touch
with. It is hard, literally, to understand, except as a kind of
enormous illusion, from which the present age is involuntarily
free. For we "know," I take it, that there is no such universal
intrinsic moral sentiment built into our hearts, no naturally im-
planted test of the good. We "know," on the contrary, that
moral judgments are the individual reflection of standards that
have been internalized from the social environment, first the
family and later the general culture, and that they therefore
differ from person to person and from culture to culture. We
know, in other words, that the whole range of moral experience
comes ultimately from without; that it is not a function of our
native subjectivity, but something we have learned. Our judgments may well have become a second nature, but they do not
derive from the first; they are sanctioned, not by biology or
divinity, but by society. Our habits automatically tell us, when
we sit down to read the moral language of most philosophers
before, say, Mill, that this language must undergo some kind
of silent translation before it will fit our assumptions. We feel
ourselves privileged to assume that those thinkers who claim
that the laws of good and bad are a part of the world, in the
same way that the law of gravitation is a part of the world,
must be suffering from a more or less benign anthropocentrism.
For the most part we silently change the old aureate coinage

into our more modest intellectual currency without much trouble. When Shakespeare or Milton or Johnson talks of the laws of Nature's God, and their reflection in the reason of the well-disposed human being, it is easy to conclude that they mean the rules and habits of Christendom, or the eighteenth-century upper classes; we read on accordingly, turning each absolute term into its relative analogue.

Now, it is possible to do the same with Emerson as well. The moral law of which he speaks with so much fervor, and which constitutes in his own eyes so critical a portion of his creed, can be read as a grand way of talking about the idealisms of a conscientious romantic with a post-Calvinist background who is committed by temperament and profession to an obsolete ethical vocabulary. When one looks down upon Emerson's ideas from a "historical" point of view, something like this is easy to say.

But once we do this, we cease to take Emerson seriously. If the moral law is not really within, as he said it was, it cannot be an intrinsic portion of the Soul. What he tells us about moral action, so far as it hinges upon his belief that such action is an aspect of independent subjectivity, would simply go over our heads. The natural impulse is to pass the question by and to concentrate once more on aspects of his creed that still ring sympathetically true.

Another trouble follows: if we look at him through relativistic spectacles, we catch Emerson in an apparent inconsistency, which further diminishes respect. For we find him preaching self-reliance and the repudiation of convention in the name of a moral law which, from a relativistic point of view, is itself a convention. If he rejects moral bondage in those areas of life where he identifies ethical behavior *as* conventional, how is it possible to go along with him when he reserves an allegiance to a superior law that he fails to see is equally conventional? His antinomianism can seem inconsistent in such a light, though perfectly consistent for him.

So far as we are controlled by such relativistic assumptions, we shall simply not have anything sympathetic to say about the doctrine of the moral law, either in Emerson or in any other of the thinkers of the long and honorable tradition who share his belief. We shall not, in the most obvious sense, be able to see what they mean. It is possible to say that Emerson's "spiritual law," or the fervency of his attachment to it, can be interpreted as a reproduction on a higher, interior level of the same kind of simpler, outward convention against which he mobilized his genius. The predicament is psychologically plausible. Rebels often internalize stiffer versions of the same expectations they externally war against. Such moral relationships would be an instance of Emerson's own law of compensation. But to comment in this vein also involves condescension. The use of psychological language, like the use of historical language, removes all ethical truth from the theory it describes. In either case one is outside Emerson looking in and still not taking what he says seriously.

Perhaps a more sympathetic view of Emerson's moral doctrine may be arrived at by making one more criticism of it. The theory of the moral law seems to embody a confusion between the motive for an action and the criterion by which the action is evaluated—between efficient and final causes, "sentiment" and "law." He speaks as if a perception of the good suffices as a motive to inspire the pursuit of it. This is a common enough muddle in everyday moral discourse; one readily assumes, for instance, that telling a child how he should behave suffices as a reason for his doing so. It is possible, though, that if one tried to point out this muddle to Emerson, he would have said he meant it, replying that the doer of a worthy action, whatever his motives, stands for the norm that justifies his action. Besides, he might say, these distinctions, together with the awareness that internal checks derive ultimately from some social context, are merely theoretical. They are facts to the intellect, but not living considerations in specific moral emergencies. In concrete moral experience, a law that upon disinterested examination may exhibit its exterior derivation will be felt as a functioning part of the relevant subject of action. Viewed from without, moral sentiments may seem conventions; experienced from within, they are a part of the self that acts, and they *feel* like motives.

The way to a sympathetic understanding of the doctrine of the moral law, then, would probably have to be through an appeal to concrete experiences of conscience. "Obedience" to the moral sentiment would mean that state of mind in which an inward judgment becomes, instead of a check or hindrance, a felt

motive for positive social action. At such moments law *is* sentiment. That such states of mind exist, even the experience of
relativists will demonstrate. Doing one's duty, however analyz-
able from without as obedience to an internalized convention,
feels from within like an access of power. The self feels its
strength immensely enlarged when it does what its conscience
says should be done. The more distinct the demands of conscience, the greater the access of liberty and confidence when the
obligation is fulfilled. Contrariwise, a man is most aware of
obligation as an imposition from without when he is failing to
acknowledge and discharge it. We are never subjectively weaker
than when we are conscious of a duty we are not fulfilling.

One might speak more positively still. No one acts clearly,
authentically, freely, unless his conscience is at rest. Guilt diminishes competence. For the man of acute conscience, no action will
be possible, or enjoyable, or his own, unless it passes the ethical
criteria he has accepted as a part of himself. Actions that do pass
these criteria will then seem to contain the principles that make
them legitimate.

In some such way one might translate Emerson's ethical language into psychological terms without the intellectual condescension that follows from using these terms to analyze the
general case. One's acts ought not to be inhibited, we could
understand him to say, either by one's internalized code or by
unworthy exterior pressure. To act without inhibition may mean
rejecting an exterior code, if this proves to contradict interior
obligation. The point would be that no one can feel free who
disobeys himself. And the call that a man obeys would feel from
within as his "true" self even though, once he stands outside his
act, it may appear as a socially derived rule or norm.

There is another element in the Emersonian moral structure
that can cause a reader some theoretical distress. This is the idea
that all men share a single sense of what is right and wrong. For
just as he believed that the Soul as mind was one, so Emerson
preached that the Soul as conscience was single: it was the same
in all men who felt it at all. From the point of view taken by
the intellect, particularly the sophisticated modern intellect, this
is simply not so. And to claim, or assume, that it is so can make
Emerson look provincial; it can seem as if he were running to-

gether the habits of nineteenth-century middle-class New England and the laws of the universe.

Again one can get out of the difficulty, if it impinges, by dropping down from the theoretical to the practical level. Assume that Emerson's claim is really a description of concrete moral emergencies, not a contribution to general anthropology, and it will hold true. All participants in an effective moral action will in fact find themselves to be sharing an ethical community, which from within is coextensive with the relevant moral universe. Unless such a community of rules is shared, explicitly or unconsciously, no *moral* action is possible at all. All practical decisions of rightness and wrongness do take place within moral provinces, which cannot be felt as provincial while the decisions are being made. Thus it has been observed that Gandhi could not have carried on his civil-disobedience campaign in India if he and his antagonists had not shared certain values in the light of which all their actions were to be judged. These values were assumed; that is, they constituted the laws of the moral universe in which all concerned were prepared to live. And all concerned could correctly presume that the values were intrinsic, that any English gentleman or Indian revolutionary could look into his heart and find them compelling.

With the assistance of such analogies, we may better prepare ourselves to extract a meaning from the best of Emerson's thoughts on the moral sentiment, whatever our resistance to the metaphysical pretensions of his formal vocabulary. "He who does a good deed is instantly ennobled. He who does a mean deed is by the action itself contracted . . . If a man is at heart just, then in so far is he God . . . If a man dissemble, deceive, he deceives himself, and goes out of acquaintance with his own being" (W.I.122). His point is that evil is privative because it diminishes the total faculty of the Soul, which can only act freely when the conscience is satisfied. The very sense of "being," of existing normally within an environment, is impugned, reduced in quality, turned illusory, when the judgments of the conscience are obscured or unconsciously defied. A modern instance of what is meant here might be psychosomatic disease, where the freedom of organic experience is interfered with because some judgment of the self upon its experience has not been accepted on the level of moral action, and so takes effect covertly upon the bodily life. Emerson would add, there are similar effects upon the intellectual life.

COMPENSATION

THE theory of compensation, Emerson's most idiosyncratic contribution to ethical thought, is harder to rescue than the theory of the moral sentiment. The very issue he wants to meet, though necessary to any view of life that associates the system of the universe with moral value, can have a musty air nowadays, when it is easiest to assume that the universe is morally indifferent and only men either good or evil. Evil is still in our world, but if its presence is man-made it will not constitute a *problem*. Part of the trouble in taking a fair account of Emerson's contribution to the age-old discussion can lie in the difficulty of accepting the importance of the issue itself. The archaic "problem of evil" can only by strenuous efforts of the imagination be problematic for minds which take for granted that morality is social.

But even when one has reached back to the significance of the issue for minds that had to reconcile divine government of the world with the sufferings of the virtuous and the triumphs of the wicked, there are still difficulties in making sense of such halfway solutions as Emerson's. For the theory of compensation is meant to stand as the liberal answer to a problem that already had, in the minds of his readers, a conservative solution. Now that both the orthodox problem and the orthodox answer are dead, his acceptance of the first and denial of the second can seem equally irrelevant. He seems to be meeting a moral case that no longer impinges.

The problem, as it traditionally appeared, assumed that the good do in fact suffer and the wicked do in fact prosper. The orthodox explanation was that perversion of justice holds only in this world; in the next, rewards and punishments will be apportioned to their proper recipients. Emerson preserves the line of this old argument while denying its premises. He dismisses the need for another world to make good the injustice of this. He also dismisses the old-fashioned God whose justice requires explanation. But, most important, he denies that it is really true that the good suffer and the wicked prosper. He asserts that the wicked are punished and the good are rewarded, not by a Personal Will but by the natural course of events in *this* world.

To understand this line of argument it is necessary to redefine the key words: reward and punishment, good and bad. If virtue is to be understood as its own reward, vice its own punishment, and misfortune advantage in disguise, then the meaning of all these words must be desocialized, interiorized, transcendentalized. We are obliged to understand the moral life as something influencing the resiliency of the individual Soul, and not as a contractual relation between members of a social group, or between man and God. Morals, in this view, turns into psychology—in the process apparently losing its independent validity.

Yet there are moments when Emerson's ethical paradoxes have a real depth, and when his tone exposes a meaning for the idea of compensation. Sentences like, "what did the preacher mean by saying that the good are miserable in the present life?" (W.II.94) or, "the fallacy [of the orthodox argument] lay in the immense concession that the bad are successful; that justice is not done now" (W.II.95) can arrest one's curiosity. Both remarks awaken attention by their literary manners—what can Emerson mean to talk like this? In the first sentence we are obliged to adjust ourselves to the obvious fact that Emerson is not in the least astonished to hear "the preacher say that the good are miserable"; what else does one expect an orthodox preacher to say? To hear Emerson's new meaning we have to redefine the word "good" to mean not the truly virtuous, who are, he implies, happy in their virtue, but the pseudo-virtuous, the mere obeyers of rules or even the hypocrites. The self-righteous are indeed miserable in the present life, for they wish to be good only for ulterior motives. A truly good person is not miserable at all, but joyful; misery is by itself evidence that something is wrong inside, not merely outside. The self-righteous are unable to feel the reality of virtue. They see it as a rule exterior to themselves to which they must conform; and therefore they feel that their conformity is a bargain requiring payment on the part of society, or God, or their conscience, or whoever else they have in mind as the person with whom they arrange their moral commerce. The preacher, then, fails to understand what is really meant by his own master word, "good." "He meant," Emerson's tongue-in-cheek tone implies, "just what you, dear reader, have figured out; but he didn't know what he was saying. I know what *I* mean by 'good,' but I don't have to say it outright; I can let him say it indirectly, by an unconscious irony, in spite of himself." Now the sentence becomes comprehensible, and indeed illuminating, though at the cost of making the truly good a rare species. How many can clear their consciences of being falsely conscientious?

Something similar happens in the second of these two sentences, "the fallacy lay in the immense concession that the bad are successful." Evidently "successful" is the word to be redefined, and, when it is, one comes out with the observation that doing something one knows is bad makes one suffer a private punishment that is exactly equivalent to the wrong done. This punishment may be no more than a temporary deterioration in morale, an uneasiness that saps efficiency in all matters related to the context in which the wrong was done until conscience feels a balance has been struck. It may be more obviously painful— there are forms of "success" the most hardened character might feel some disillusion about. The actor of evil, in other words, suffers a compensatory loss or injury so long as and to the degree that he responds, however unconsciously, to his own crime. This does seem true to our moral experience.

But what about the doer of evil who is not aware in any way that he has behaved badly? A well-brought-up New Englander could be depended on to have an oversupply of scruple; such a man could not help but punish himself for any wrong he did. But how could the man without a conscience, or with a limited one, suffer a punishment of this interior sort? Of course one could say that the possession of such a bad character was itself a complete punishment. But is the psychopath really punished by being a psychopath? The psychopath himself would not think so, nor would his victim. Emerson's answer would be, the psychopath is deceived; he is a very partial self, who lacks an essential faculty and, though he does not feel his incapacity, *we* know that his Soul is not complete.

The presence of the victim is another factor hard to assimilate to the theory of compensation. He who suffers evil can scarcely ever be said to get an equivalent in return—unless we think of his suffering as the consequence of some previous act of evil of his own. Common sense would indeed say that suffering tends to breed additional evil, that the character of victims is more often deteriorated than improved by their sufferings. Here too Emerson would presumably reply that a victim who allowed suffering to deteriorate his character was failing to use the resources of the Soul, and that weakness would be, ultimately, *his* responsibility.

Another difficulty in making sense out of the theory of compensation follows from the instinctive tendency to think that reward and punishment should bear a specific, direct, and reasonably immediate relation to the acts they compensate. Unless there is a visible *quid pro quo,* a reciprocity of performance and consequence, one does not feel that justice, in the primitive sense of the word, is taking place. Very little experience suffices to show that justice in this sense is not done. Emerson would agree. He wants to make the word "justice" mean a moral equivalent to the physical law which states that every action has an equal and opposite reaction; but he also reminds his reader that the reaction, in the moral context, need not take place right away, or in the dimension of life where you are on the lookout for it. The other half of the event will show up, he is saying, in odd ways and at odd times, and from a sufficient distance an informed eye could see the complementarity of the parts, even though the victim and bystanders may see only undeserved bad or good luck.

In all this Emerson is anxious to demoralize "morality." He wishes to turn reactions into comprehensions, guilt and complacency into watchful curiosity, prejudice and expectation into alertness of mind, inhibition into choice. There is something adventurous in the endeavor.[16] An important truth is adumbrated —but the doctrine of compensation is perhaps not a sufficiently explicit way of formulating it. One ends up, even when one thinks one sees along the Emersonian oblique, with a truth that turns as one regards it into truisms: "things happen," or "feelings have consequences." How far does this doctrine help one to make

judgments or solace somebody stung by any of the thousand effects of life? It may in those cases where the somebody in question has not exhausted his power to take responsibility for his
existence. For him the Emersonian "compensation" contains
a saving sting of truth. To learn that every man sooner or later
profits or suffers from what he does can be a real discovery when
the connection is made in specific instances. Consciousness, when
it advances, when it becomes itself, is always a true good.

A man does not see that as he eats, so he thinks; as he deals, so he is, and
so he appears; he does not see that his son is the son of his thoughts and of
his actions; that fortunes are not exceptions but fruits; that relation and
connection are not somewhere and sometimes, but everywhere and always;
no miscellany, no exemption, no anomaly,—but method, and an even web;
and what comes out, that was put in. As we are, so we do; and as we do,
so is it done to us; we are the builders of our fortunes. (W.VI.220-221)

The repetition, the inability of the language to get up the flying rhythm intended, suggests that the expression here is still
unclear—though what the passage would say if it *were* clear
could be a useful truth. As the language approaches explicitness,
though, paradox increases; the more succinct Emerson's expression of what he means, the less meaning his words seem to bear:
"Every secret is told, every crime is punished, every virtue rewarded, every wrong redressed, in silence and certainty" (W.II.-
102). An effort to redefine the key words here so as to read out
a new and reasonable meaning is hard to make; the words
crumble and lose their ordinary sense, but acquire no others.
If *every* wrong is redressed, does not the word "wrong" or "re-
dress" lose so much of its meaning that close to nothing is said?
One seems to be counseled to cease thinking in terms of reward
and punishment, which may be wise advice; but it is hard to
accept it if the advice itself is still couched within these terms.

The best way to rescue the truth in Compensation is to bear
in mind the basic conception of the active Soul. Emerson's most
constant moral objection is to that species of conventional morality which expects a material compensation for outwardly virtuous
behavior. Emerson wants to remind us that the wish for material
advantages, or the power to enjoy them, engages only a portion
of the Soul. Real virtue is not the possession of such things, he
would say, but the action of faculties higher than those employed

in such desiring and having, or in chaffering about things that may be desired or had. Virtue is not a bargain, or a self-pitying expectation, but a positive deed. And such a deed, like all other positive acts of the Soul, is its own reward. On an organic scale, the evil action is simply one that fails to engage much of the Soul, and the punishment suffered is a diminishment of one's native power to act relevantly in the world. To do ill is to release traits that poison the life of the doer and lessen the security of his grasp on reality. To do well enlarges life, by increasing the energies and responses that may be enjoyed. "There is no penalty to virtue; no penalty to wisdom; they are proper additions of being. In a virtuous action I properly *am;* in a virtuous act I add to the world" (W.II.122). By throwing the attention back upon the quality of the subject's activity, questions of objective reward and deprivation become trivial materialism. Emerson is interested in psychology, not commerce: "All the good of nature is the soul's, and may be had if paid for in nature's lawful coin, that is, by labor which the heart and the head allow" (W.II.122-123).

THE WHOLE SOUL

By NOW we have reviewed in schematic sequence all the distinguishable dimensions of the Soul, organic, aesthetic, practical, intellectual, and moral, arranging them very much in the way Emerson himself ordered them in *Nature*. One might in fact, following that essay, take Emerson's own term "discipline" as a general name for the "use" of each of these agencies, to remind us that each has its final relevance as a functioning part of a putative whole experience made up at once of enjoying, handling, knowing, confronting, judging, doing. For (substituting the word "Soul" for "mind") "how can we speak of the action of the mind under any divisions, as of its knowledge, of its ethics, of its works, and so forth, since it melts will into perception, knowledge into act?" (W.II.325). Still, it was usually easier for Emerson to

Dimension	Faculty	Object	Office	Heroes
moral	moral sentiment, conscience, will, character	the good	prophet, seer, preacher, reformer, friend, hero, gentleman	Christ, Washington, Lovejoy, Swedenborg, [Emerson]
intellectual	mind, genius, intellect, reason	the true	scholar, naturalist, historian	Plato, Newton
aesthetic	imagination	beauty	poet, orator, writer, artist	Shakespeare, Raphael, Michelangelo, Goethe, "Saadi"
practical	talent	skill	farmer, sailor, businessman	Napoleon, Columbus, Webster
organic	instinct, sensibility	pleasure	lover	

THE SOUL

express one or another aspect of man's disassociated sensibility at a time, while suggesting, by the way he defined each, those other ranges of life that in an ideal self would not have to be omitted. In practice, as Emerson like all other romantics painfully knew, the whole Soul rarely has a chance to come into entire and authentic action, even linguistic action: "a man," any man, is most often found to be acting "not from one nature, but from many shifting fears and short motives; it is as if he were ten or twenty less men than himself, acting at discord with one another, so that the result of most lives is zero" (W.X.224).

The definable "faculties," then, are always diminished versions of themselves. Thus fancy is the metaphor-making power abstracted from its natural relation to the moral sentiment, the active presence of which would turn it into live imagination. Similarly, the understanding is intellect divorced from the vital sensibility that would transmute it to reason. An infrequently consulted essay on "The Comic" is serviceable for its unexpectedly interesting exploration of the way in which ludicrous occasions involuntarily expose the human gap between the partial appearance and whole ideal reality. We laugh, says Emerson, when we see somebody who covers his vacuity with a mask that

Typical Action	Consummation	Product	Typical Essays
affirmation, resistance, self-reliance, probity	enactment of law	convention, church, institution	Divinity School Address, Self-Reliance, Man the Reformer, The Transcendentalist, Compensation, Heroism, Character, Manners, Politics, Swedenborg
classification, explanation, insight	perception of law	system, formula, fact	The American Scholar, Literary Ethics, The Method of Nature, History, Intellect, Education, Plato
creation, expression	harmony	work of art	Art, The Poet, Shakespeare, Goethe
work, concentration	efficiency	property, "results"	English Traits, Wealth, Napoleon
enjoyment	satisfaction	death, temperament, illusion	Experience, Race, Fate, Power, Beauty, Illusions, War

counterfeits the absent power. Man is entitled to the whole action of the Soul; but he is perpetually inclined to lapse into some partial action, which to maintain social credit he calls entire. When the cheat is discovered, our sympathies find the inadequacy painful; but the intellect finds it ridiculous. Thus Emerson is able to borrow the classical doctrine, that comedy is a defense of man's proper being against those who betray it, and to apply this traditional technique to his own romantic ends.

The entire public work of Emerson, therefore, may be organized in one's mind as a display of the whole Soul in its several distinguishable manifestations—that is, as *Nature* writ large. The early essays tend to be named either after abstract representatives of the Soul in some one of its potentially creative contexts of action ("The Poet," "The American Scholar," "Self-Reliance"), or after the context itself ("Prudence," "Heroism," "Politics"). No one essay, though, is exclusively devoted to its chief representative protagonist or context. Within any one context, the entire subjectivity, or man with reference to that particular context, may appear as a faculty ("The Moral Sentiment"), an abstract figure ("The Preacher"), or the typical hero of some Plutarchian anecdote (Luther, Father Taylor). In the first case, the necessary inwardness of the Soul, and its availability to all, is emphasized; in the second, we are implicitly reminded of the essential idea that the human possibility in question appears in life as a generalized norm; in the third, the practicability of psychic action is established by the presence of history of its personal representatives. What is said in particular of the Poet is true in some way of every hero, abstract and concrete: he "stands among partial men for the complete man, and apprises us not of his wealth, but of the common wealth" (W.-III.5). Such a way of organizing Emerson's major statement can be put in the form of a chart.

The whole Soul is often better imagined as a criterion for judgment than a description of a possible protagonist. It can never be seen in its entirety except through instances that symbolically demonstrate the style of the whole in one or another partial context. What we face in actual life are at best its "representatives." Mediating among these is Emerson's familiar strategy of polarity, or the dialectic, his way of enforcing upon the reader a proper respect for the manifold inclusiveness of the Soul's authentic action. "Polarity" allows Emerson to stress first one aspect of the Soul and then another, the pair appearing, to the understanding, mutually opposite but, to the reason, complementary parts of a whole. Thus his essays are constructed, and thus essay is related to essay in each *Series*. In the implied equilibrium of a mind prepared to acknowledge simultaneously the opportunities of experience and thought, matter and spirit, prudence and heroism, conservative and transcendentalist, law and instinct, society and solitude, conscience and intellect, Yankee and mystic, Emerson adumbrates at the level of ordinary human possibility the unfulfilled grandeur of the totally active Soul.

At this point of appreciative balance, in later life, Emerson is inclined personally to remain; "Montaigne," or the skeptic, is the name of such a position in literary history and prototypical abstraction respectively. In his earlier phase, especially at times of moral optimism and imaginative "saliency," Emerson presents an "ascent" from one level of the Soul to the next. The full Soul comes into being when the line of experience spirals up from the instincts into the intellect and the moral consciousness. This ascent is what the early Emerson means by the term "culture."[17]

Each turn of the developmental helix fits the circle below by virtue of that correspondence by which events in one dimension parallel and illustrate events in another. When this parallelism is moved into language, we have metaphor: the actions of one faculty of the Soul prove their authenticity by being described in terms of another.

The remainder of this part of my book, therefore, is devoted to Emerson's efforts to show the relations among the faculties of the Soul, one to the other, and to the individual self.

THE VITAL MIND

HIERARCHICAL ascent is the chief means Emerson uses to demonstrate such relations among faculties. A striking general instance appears in his continual attempt to link intellect with the organic faculty. We have already observed some examples. He knows that too exclusive a commitment to the intellectual mode by itself can be a disguise for pride, which interferes with precisely that truth the mind is in search of. Victimized unconsciously by mere selfhood, the truths that isolated intellect can perceive will seem opposed to the other goods of the Soul. Consciousness will act in fatal separation from the very nature that belongs to it. "Each and All" is a good parable of such a state of affairs. Toward the close of that poem an assertive speaker claims

> I covet truth;
> Beauty is unripe childhood's cheat;
> I leave it behind with games of youth

But the false independence of this speaker is rebuked immediately by the details of the scene around him:

> The ground-pine curled its pretty wreath,
> Running over the club-moss burrs;
> I inhaled the violet's breath;
> Around me stood the oaks and firs; (W.IX.5-6)

Organically interrelated, each detail of the environing scene separately and together is witness to the "beauty" that the ar-

rogant intellect would repudiate. The speaker then "yields" himself to the "perfect whole." His sensuous experience of organic
beauty dissolves his solitary partiality, and at the same time
satisfies the legitimate demands of the mind. For the proper goal
of intellectual effort, the poem concludes, is precisely a perception
of that unity which the speaker learns to let himself enjoy
through a more primitive faculty of the Soul. The mind is the
Soul's true agent when it converts to intellectual truth the instinctive experience of organic relatedness.

In the prose this important connection between aesthetic and
intellectual experience is entrusted especially to metaphor. By
persuasive references to the vital texture of organic life, the
propensity of solitary mind to track its "violent railroads of
generalization" (W.X.226) is imaginatively brought back into
healthy relation with nature. The prevalence of this linguistic
device has been pointed out by R. P. Adams, who weighs the
effect of images drawn from organic life upon the different varieties of intellectual action.[18] His main piece of evidence is the
famous passage in "The American Scholar":

Nature hastens to render account of herself to the mind. Classification
begins. To the young mind every thing is individual, stands by itself. By
and by, it finds how to join two things and see in them one nature; then
three, then three thousand; and so, tyrannized over by its own unifying
instinct, it goes on tying things together, diminishing anomalies, discovering
roots running under ground whereby contrary and remote things cohere
and flower out from one stem. (W.I.85)

The Soul here manifests itself as the intellect, which classifies
the objects of the universe by comparing one to another and
generalizing in the shape of some law the relations it perceives.
Thus "nature," in this context the idea of an objective universe,
is built up into an imaginative structure of explanation. The
passage continues by dwelling upon the degree to which this act
of explanation defines both the outer world and the mind that
knows it, so that the "law" arrived at is seen simultaneously to
be true of the world and a creation of the faculty which makes
that world intelligible. Then we get: "But what is classification
but the perceiving that these objects are not chaotic, and are not
foreign, but have a law which is also a law of the human mind?
The astronomer discovers that geometry, a pure abstraction of

the human mind, is the measure of planetary motion" (W.I.85-86). So far Emerson is describing the act of intellect in a familiar way.

But the language of the first fragment I have quoted here is interesting beyond its power to convey a thought about the way the intellect works. As Adams has pointed out, this language is richly informed by an organic metaphor. The mind appears in this account of its behavior as tyrannized over by an instinct that forces it to act like an active vegetable, a vine, which in turn coalesces with the roots and stem it "discovers," so that the known universe and the faculty which knows it acquire a joint new identity as a single living creature. The mind thus becomes dangerously vital. The reverse happens too; the power of life becomes, by a reciprocal effect of the same metaphor, something that grows or develops toward consciousness. Intellectual awareness, the metaphor implies, should risk coincidence with the force of life itself.

Emerson's language, then, links two aspects of the Soul, mental subjectivity and vital subjectivity. It is a powerful combination. We cannot trust the mind, the general implication would run, when it does not flower out of the instinctive vitality of the living organism. Like all romantic thinkers, Emerson would affirm that when you separate out the mind you have merely the understanding, whose actions are death. What is particularly interesting, though, is that the link, the association of the two agencies of the Soul, is accomplished *through* language—in this case, through metaphor. The words are literally "loaded with life" (W.I.95); "in his every syllable / Lurketh Nature veritable" (W.IX.134). And we have no trouble, once we have identified this particular use of the metaphor, in finding it elsewhere in similar contexts.

Some useful consequences follow from the use of an organic nexus as a typical image for proper intellectual action. The organic image illustrates more "naturally" than the act of Linnean classification the informing relation of the active mind to the parts of experience that it organizes. It does not imply, as the idea of a classification chart does, a notion of an abrupt discontinuity between one fact and another, or between all the facts and the law that generalizes them. More positively, the organic metaphor connotes concreteness and exteriority; a classification may be frivolous or pedantic, but an organism must be independently alive and real. Most important, the metaphor redefines the intellectual subject of action as identical with the spirit of life itself: radical, unconscious, and inalienably present. The effect is in sharp contrast to the rationalistic implications left behind by purely scientific examples. Finally, as Adams observes, the idea of organism could help Emerson to see unity even in extreme particularity. The organic image allowed him to be confident that the slightest fragments of truth he did see would form a whole with others he did not see.

In many places we can pick up Emerson's endeavor to transfer the vitality of the Soul in its organic manifestation to the characteristic actions of the Soul as intellect. Thereby he ensures that the transmutation of experience into thought, of circumstance into consciousness, will preserve, at least in our imaginable idea of that ascent, the principle of life. Each event, as it becomes an object of contemplation, will still be a "ripe fruit" (W.I.96), the product of a continuous natural process. Metaphors drawn from nature for the typical products of the intellectual life are one literary guarantee of this continuity. Another is the identification, within the process of intellection itself, of a "great principle of Undulation" (W.I.98) in accordance with which life and thought alternate rhythmically within the experience of each man who enjoys both. "The mind now thinks, now acts, and each fit reproduces the other" (W.I.99).

Still another mode of registering a proper organic response is exhibited by Emerson's continuous reminders to himself and to us that thinking is never genuine unless it emerges spontaneously from the whole heart of the experiencer. It is one of his objections to the rigorous intellectual mechanisms of such men as Swedenborg and Cousin that they miss that derivation from life which gives ideas their claim to truth. "Truth will not be compelled in any mechanical manner. But the first observation you make, in the sincere act of your nature" (W.I.171) will open genuine views. The use of "sincere" here enables Emerson to establish additional connections between the organic instinct and the virtues of honesty, directness, and simplicity—virtues held in common by the mind and the moral sentiment. Think in the sincere act of your nature, and there will come the "profound thought" that lifts Olympus, which in its turn "warps and shrinks away" (W.I.172) upon the emergence of a new thought of the same kind. This is intellectual growth. "The power of mind is not mortification, but life" (W.I.194).

No one is better than Emerson at catching and expressing the quasi-physical agility of the free mind. For insight, he says, one needs "a readiness, open eyes and ears, and free hands" (W.XII. 412). He is wonderfully sensitive to the perennial opportuneness of life, on the pulse of which depend the dangers and honors of high consciousness. "Knowing" is not something that happens when a switch is turned on at administrative moments; the real and vital world is "arrived at by untaught sallies of the spirit, by a continual self-recovery, and by entire humility" (W.I.66). The Soul, for Emerson, has always a lively and loving style. He knows intuitively the limits and feel of knowledge, the inevitable bafflements, the blur and grace, far better than such latter-day thinkers as Henry Adams and Percy Bridgman. He can feel these conditions as a whole, directly, humorously—not as a "technique" to be used.

Emerson's tact is just as sharp when he is interested in nature itself. As the Soul is always vital, so nature is perpetually "unattempted" (W.I.168). Nature escapes into distances ahead or slips aside; the "goddess . . . coquettes with us, hides herself in coolness and generalities; directly confronted, nature has only the thickness of a shingle or a slate" (J.VI.490-491).

One resource, he says, is to relax the strained attention and remain voluntarily in that state of mind in which the message of the tree and the river is not yet "made out"; they are nonetheless "by no means unimpressive. I wait for them, I enjoy them before they yet speak" (W.XII.5). To go beyond the apparent tree and river, actually to know, can be to lose something valuable in the more closely organic experience of frustration: "Will these fields stretch so immovably wide, these leaves hang so individually considerable" (W.II.303), once we have risen to the discovery of the laws which explain them? It is one of Emerson's best traits to feel acutely what one fails to know by only knowing, what a man cannot know when he becomes overconscious of how he knows.

Yet Emerson believes, of course, in going on. The Soul should "be the only fact" (W.II.104). Nature as something forever independent of explanation would be anomalous, however habitually present, and the mind endeavors to bring it in if only to recognize itself. For if nature exists objectively in the act of contemplating it, the mind exists subjectively as a function of the facts it has seen and understood. We "study the mind in nature" (W.I.197) because it is not experiencable in any other way. One builds one's own consciousness, and that of the race; that of God (if one likes to use the name) is built only by understanding what is there to be understood in the midst of the experience through which one lives.

THE INSTINCTIVE CONSCIENCE

THE relation between the Soul as moral sentiment and the Soul as organic faculty is as important to Emerson as that between the latter and the intellect. But it presents him with a problem, and his solution to it is itself problematic. For he wants to be able to say not merely that the conscience is a part of the subject of action (a position that we have seen involves its own theoretical difficulties), but also that this interior agency is or ought to be bound up with the instinctive life of the individual within whose experience it functions. For him the sense of true virtue grows out of the sense of life and is as "natural" as that: "For the origin of all reform is in that mysterious fountain of the moral sentiment in man, which, amidst the natural, ever contains the supernatural for men. That is new and creative. That is alive. That alone can make a man other than he is. Here or nowhere resides unbounded energy, unbounded power" (W.I.272).

Such expressions might be found wherever the moral faculty is discussed. Yet such an effort to link the moral and organic dimensions contains within itself a persistent practical contradiction. Thus in the poem "Grace" we find Emerson congratulating himself on the power of his Calvinistic moral inheritance to check his bodily impulses; but "Self-Reliance" is full of appeals to break through just such chains. The poem "Give All to

Love" advocates abandonment for three stanzas and reserve for three more. The conflict, or "polarity," appears everywhere one looks: he is deeply puritanical about matters of diet and sensuality whenever they come before his attention, yet at the same time he is entirely open to the physical luxury of a solitary walk in the woods. In one context, the moral law appears in its traditional way as a check upon the appetites of organic man. In the other, the same law is felt to spring from and be entirely congruous with the freely operating instincts. We saw earlier how beauty could be reconciled with intellect. Emerson wished to achieve a similar connection between beauty and the good, but for the heir of Puritanism this could not always be easy. The poem on "Beauty," like the references in the essays to the same aesthetic quality, contains mixed attitudes:

> I drank at thy fountain
> False waters of thirst;
> Thou intimate stranger,
> Thou latest and first! (W.IX.87)

We may guess that it was the latent erotic undertone in the experience of beauty (obvious enough in these lines) that made Emerson chary of embracing it when its possible connections with the conscience were bruited, though in other connections he could be sure he was naturally its devoted lover.

Inconsistency, of course, is not always a contradiction; given the right circumstances, it can be doubleness or irony or surprise. This particular inconsistency becomes something close to a great rhetorical success at one famous moment. The "Divinity School Address" is the *locus classicus* for the link between organic responses and the moral sentiment, and the opening paragraphs of the essay are well worth looking at in some detail to see what the polarity between Emerson the liberator and Emerson the conservative can become when the topic and the occasion set the electricity flowing.

The opening paragraphs, to start with, exhibit a sort of concentration of the argument of "Nature." The different agencies of the Soul are laid out in hierarchical order, starting from the physical sensibility and moving up through the practical faculty to the intellect and thence to the "sentiment of virtue." We have the whole spectrum of the Soul, except perhaps that portion of it occupied by the convention-defying self. The social context of the address, if not the notions expressed, amply supplies this omission. For a brief exhibition of what the Soul is to the early Emerson, one could not go to a better pair of pages. Here is half of the first paragraph:

In this refulgent summer, it has been a luxury to draw the breath of life. The grass grows, the buds burst, the meadow is spotted with fire and gold in the tint of flowers. The air is full of birds, and sweet with the breath of the pine, the balm-of-Gilead, and the new hay. Night brings no gloom to the heart with its welcome shade. Through the transparent darkness the stars pour their almost spiritual rays. Man under them seems a young child, and his huge globe a toy. The cool night bathes the world as with a river, and prepares his eyes again for the crimson dawn. The mystery of nature was never yet displayed more happily. The corn and the wine have been freely dealt to all creatures, and the never-broken silence with which the old bounty goes forward has not yielded yet one word of explanation. One is constrained to respect the perfection of this world in which our senses converse. (W.I.119)

Taken by itself, this is perhaps over-rich, though I think the excess has a special point, given the dramatic situation. "Refulgent," in that first sentence, is unusually aureate, even for Emerson's most lavish mood. The kind of experience described consists of the simplest organic responses: breathing, growing, bursting, bathing, drinking. The language makes all these more sensual than sensuous. No voluptuary could more unreservedly recommend the life of the senses.

Emerson put this luxurious scene together with some care; he was inspired in part by the unusual quality of the summer of 1838, which had seemed strikingly pleasant after the damp and chilly spring of that year. But he had also worked back while composing this paragraph to a note of March 1836, from which in turn he recovered something written in June 1835, praising the luxury of that earlier season. He meant, then, to make his picture of the physical operation of the Soul as lush as he could. The immediate rhetorical motive, evidently enough, is shock: an address to a small group of graduating divinity students is not supposed to begin by an appeal to the sensual man. Presumably he wished to imply an argument through the substitution: the Soul, his words here say for him, is to start with the physical power of life, the power to be erotically pleased within an environment that generously nourishes every living being. This presentation is made with entire blandness, as if Emerson did not in the least know what he was saying—until we get to the climax, the final sentence of the passage just quoted. "One is constrained to respect the perfection of this world in which our senses converse." *Constrained to respect* is the drily humorous understatement he needs to bring himself and his audience back to dramatic reality.

The new tongue-in-cheek tone introduced by the phrase redefines the picture he has just painted; it was done, as if in a conjuring trick, with words. After all, the senses do not literally "converse" with nature—they merely enjoy it, so long as it is enjoyable; conversation is exchanged through other faculties. A clerical New Englander tips his hat. The speaker does not intend to fool himself or the more fanciful among his audience about the exact terms upon which he and the summer season communicate.

The skeptical tone obvious here is already present in the sentence immediately preceding: "The never-broken silence with which the old bounty goes forward has not yielded yet one word of explanation." One can hear how that patronizing "old" puts him at a certain distance from lavish nature: an affectionate distance, but real. After this dry shift of tone, then, Emerson returns to fullness of praise:

How wide; how rich; what invitation from every property it gives to every faculty of man! In its fruitful soils; in its navigable sea; in its mountains of metal and stone; in its forests of all woods; in its animals; in its chemical ingredients; in the powers and path of light, heat, attraction and life, it is well worth the pith and heart of great men to subdue and enjoy it. The planters, the mechanics, the inventers, the astronomers, the builders of cities, and the captains, history delights to honor. (W.I.119-120)

This ends the first paragraph with an easy catalogue, following the pattern of *Nature*. This part of it gives room for us to imagine the practical response to nature, nature as "commodity," just as the beginning of the paragraph shows nature as beauty. It is the privilege of the man of power to "subdue and enjoy" the richly sensuous world he has described and to govern the "powers and path" of heat and life.

Once again the actual audience and Emerson himself, none of them practical men of power, are ironically placed. And the opening of the second paragraph makes a further turn that confirms the earlier shift of voice, spelling out the promise made in the middle of the first paragraph by tone alone: "But when the mind opens and reveals the laws which traverse the universe and make things what they are, then shrinks the great world at once into a mere illustration and fable of this mind" (W.I.120). Is that "mere" a little ungrateful? Yet he has just made good what he speaks of; the rich description has in fact been an illustration of his own mental fancifulness. And if the whole of actual nature, not merely the nature constructed out of lush images, but the silent inwardness and outwardness for which the lavish words are an old-fashioned flourish of respect, is simply an "illustration and fable" for some mind for which he, as an artist in words, stands here as a speaking representative, then so much the more is that mind dignified. Let the imagination open, let it reveal within itself the laws that govern the reality of the world without—then the mind has indeed put a lever under the whole of organic experience.

The remainder of this second paragraph does further justice to the Soul as intellect and ends with another wry drop in tone: "These works of thought have been the entertainments of the human spirit in all ages." *Entertainments,* once more, is a tonal joke; it is only from the point of view that sees all the actions of the Soul together that the admirable work of the mind can properly seem a mere entertainment. After all, Emerson is a serious scholar; and so, again, are his hearers.

Then comes the climax, of which the remainder of the address is a development—the Soul as moral sentiment is evoked:

A more secret, sweet, and overpowering beauty appears to man, when his heart and mind open to the sentiment of virtue. Then he is instructed in what is above him. He learns that his being is without bound; that to the good, to the perfect, he is born, low as he now lies in evil and weakness. That which he venerates is still his own, though he has not realized it yet. *He ought.* He knows the sense of that grand word, though his analysis fails to render account of it. When in innocency or when by intellectual perception he attains to say,—"I love the Right; Truth is beautiful within and without for evermore. Virtue, I am thine; save me; use me; thee will I serve, day and night, in great, in small, that I may be not virtuous, but virtue;"—then is the end of the creation answered, and God is well pleased. (W.I.120-121)

The language here is deliberately connected to the previous remarks about the intellectual action of the Soul, and the organic action earlier. Here too the subject of action is conceived of as "opening" itself to floods of nourishment from without. The faculty now in question is presented as innate, a right to which man is "born." "That which he venerates is still his own, though he has not realized it yet. *He ought.*" It is, of course, "realize" that gets redefined in this sentence, and the pun functions as it has elsewhere, imparting an argument: to venerate is to experience an appreciation for some virtue that must be implicit in the venerator. If this admired virtue is then made actual in the affairs of life, the practice of it will feel like a development of an inborn readiness. Let a man understand the commitments his admirations imply, the sentence says, and he is halfway to the freedom he needs to bring his judgments into effective action within his moral experience. And that freedom will seem a natural development from the experiences of the sensuous and intellectual man.

This sort of connection between the organic and the moral is revolutionary, like all ethical appeals to vital experience—as revolutionary as Blake, for instance, though Emerson might have been as uneasy at the comparison as some members of his audience were shocked by him.[19] All romantic radicals have a basic strategy in common. They assume that the way the organism acts in its natural environment is continuous with the way the mind should act when it comprehends nature and the way the self should act when it engages with society. The operations of the biological subject, then, provide the sanction for all authentic actions. Which biological operations seem most crucial is relatively less important, though the choice obviously determines the tenor of a man's thought. For Lawrence the key organic act is sexual love; the social resonances of this, achieved and denied, form the moral topic of his novels. For Blake the important part of the organic spectrum seems to be the sensation of desire. For Wordsworth the key action is probably bodily movement through a living scene. For Emerson, as we have seen, this last is significant, but probably less typical in the end than the most primitive organic action of all, the absorption of the scene by breathing or "drinking it in." But all these thinkers share the instinct, too primordial to be called a belief, that the higher actions which reveal the Soul to the world ring true and free only when they work coincidentally in their several contexts with the key motions of organic life.

This conviction puts all romantics in automatic conflict with the social order, which always assumes that organic actions are or should be governed by some set of exterior social norms, and that these norms maintain themselves in ceaseless opposition to the impulses of the natural organism. "Traditional" morality, that is, all socialized morality, must in the nature of the case assume that man's animal nature is civilized against its will. Hence when Emerson starts his speech with a voluptuous image of sensuous pleasure (modest as this species of luxury may seem), the issue is powerfully if covertly joined. The actions of the Soul, he is saying, are essentially one: "in the game of human life, love, fear, justice, appetite, man, and God, interact" (W.I. 121). If this was what "Uriel" had to say, the "stern old war-gods" were right to be shocked.

SELF-RELIANCE

THE connection between morality and organic experience can only take place, according to Emerson, within specific acts of individual persons. The effort to establish the connection rhetorically is bound up with Emerson's urgent stress on the extreme value of the private self; for all worthy combats between the individual and "society" have their sanction in the connection only individuals can make between an ethical injunction and an immediate instinct. The world's imperatives always confront us as naked moral demands. Our resource against them is, he says, so much of a higher norm as we can connect with the principle of life. The argument of "Self-Reliance," where this aspect of the Emersonian warfare comes most acutely to a head, is not only the indispensability of all the Soul's faculties, but the impossibility of engaging their harmonious action outside the sphere of oneself as a particular individual. Specialized subjects of action may be separately conceived as abstract entities, but no coincidence of energies is imaginable outside personal hearts. Only individuals, as Emerson said to explain his pursuit of the extraordinary Englishmen he looked up on his first visit to Europe, "can give an inside to the world" (W.V.4). And inside each admired individual in turn is always the Soul of their admirer. "Nothing is at last sacred but the integrity of your own mind" (W.II.50) is a familiar (if powerfully ambiguous) Emersonian truism. It can be true so far as the "nature" on which one is urged to rely —the spontaneous motions from within, unpredictable and unselfconscious—is uniquely personal. The resistant factors, correspondingly, are social, exterior, "dead," mere interferences with the private "sense of being." "There will be an agreement in whatever variety of actions, so they be each honest and natural in their hour" (W.II.58-59). One's own instinct is thereby made the source of moral independence. "When you have life in yourself" (W.II.68), count yourself free.

It is this emphasis on the natural individuality that gives the early essays their revolutionary undertone. "Your local unregenerate individuality may after all manifest the Universal Spirit" is the constant secret promise. The entire Soul-Nature relation can only become *emotionally* interesting when Soul seems to mean Self and Self means Me. We cannot take the impersonality of spirit seriously until it becomes a personal event.

In his liveliest moments Emerson is fully aware of this paradox, not to say pleased with it. "What each does" in the common realm of impersonal action is what he as a private party can do, what is "proper to him" (W.VI.40). Private life ripens truths that cannot have meaning when they are presented from without in generalized or conventional form. When the moment of insight arrives within the economy of the individual self, a truth of the Soul will be spoken in a local dialect. A neat resolution of the potential conflict between Soul and Self comes in a journal entry mediating upon the jump of heart with which we see in another's work a resemblance to something genuine in our own past that we neglected to report to ourselves, and so lost the value of. The other person's noticing then stands as a lesson to us of the impersonal value of our personal lives:

It admonishes us instantly of the worth of the present moment. It apprises us of our wealth, for if that hour & object can be so valuable, why not every hour & event in our life if passed through the same process I learn (such is the inherent dignity of all intellectual activity) that I am a being of more worth than I knew & all my acts are enhanced in value The deepest pleasure comes I think from the occult belief that an unknown meaning & consequence work in the common every day facts & as this panoramic or pictorial beauty can arise from it, so can a solid wisdom when the Idea shall be seen as such which binds these gay shadows together. (J.IV.100)

Any meaning or beauty that is found must ultimately be impersonal, for no merely private sense for words like "meaning" and "beauty" is imaginable for Emerson or for anybody else: all experience dominated by such words is objective. Yet the shadows are gay because of the private sense of life. The almost truculent pleasure in the opportunities offered by his own identity is more characteristic of Thoreau or Whitman than of Emerson, but in the master as well as in the disciples the note is struck everywhere now and again, and can be heard for pages together in essays like "Self-Reliance," "Few and mean as my gifts may be, I actually am, and do not need for my own assurance or the assurance of my fellows any secondary testimony" (W.II.53).

Better evidence still of his quick courtesy to the ongoing course of his experience as an individual self occurs in a journal entry, reproduced here in Emerson's own hand (from Journal TU, pp. 284-285). In October 1849 he wrote, under the heading "Symbolism," the following passage.

The phrase "& believing that," added afterwards so as to intervene between the already written "for me" and "& hints," is perhaps but one instance of second thoughts. These are more regularly recorded in a second draft composed in December of the same year (Journal AZ, p. 151), which is the same up to the word "Fatebook," whence it continues, incorporating the changes smoothly: "is Fatebook enough for me; believing that hints & telegraphic signals are arriving to me, every moment, out of the interior eternity."

Emerson's rhetorical care was worthwhile, for the result (it may be found in a cleaned-up version in J.VIII.63-64) is a central and one of the most attractive renderings of the Emersonian venture. The lively beginning, "What I want to know is," imitates an assertive practical man, the kind of man who takes for granted that his private Mondays and Tuesdays are far too large, diffuse, actual, and banal to be worth trying to clarify and articulate. The quieter voice that takes up after the opening phrase is a part of the answer to such an attitude; what, it asks, about all those bothers, anxieties, flashes of fear or fantasy that interrupt the boring course of the working day? The socialized man disbelieves in them; or if he is neurotic enough to be unable to ignore them, he wishes they would go away. But they do not go away; they continue, "hints and telegraphic signals" that must be read if health is ever to be recovered. Health, indeed, *is* the act of fully and committedly reading them.

Within the most private experience, then, is found a man's true "subject." Let him therefore employ "just observation not in odd moments but in sane moments" (J.V.314), to "choose among what he calls his experiences that which is really his experience, and record truth truly!" (J.V.516). It is one of the special honors due transcendentalism that it could turn a man back to those "own facts" in which the perception of vital truth might be latent. An explanation of a private experience must be a public statement, and the mind which finds it true and knows it to be true acts impersonally, for that mind may be shared by more than one person; but the case to be explained, the memories and purposes, must always be within the actual predicament of a concerned individual. No one can know the meaning of any life that is not first his own.

There are many chances to see how attentive and courteous
Emerson could be to the fragments of experience just below
meaning, how neatly he could register experiences of "dim
anticipation of profound meaning, as if, by and by, it would
appear to me why the apple-tree, why the meadow, why the
stump standing there, and what they signify to me" (J.V.76).
To be sure, the "why" here is dangerously susceptible to an
orthodox or Swedenborgian answer; but it is just possible that
an honest, "natural" one might be developed. We are closest to
the kind of approach that might bring such an answer when
Emerson thinks not of exemplary portions of visible nature, but
of the unaccountably brief and insignificant memories that stay
with him as signs of the state of feeling he was in, for instance,
on those visits to court his first wife: "The little piazza, a piece
of silk, the almshouse, the Davison girl" (J.III.437) stick with
him like fragments of an uninterpreted language.

The more immediate and concrete the experience, the more
trustworthy its moral interpretation will be. Everyone's life is at
least as available and particular as his neighbor's. If "the moral
influence of nature upon every individual is that amount of truth
which it illustrates to him" (W.I.42), much will depend on the
sharpness with which the random fragments of "it" are grasped
and understood, on an independent willingness to risk exploring
the random resources of the personal life. The stress on character that increases in the later essays may be read as a somewhat
conventionalized development of this ethos, for character is the
habitual knack of converting "all impediments into instruments,
all enemies into power" (W.VI.166).

One good final set of instances of Emerson's scrupulous regard
for the personal quality of the Soul's predicament appears in the
sensitive accounts of dreams that run through the journals and
appear now and again in the essays. There is always a fine sense
of the potential meaningfulness of dreams, of the quick way they
escape from the waking mind, of the curious sense a dreamer has
of not being fully himself, yet related to himself; of the odd discontinuity between the dreamer and the scene he seems to be in
the midst of, as if his environment did not fit him. Emerson
knows well that dreams hint of private truths: "They are the
maturation often of opinions not consciously carried out to statements, but whereof we already possessed the elements" (W.

X.8). They are protoverbal, that is, and therefore allied to the near-verbalized everywhere. When Emerson comes to write a dream down, it is often the *way* he has dreamt, or ceases to dream, that remains memorable:

There is an air as if the sender of the illusion had been heedless for a moment that the Reason had returned to its seat, & was startled into attention. Instantly there is a rush from some quarter to break up the drama into a chaos of parts, then of particles, then of ether, like smoke dissolving in a wind; it cannot be disintegrated fast enough or fine enough. If you could give the waked watchman the smallest fragment, he could reconstruct the whole; for the moment he is sure he can & will; but his attention is so divided on the disappearing parts, that he cannot grasp the least atomy, & the last fragment or film disappears before he could say, I have it. (J.X.314)

This is good observation, much harder than reporting the content of a dream. It is good enough for a reader to take as a clue to his own best way to read Emerson. For here is the necessary reminder that it is the awakening of awareness that intrigues, that "imports," as Emerson would say. The experience of coming out of a dream is a dramatic instance of a quickened sense of meaningful mystery in one's individual experience, detached enough from the pressures and habits of ordinary life to reward respectful inquiry—to prompt, indeed, new *self*-respect. Waking experience, like dreams, should alert the Soul to its practical opportunities and enlarge its hold on nature.

PART II

The Soul's Emphasis

THE LITERARY TEST

In *Psychoanalysis and the Unconscious* Lawrence has a good remark about the evil done by people who bully others through what he calls, scornfully, idealism: "the motivating of the great affective sources by means of ideas mentally derived."[1] Could Emerson be called an idealist in this malignant sense? Lawrence (who did not discuss Emerson in his *Studies in Classic American Literature*) would have taken it for granted that he was. And it is possible to find in some of Emerson's remarks about the intellect, and especially his remarks about the moral sentiment, a serious ambiguity about the way in which they are to be read. Should the use of organic language to describe these faculties be taken as testifying to a belief in a natural ascent from instinct toward the "higher" faculties, which would work freely only when their activity takes off from the satisfaction of the "lower"? If so, Emerson is not merely clear of the Lawrentian accusation, but a fellow warrior in the same romantic cause. Or is the use of this language rather a sign of an unacknowledged *de*-cendental-ism, a covert effort to enforce conventional standards of conscience and consciousness on the primordial sense of life? If so, he is guilty. Both interpretations are sometimes possible, but the first is always Emerson's intended meaning, whenever he is aware of the issue. The ambiguity arises because he is not always aware of the issue; and ministerial conventions and the need to say something uplifting can occasionally get the better of his truer doctrine, turning it into its subtly sinister opposite.

Our best resource, as always, is to take Emerson at his better moments and to allow for the worse in the light of those. These best moments will be passages in which the presence of organic language is no mere gloss of rhetoric over a strained elevation of mind, but a reminder of ranges of possibility excluded by the necessary narrowness of individual experience.

The test at bottom is literary. For the literary event is the best mediator between otherwise separate faculties of the Soul. By tone, for instance, we are reminded in the midst of some superficially impersonal remark of the presence of a person. By tone, then, a self appears in coincidence with mind. If that tone has authority, strength, and range, the statement in question gains immensely in authenticity. By metaphor, similarly, dimensions of experience are combined and simple actions doubled. And by rhythm, especially, the most rarefied idea can be imbued with an intrinsic reminder of elementary cycles of vitality. To feel a rhythm is to feel life, for life is rhythm. Thus the resources of literature can practically recombine the existentially alienated faculties of the whole Soul in a context of words that makes their coincidence available to the imagination—and thereby credible as a possibility for experience outside words.

The literary actuality is intrinsic to the very point about the Soul Emerson wishes to make. The credibility of his major idea is profoundly bound up with the quality of his literary achievement. At the same time, Emerson the artist, the man of words, tends perpetually to escape the alertness of his best readers. Yet this is the Emerson that counts. He would have been ready to agree that "an immense deduction is to be made from the doctrine of the wisest man to arrive at his truth" (J.VI.183). The live "truth" about the whole Soul is always an *expressed* truth.

To distinguish the "literature," the "excitement," or "awakening" (J.X.317) from the "metaphysics" is then his reader's best task and pleasure. To catch Emerson at work acting out his doctrine verbally; to discover the meaning of his prime insight over again from the beginning, as far as the artist can make it knowable and present within a set of words; to change "Emerson," that label for a notional construction, back for a fractional moment into a voice speaking distinct words—that is, into himself; this is the ultimate critical task. Only the poet, the creator in language, "is in the natural attitude" (W.XII.14) and "writes the adequate genesis" (W.VIII.71). Life is the essence of the Soul, and literature is the only verbal imitation of life. A defender of the Soul who cannot render his thoughts about it in words must expect finally to be repudiated—or at best "classified," as I have just tried to do.

Knowing this, Emerson is always jogging his own elbow, reminding himself that "the thing set down in words is not affirmed. It must affirm itself" (J.III.10), or, more positively, that "poetry makes its own pertinence" (J.V.343). His ideas could have no final truth independent of his immediate expression of them; the minute what he wished to say ceased to be said well, it ceased to be worth attending to seriously. This obligation was of course especially binding on someone whose "something to say" was in so great a part an insight into the perpetual conditions of saying, of putting life into letters.[2] "Beauty is the only sure sign, so that if your word threatens me, I know it is a bully, I know that it is weak, I know there is a better word discoverable & returnable. That word only which is fair & fragrant, which blooms & rejoices, which runs before me like verdure & a flowering vine, sowing an Eden in the path, is truth" (J.V.537-538). This last sentence thoroughly illustrates its own point.

Emerson's criticisms of other writers can often be read as covert descriptions, good or bad, of his own creative activity. There are many striking comments on his own expectations and prowess as a reader, for he depended on his reading for echoes, presentiments, and parallel formulations of his own truth. In a modest moment he could call himself a "natural reader, & only a writer in the absence of natural writers. In a true time, I should never have written" (J.IX.181), yet his remarks about reading are among the most distinguished examples by which to show how naturally the two activities can be combined. A writer of sentences, it is for sentences he read, to which he "yields" (J.VIII.56) when he can—as he implicitly requires his own reader to yield when life appears. "In the book I read, the good thought returns to me, as every truth will, the image of the whole soul" (W.II.280).

This last sentence conveys succinctly what he wished his own writing to do. "Whole soul," for example: Emerson is asserting that the "good thought" is precisely that which liberates in the reader powers beyond those exercised by his ordinary self or even those of the writer whose good thought it was. An interesting sentence generates the very mind that grasps it; it provokes the mind to act. The whole soul then would be the healthy soul, the soul without private defensiveness and therefore free to act, to perceive that a truth is a truth. All acts of recognition liberate persons from partiality, and in the course of doing so they remind the recogniser of the power that in ordinary and vain moments he forgets he has permanently at his disposal: to live simply for what is truly there.

Yet there can be an ambiguity in the phrase "good thought," which will work in Emerson's favor only when it is resolved in a single direction. If in "the book I read," I read a good thought, I may be participating imaginatively in a piece of fine action, a positive accomplishment of the Soul, however minor; if so, the thought in question is "good" because it is authentic, available, and exciting to me. An act, not an object, such a thought would indeed "image" the whole soul because, according to Emerson's theory, it is just at such moments that one is put into connection with the potential and proper entirety of the Soul. A reader participating in such acts of recognition possesses for a moment an aroused consciousness capable ideally of regarding all facts with equal insight.

But it is also, distressingly, possible to think that Emerson could have intended by "good thought" something as weak as "fine sentiment," in which case the reader the sentence describes would be congratulating himself on encountering an image of his own moral complacencies. The first of this pair of alternatives is itself an example, it seems to me, of the good thought Emerson wanted to mean; the second exemplifies the kind of lapse into conventionality that is almost always possible. The half-life of the first, or active, sense can be dreadfully brief; one frequently finds oneself with only the lead into which the radium has changed.

Such ambiguities of interpretation can serve representatively to "return an image" of Emerson's struggle against his tradition, his environment, his disciples, his own benign impulses, the entropy of his creative impulse. The sentence following the one just quoted helps to confirm one's instinct that Emerson the writer would support, on behalf of his own work, the same radical measures he recommended for the books of others: "To the bad thought which I find in it, the same soul becomes a discerning, separating sword, and lops it away" (W.II.280). The whole soul, once expressed and enjoyed, constitutes the standard by which a reader may distinguish reality in words from pseudo-statement. One must, he observes decisively, "be an inventor to read well" (W.I.92). "Invent" is of course used in its Latin sense and means to find or re-create the full existence of, not to substitute fancifully—though it is possible to think that many an attempt at invention in the higher sense ends in a self-flattering inventiveness in the lower.

There is a fine paragraph in "The American Scholar" where invention is firmly attached by the context to its best Emersonian meaning:

> When the mind is braced by labor and invention, the page of whatever book we read becomes luminous with manifold allusion. Every sentence is doubly significant, and the sense of our author is as broad as the world. We then see, what is always true, that as the seer's hour of vision is short and rare among heavy days and months, so is its record, perchance, the the rest he rejects, were it never so many times Plato's and Shakespeare's. least part of his volume. The discerning will read, in his Plato or Shakespeare, only that least part,—only the authentic utterances of the oracle,— all (W.I.93)

To be sure, the references to Plato and Shakespeare limit the application of the insight, for something of what is important in *Hamlet* or the *Republic* is going to be lost if you make Shakespeare, or even Plato, a "seer." Yet the advice is good guidance for readers of books that set out to speak oracularly to start with. We are urged not only to lop away inauthentic utterances (a readiness to recognize the real thing will ignore banalities without conscious striving), but to attend closely to the potential meaning locked within superficially inactive remarks. The record of vision will be, he says finely, "words overheard at unawares by the free mind" (W.VIII.204).

We know that original composition came close for Emerson, in association and often in time, to successful reading: example prompted the power and will to try a like statement. "There is at this moment there is for me an utterance undoubtedly bare & grand as that of the colosal chisel of Phidias, or trowel of the Egyptians, or pen of Moses or Dante, but different from all these. Not possibly will the Soul deign to repeat itself, but if I can hear what these Patriarchs say, surely I can reply to them on the same pitch of voice" (J.V.184). To find and hold this pitch, though, was hard: "All the conditions must be right for my success, slight as that is. What untunes is as bad as what cripples or stuns me" (J.X.44). This was so, one may guess, partly because it was precisely the "all" of the "conditions" Emerson hoped to turn to music. If one supposes a Soul with words at its disposal, surrounded and interpenetrated by all that is instantaneously perceptible, the act of separating, ordering, naming will approach impossibility. Emerson envied the sculptor of the Egyptian obelisk who, he quotes Greenough as observing, created a sign that did in fact *say* something—"Here!"—and said it "very loud," for a stone shaft could exclaim more sharply than any verbal equivalent.

His own moments of success could often be almost as brief. It is not true that Emerson is literary only in single sentences. There are continuities of excellence longer than paragraphs, though none, in my judgment, that exceed a page or two of sustained utterance. But sentences are the first examples of success a reader will encounter, and the convention of criticism from Carlyle to the present that has made Emerson especially important as a worker in sentences and single verses is broadly right. Mark the first case of interesting expression in any essay, and the chances are it will separate from its context as a sentence, the smallest grammatical unit that can put into words the present moment of any actual speaker. One understands sentences at once, and altogether; all parts make a whole in an instant of apprehension. We literally hold the universe in these grains of sand, for the "universe" becomes, is re-created as, just one grain in the moment of our experience of it.

Then, too, a sentence is the smallest complete unit; it brings into imaginative existence, as isolated words cannot, an activity, a dramatic situation. A speaker addresses a listener, and some kind of referent is evoked, a possible universe to be communicated. Emerson's recognition that the essential act of life can be "imitated" within this narrow limit makes him speak of sentences as other writers speak of entire works of art—which, for him, they are. The worth of good sentences "consists in their radiancy and equal aptitude to all intelligence. They fit all our facts like a charm. We respect ourselves the more that we know them" (W.VIII.191). We respect ourselves because in understanding them we taste the flavor of the act of experiencing; we share with the speaker a mutual rediscovery of the whole Soul. A writer has a million opportunities: if he "has messages to men," "truths to impart," he should not "scribble flourishes," but strive to "write that which cannot be omitted, every sentence a cube, standing on its bottom like a die, essential & immortal" (J.IX.423).

But if a sentence is a die, the writer is a gambler, who may need to make his throw over and over before that expression is found which will mean what it says. Emerson's literary method, at once his strategy and his fate, allowed him to repeat a single attempt at expression from one version to another through successive pages or volumes of his journals, or from journal to lecture to essay; in such a system of composition, a writer gives himself more than one chance to "throw" or, to double the metaphor, to "cast": "It is one of the laws of composition that let the preparation have been how elaborate, how extended soever the moment of *casting* is yet not less critical not the less all important moment on which the whole success depends" (J.III.446). He wrote this observation early, while working presumably on *Nature,* his first finished piece of prose, but his career gave him opportunities enough continually to test its truth. The earliest versions of any particular statement are on the whole, it is worth repeating, the less successful ones. Even such continually repeated themes as compensation are less impressive verbally in the journal than in the essay, just as the finished essay is itself less impressive than the fully achieved passage it may contain. The last is the best.

This elementary but crucial predilection for brief achievement is supported by a sharp sense of the evanescence of any experience of meaning. A new and shocking remark comes "like an abyss of scepticism" to those who are used to other terms, but "the eye soon gets wonted to it, for the eye and it are effects of one cause; then its innocency and benefit appear," but "presently, all its energy spent, it pales and dwindles before the revelation of the new hour" (W.II.305-306). Nothing is said once and for all; no literary success *stays.* The extreme pleasure offered by a new thought in good words is followed (and anticipated) by the repeated discovery that its virtue evaporates: "After a few months, I come again to the record, and it seems a mere bit of glistening tin or tinsel, and no such world wisdom" (J.VIII. 278).

This sense of meaning's mortality is reinforced by a more radical suspicion, never entirely suppressible for longer than it takes to make single affirmations, that verbalization fatally qualifies the experience it purports to express. If, in a state of rapture when the imitation has worked, Emerson can assert that "all Experience has become mere language now" (J.VI.62), he more frequently and tartly stresses the pessimistic complement, the sigh that comes as the ink begins to dry. "Every act hath some falseness of exaggeration in it, every sentence For the infinite diffuseness refuses to be epigrammatized, the world to be shut in a word. The thought being spoken in a sentence becomes by mere detachment falsely emphatic" (J.VI.65). *Mere detachment:* any sentence becomes detached from its possible context if it is to exist at all; any statement will be at a distance from its possible referents if it is to appear before the mind as a sensible set of words. The existence of words as words displays the impotency as well as the triumph of all expression.

One resource, when words are a failure, is to live, to escape from "subterfuge" and fall back upon "virtue" (J.V.102) or the "insight" that comes after one has completed a piece of writing which is in itself a "confusion" (J.X.48). That "joy which will not let me sit in my chair, which brings me bolt upright to my feet, & sends me striding around my room, like a tiger in his cage" should not require the justification of an expressive "book or line"; the "affirmative experience" (J.IX.221) is its own reason for being. But Emerson's very statement here contradicts him; the pacing back and forth is itself a translation of the inner experience into a language less satisfactory even than words. A tiger in a cage is longing for freedom. A man of letters cannot withdraw from words. There are, after all, degrees of "remoteness from the line of things in the line of words." He who is prepared to wait for the "by & by" in which there "comes a word true & closely embraces the thing" (J.III.49) can find himself satisfied. Emerson's hope of speaking such satisfactory words depended on his preserving a practical faith in language that he would not have maintained theoretically. "A man can only speak so long as he does not feel his speech to be partial and inadequate. It is partial, but he does not see it to be so whilst he utters it." You cannot write at all unless you are able to think that what you write "is for the time the history of the world" (W.III.189), an adequate re-creation of life.

WORDS

EMERSON's admiring selection of a remark made by Mirabeau about Robespierre can illustrate his own literary hope in miniature. "That man will go far, he believes what he says" (J.VIII. 419). The necessary special emphasis on "believes" here is a quick example of the "word" as Emerson himself was accustomed to await it. For though words do not alter—"the word beats all the speakers & definers of it, & stands to their children what it stood to their fathers" (J.VIII.100)—yet "every word admits a new use." The double presence of an inherited meaning and an immediate overtone stimulates that "instant activity of mind" (W.VIII.17) which raises common speech to poetry, and hence to a provocation of the Soul in the alert reader. The elementary literary event is therefore the pun, and Emerson, always reverting to the initial position, always starting anew, is ever the re-emphasizer, the redefiner, of single words.

Sentence after sentence is interesting through this tactic. Some, like "He is weaker by every recruit to his banner," are openly paradoxical, evicting the expected word ("stronger" in this case) in favor of its opposite. More frequently, sentences are smooth except for a wrinkle at the one or two words over which the mind must hover. "If only he *sees,* the world will be visible enough" is a crude but typical example of this mode of literary action, pressing out two of the meanings of a peculiarly important verb. To recover the proper tone, one need hardly say, this sentence should be heard without the ostentation of stress indicated by Emerson's italics. Even with such a reduction, it is a question whether the remark is a vapid truism or a wise truth. As we opportunely redefine "see" in the direction of "have insight into," it momentarily shifts from banality to suggestiveness; though always capable of lapsing, as Emerson has warned us, back to banality. As we think of the matter again, though, it is not so much that a new sense is being found as that the primary meaning is being recovered. "See," we can find, does mean *see*.

Since the word "property" can move in one direction toward commerce and in the other toward technical philosophy, it is a favorite node at which to alter the direction of sentences. I doubt if Emerson ever uses it in his most deliberate writing without gathering a double meaning as he goes. A familiar paragraph from *Nature* begins, "We are taught by great actions that the universe is the property of every individual in it. Every rational creature has all nature for his dowry and estate. It is his, if he will. He may divest himself of it; he may creep into a corner, and abdicate his kingdom, as most men do, but he is entitled to the world by his constitution" (W.I.20). The ambiguity of "property" in the first of these sentences represents within the arena of a single word the affirmation made at large by the several sentences together, indeed by the whole of this fundamental essay. The outer (and inner) world can be called the possession of its inhabitant just so far as it provides an arena for the active presence of a master faculty, or "property," of the mind. The pun demonstrates the heart of the Emersonian insight in little. It is the universe in the smallest conceivable grain of sand.

The other sentences display their own examples of the same action: "will," for example, in "It is his, if he will." That the world belongs to those who exercise moral determination is certainly one meaning. Emerson is also, I submit, uncovering the corner of a slighter, more flexible and also more radical attitude: "will" also means *wish*. The universe we face, the sentence would then say, is our own when our desires are engaged—provided, to put it in its barest form, we like. Here, as with "property," the two meanings of a single word make an argument; moral effort succeeds when it is founded upon spontaneous desire, and vice versa; then only is will informative, exploratory, world-making. "Constitution" is the last of the puns in this series; the same action appears there in the shape of a tongue-in-cheek joke linking a moral norm with a physical predisposition.

It is worth reading the original version of these elegant sentences as they appear in one of the early lectures:

Every rational creature has all nature for his dowry and estate. All nature, nothing less, is totally given to each new being.

It is his potentially. He may divest himself of it, he may creep into a corner and abdicate his kingdom as most men do but he is entitled to the world by the constitution. He is entitled to it; only he must come and take it. (E-L.I.384)

Did Emerson really say this flat sentiment aloud? There are weak stresses, which show what he wanted and failed to do, in the gasps of effort at the beginning of the second sentence: "*All* nature, *nothing* less, is *totally* given." But there is no achievement. It is only when the significant single words are brought forward and exposed that the wit and smoothness and security of the final version appear. There is usually a considerable literary gap between the early lectures and the first published work, though they come close in time and share the same themes.

One can more easily perceive the necessary double meaning when tone makes a pun a real possibility. We can hear Emerson decide not to join the social experimenters at Brook Farm because of a "preoccupation of mind" (J.VI.482) and hear him observe sharply that "It is easy to live for others: everybody does" (J.VII.46). So too with "The reason why we feel one man's presence and do not feel another's is as simple as gravity" (W.III.95). The pun on "gravity" is presumably the place where the joke starts; discovering it allows the reader to awaken a sleeping metaphor in "feel." A further didactic implication emerges, as with a smile, from behind the obvious untruth of the assumption: gravity is not that simple, really, either the Newtonian or the moral variety. Yet both, as forces of nature comprehensible through the creative mind, operate all the time; we are always falling with our full weight, physically and spiritually.

I suspect that the action of redefining words to provide alternative readings for single sentences is the literary tactic that most fundamentally corresponds to an essential part of Emerson's whole attack upon his reader's hopes and knowledge of the world. Puns play upon the difference between what is and what ought to be, what our mind sees to be so and what our "moral sentiment" would prefer. The meaning you must make out to preserve the direction of a sentence will be the "ought" meaning;

for a moment, "ought" replaces "is"; in the reader's consciousness a world is converted, and intellect and conscience reconciled.
Yet, on second thought, it is seen that this is not exactly what has
occurred: "ought" only illuminates an unperceived condition of
"is." The redefinition does not so much replace one meaning
with another as alter our feeling for what we are saying when
we make the ordinary statement, the statement that simply
accepts a condition. We are freed to re-encounter the world as
it is with more of ourselves.

The literary clue to this demonstration of the Soul is doubleness. A word acts itself twice over. Redefinition of language
triggers a small but giddy realignment of forces within silent
experience. Wit engages more of us, forcing us to use more of
the Soul. Verbal reduplication is therefore both art and morality.
"Our strength is transitional, alternating; or, shall I say, a
thread of two strands. The seashore, sea seen from shore, shore
seen from sea; the taste of two metals in contact" (W.IV.55)—
the taste, that is, of electricity.

RHYTHM

DOUBLENESS is typical of literature in all its most obvious
manifestations—tone, metaphor, rhythm. Of these, rhythm is
the most primitive, since it reflects most directly the fundamental
mode of action of what I have been calling the organic faculty.
Rhythm appears, in the shape of "polarity," as an organizing
principle for whole essays, for these are typically ordered so as
to place various topics before alternating points of view. It is
reflected generally through the Emersonian world view in the
dialectic between such paired opposites as prudence and heroism,
reason and common sense, commodity and spirit, life and
thought. But the most relevant appearance of "the earth-beat,
sea-beat, heart-beat, which makes the tune to which the sun
rolls, and the globule of blood, and the sap of trees" (W.IV.
141) is the style itself. "Every good poem that I know I recall

by its rhythm also" (W.VIII.49), Emerson says in his last, long, undervalued essay on "Poetry and Imagination," and the truth holds still more subtly for readers of his prose.

It is by appealing to metaphors of physical motion that Emerson expresses for himself the experience of rhythm in words. "In reading prose," a frequently quoted sentence puts it, "I am sensible as soon as a sentence drags, but in reading poetry, as soon as one word drags" (J.IX.214). If he has his own writings in mind, he is overmodest, for it is in prose that he best shows his acute knowledge of how a word can drag and stop the motion of a sentence "as if Nature had sprained her foot," turning a connected statement into a "plenteous stopping at little stations" (W.XII.49). Rhythm is always for Emerson a healthy sign of intellectual venturesomeness. The association comes out in his praise of his literary friends. "I hate circular sentences, or echoing sentences, where the last half cunningly repeats the first half," he wrote to his German friend Grimm, reflecting presumably on the antithetical sentences characteristic of the rhetorical manner in which he had been brought up; "but you step from stone to stone, and advance ever."[3] Reading Thoreau's journal after his friend's death, he found "the same thought, the same spirit that is in me, but he takes a step beyond, and illustrates by excellent images what I should have conveyed in a sleepy generality" (J.IX.522). And Elizabeth Hoar appealed to him because of a "certain forward motion of the mind" (J.VIII.498-499) apparent in her manner of speech, which he associated with lack of egotism—that is to say, with presence of mind.

More than once in the journals the "essential act of life" (J.VIII.501) is described as a movement forward past inhibition into grace. "This creative saliency, this saliency of thought, this *habit of saliency,* of not pausing but going on" is a chief symptom of the presence of divine strength (J.VII.317, also W.XII.59 and W.VIII.72). The very momentum he prays for exists concretely in these words as the repetitions build and a trajectory begins to be traceable—though italics, as always, must be read as a partial confession of failure.

A better success is a sequence where the breaking in of metaphor liberates a steady pacing rhythm. It is, he says, the "uncontrollable interior impulse which is the authentic mark of

a new poem, & which is unanalyzable . . . & which is felt in the per-
vading tone, rather than in brilliant parts or lines; As if the sound of
a bell, or a certain cadence expressed in a low whistle or booming, or
humming, to which the poet first timed his step, as he looked at the
sunset, or thought, was the incipient form of the piece, & was regnant
through the whole. (J.X.267)

The march of these images more fairly expresses the run and
check of prose rhythm than that of poetry, though in both poetry
and prose a "certain cadence" is felt to exist.[4] In poetry this is
meter, the expectation that a certain established number of syllables, and an established distribution of artificial stresses within
these syllables, will persist through the actual words before the
end of a line or stanza is reached. In prose the question of
rhythm is more complex, partly because, though they exist, the
analogous norms change so quickly and partly because our consciousness of them is far less developed theoretically.

The simplest variety of prose rhythm seems to occur when an
identical repeated form persists within a clutter of superficial
differences. Thus the expression "a certain cadence" in the passage just quoted is rhythmical provided that one feels a formal
identity in the stress patterns of the words "certain" and "cadence," an identity that persists in spite of obvious differences in
sound, meaning, and grammatical function. By itself the word
"cadence" is apt to be more distinctly articulated than "certain,"
whose final syllable is commonly swallowed. But when the words
occur together, especially as a rhythmical fragment of a larger
rhythmical whole, the weaker word has to be articulated as
firmly as the stronger to bring out the form they share. One
makes sure of saying "a CER-tain CA-dence." The form here
might be called, borrowing a metrical term from poetry, a trochaic foot.

Prose rhythm, then, matches the differences between the variously stressed syllables of ordinary discourse against a limited
imaginative design, the felt presence of which influences the way
the words in question are pronounced. So far prose rhythm works
in the same way that poetic rhythm does. But in prose a single
norm persists no longer than those words to which it particularly
applies. Thus the trochaic norm just mentioned is immediately
lost as the sentence proceeds: "or a certain cadence expressed in

a low whistle or booming." Rhythm next appears in the way we read the pair of words "low whistle." To my ear, the two words are *formally* identical and constitute a pair of equal feet in rhythmical time and space, each of which consists of a single accented syllable. The second syllable of "whistle" is not formally present, though it is actually; it is therefore correct to swallow it in reading, as it would not be correct to swallow the second syllable of "certain." Such rhythmical norms of stress usually come in pairs or triplets; they cannot persist longer than a brief series.

This brings us to a second aspect of prose rhythm. The felt presence of rhythm is evidently closely connected with the way we hold on to the syntactic order that organizes our understanding of a sentence. Syntax, after all, is the first "form" we must keep in mind; without it, a sentence will simply be a random trickle of words out of the dictionary. Before we can become conscious of rhythm, then, we need an assurance that the sentence we are in the midst of is going to come out right grammatically. We must believe that our notion of the syntax ahead will not be contradicted. Once we are sure about this, rhythm can begin to be possible, for we are in a position to understand that the clause we are on the verge of reading acts in the sentence in the same way as the grammatical unit we have just assimilated. We can realize that we are in the presence of two nouns, or two verbs, or a pair of alternative prepositional phrases, which act grammatically in the same way within their sentence, though the number of words and syllables may vary. This grammatical identity may then begin to constitute a rhythmical form, like stress in the simpler case. Rhythm appears when we can begin to take pleasurable notice of the precise way in which our syntactic expectations are fulfilled consubstantially with the shuffling and crowding of actual words and syllables.

These general observations may help to explain why walking is a prime metaphor for Emerson whenever he discusses or exemplifies rhythm. The pace of a man striding is the best possible analogue in bodily motion to the mental motion of a rhythmical sentence. The repeated unit of progress in walking is the single stride, each of which is "the same" though each passes over a different patch of ground and may be short or long, quick or slow, easy or hard, according to the terrain and the condition of the walker. This repeated organic form corresponds to the syntactic paralleling of accentual or grammatical units that guide the reader's consciousness as he assimilates the quantity and meaning of the words in each individual phrase. Thus rhythm is present in the sequence, "as he looked at the sunset, or thought," to the degree that we are prepared to notice that the unit "or thought" is grammatically the equal of the whole phrase "as he looked at the sunset," and are therefore ready to accept it as a rhythmical equal. If we are, the later and shorter of the two phrases will be heard in the inner ear preceded by a hesitancy of voice, in order to match the time taken to pass through the longer phrase that precedes it.

Rhythm is therefore not built into the structure of prose as it is, by meter, built into that of verse, for a sentence that a sensitive ear will find rhythmical can usually be read unrhythmically if one responds only to the fall of syllables and does not feel the presence of a form over and above the patter of vowels and consonants.

So much is Emerson attached to the walking metaphor that he can scarcely mention a literal walk in the woods without cadence breaking into his description. Furthermore, the connection becomes moral: the self-reliant man, he says, "walks in a long street" (J.VIII.562), and the delight of language is "the hint or advertisement it gives us of our constitution"; we men are a "marching fraternity—we are bound on a long tramp" (J. VII. 49). The interconnections between walking and writing may be elaborated. Both actions are linear, and so both contrast with the "broad, radiating, immensely distributive action of Nature, or Spirit" (J.IX.114) within which one walks and about which one strives to write. To take a walk in some specimen countryside is thus a halfway step from inexpressible experience to a world made up by ordered language, from life to literature, from the organic to the intellectual action of the Soul.

We know that for Emerson, as for Channing and Thoreau, a walk customarily preceded each deliberate act of composition. In all three writers the walk was a prime subject, suggestively emblematic in several of its particulars of the transcendental approach to any subject. A walk is a fragment selected from the continuum of experience, purified by separation from society and by contact with nature, made vivid by the consequent pacification and opening of all the faculties, and centered on the singularity of an individual observer. The walker is away from his job, his family, his friends, and therefore away from the words of others as well as their wills. He is in the presence only of his sensibility and the scene. On a walk one experiences deliberately and casually, focusing, glancing, and gazing steadily before passing by, all the while striding, trudging and stopping, running and sitting still. The eye, mind, and muscles interact as the legs warm up and the attention liberates itself. A walk is thus a kind of model for the action of the whole Soul. A devout walker who is also a good writer (and has walking, as opposed to pedestrianism, ever been attractive except to highly verbal *isolatoes,* temperamental transcendentalists?) would find it natural to link the two actions when he came to describe that air of success for which his physical movement were both stimuli and model. "The perception creates the strong expression of it as the man who sees his walks in it" (W.VIII.30).[5]

We can find other physical images besides walking for the organic dimension of prose. Once Emerson recalls a singer in church whose "angel voice goes choosing, choosing, choosing on, and with the precision of genius keeps its faithful road" (J.IV. 468), and a "bird moving thro' the air by successive dartings" teaches him that "there is a beyond to every place" (J.IX.209). Yet these two are obviously variants of the simpler mode of organic motion, like dancing or skating, which also occasionally appear in images for his own or another's literary style. Thus in one place he desires a dance that will express the solar system (J.VII.228), and in another calls the writer "a skater" who "must go partly where he would, and partly where the skates carry him" (W.VIII.31).

To get the elements of experience out of "kitchen order" into "true order" (J.VIII.389); to establish continuity and to guide while altering expectation; to create, above all, contexts of aroused sensibility for the surprise of insight; these are obvious contributions of rhythm. Doubling is still the clue to its interpretation; rhythm doubles felt form just as puns duplicate meaning. When you do an act once, your attention is fixed upon the purposes of the act; when you do the same act once again while still maintaining the same degree of consciousness, you will notice the purpose as before but you will also notice the means by which the purpose is fulfilled. This is the beginning of aesthetic experience and of the contribution rhythm makes to its creation.

The simplest rhythms (and with rhythm, as with all the resources of rhetoric that Emerson made his own, the simplest case is always the one most consciously dwelt upon and enjoyed) are to be found in series. A series repeats an identical form of grammar several times running in the midst of an ever-varying actuality of utterance, and Emerson delighted in them. "Bare lists of words are found suggestive to an imaginative and excited mind" (W.III.17-18). Something similar can happen where the units of a series lengthen out, grow to independent sentences, drop all but the slenderest syntactical analogy with their fellows, and yet still maintain a striding action, an impression of a continuing ideal order prevailing over actual irregularity. The perception of this awakens the sense of anticipation. When we guess that something is coming, the intermediate material can become organized into steps toward the predicted end. Thus sentences grow organically into paragraphs. "There beside me," Emerson says, thinking of the advantages claimed for travel, "is the stern fact, the sad self, unrelenting, identical, that I fled from. I seek the Vatican and the palaces. I affect to be intoxicated with sights and suggestions, but I am not intoxicated. My giant goes with me wherever I go" (W.II.82). Rhythm may be defined here as that which gives the sentence in the middle its tone: "I seek the Vatican and the palaces" is toneless information out of context; in context it becomes an expression of a hurried, raised, anticipatory state of feeling; the reader knows that the sentiment expressed is an affectation and that there is a conclusion coming which must show forth the truth this hasty speaker neglects. When the conclusion arrives it is good because, while it fulfills expectation, it also surprises; there is, I think, a slow, resigned, affectionate wisdom to "My giant goes with me wherever I go" that could not have been predicted. This is surely a great part of live rhythm, as it is of the walk: there is something at the end of the journey worth getting to, some experience of meaning that can climax, reverse, and reinterpret the preceding elements.

But, as in a walk, we should not feel ourselves hurried blindly to the climax; we want to observe as we go and can tolerate any amount of divagation, irregular eye-castings, movements of branches, duckings of head, and leaping of wet patches, so long as they do not interrupt our progress toward the next vantage point. One learns, in the observations just quoted about travel, something real about the "I" and its relations to its own powers, its "giant"; one learns more and more as the sentences go, and most at the end. Everything is provisionally good as an excursion around and toward the nature of the Soul, about which the word "giant" does finally have something to say.

METAPHOR

IF PROSE rhythm is, in the terms I have been using, the organic dimension of the whole Soul's activity imitated in literature, metaphor is just as clearly the characteristic literary manifestation of the Soul as intellect. And if the Soul as intellect is what Emerson proves to have so much to say for and about, and if further the action of the intellect is in itself intrinsically metaphoric, then it cannot be surprising that his writing should contain very rich and interesting examples of metaphor in the ordinary literary sense, as well as very acute comments on the profound significance of metaphor in general. One could indeed almost derive the whole of what is most original about Emerson, what is to a modern reader perhaps almost too exclusively relevant about him, from this side of his literary achievement alone. So much so that one should, I think, be on one's guard against the temptation to read him virtually exclusively as the hero of metaphor, the Representative Man of symbolic action.

From the beginning of his creative period, Emerson was extremely conscious that he was committed in a special way to metaphor. "I believe I never take a step in thought when engaged in Conversation without some material symbol of my proposition figuring itself incipiently at the same time" (J.III.527), he says in an early journal. He goes on to instance a conversation about Plato and Aristotle, in the course of which he remembered "The old pail in the Summer Street kitchen with potatoes swimming in it some at the top some in the midst & some lying at the bottom; & I spoiled my fine thot by saying that books take their place according to their specific gravity 'as surely as potatoes in a tub' " (J.III.528). The "spoiled" here is mostly tongue-in-cheek, even at this early time in his life; his firmer opinion is expressed in such a later entry as the one claiming that "the meaner the type by which a spiritual law is expressed, the more pungent it is, & the more lasting in the memories of men" (J.VI. 24). One can see why—the meanness of the trope is a guarantee of the connectedness of the intellectual "law" with organic reality.

Emerson could be dogmatic about his awareness of this procedure: "Imagination is the nomination of the causal facts,—the laws of the soul—by the physical facts. All physical facts are words for spiritual facts, & Imagination, by naming them, is the Interpreter, showing us the unity of the world" (J.IX.127). But to put the matter dogmatically is to impugn the excitement of the metaphoric act, or to reduce it to a merely ingenious correlation of the "laws of the soul" (already, by implication, well rehearsed in abstract language) and the "physical facts" (to be borrowed from one's reading in popular science, if no pails of potatoes come to mind). The rigid allegoricalism implied by such remarks as "every aster in my hand goes home loaded with a thought" (W.IX.119) does not represent his best instinct. Metaphor is more radically defined when "imagination" demonstrates itself directly in "nomination." In Plato's "broad daylight," for instance, "things reappear as they stood in the sunlight, hardly shorn of a ray, yet now portable and reportable. Before, all things stood enchanted—not tangible. He comes, & touches them & henceforth anybody may" (J.VII. 45). "Reportable" embodies a redefinition, a metaphoric doubling of physical and intellectual, of the plainest and neatest kind: one can *carry about* only those parts of the world that have have been *reported on* or named.

A more formal consideration of literary metaphor might well start with a famous passage from "Education." Its gross metaphor is characteristically organic—the image of absorption, or drinking in the universe, already commented on. But this image stands as it were behind some more explicit lesser metaphors, which are interesting in their own right for the comment they make on the metaphoric structure of intellectual action generally:

> In some sort the end of life is that the man should take up the universe into himself, or out of that quarry leave nothing unrepresented. Yonder mountain must migrate into his mind. Yonder magnificent astronomy he is at last to import, fetching away moon, and planet, solstice, period, comet and binal star, by comprehending their relation and law. Instead of the timid stripling he was, he is to be the stalwart Archimedes, Pythagoras, Columbus, Newton, of the physic, metaphysic and ethics of the design of the world. (W.X.131)

We can notice delicate shifts in the terms assigned to the action Emerson wants here to recommend. At the beginning, the Soul's act of understanding nature, of explaining it, is a "taking up"; this verb is exchanged for the mining operation implied by calling the universe a "quarry"; it is metaphorized once more in a different image by "representation," and thereafter three times anew by "migrate," "import," and "fetch away," before returning to the abstract term "comprehending."

These shifts of illustrative terminology embody the ideal act of knowledge more directly than the sentences express it discursively. Metaphors are *how* "the man" takes up the universe into himself when he acts as mind; this is the way that Soul and Nature come together. We can understand the nature of the act that the astronomer performs as he mathematically "comprehends" the facts presented to his eye by his instruments when we become aware of the metaphoric nature of that act. And the way to keep this awareness alive if you are writing English prose is to use metaphors yourself: what you are doing in words will then exemplify what "the man" does by way of the terminology and technique appropriate to his science.

This strategy of demonstrating an insight into the metaphorical character of the acts of intellect by talking about them in language that is itself charged with illuminating metaphor is, I believe, one of the defining idiosyncrasies of Emerson's genius.

There could be more to notice in this particular passage—let me call attention only to the phrase, "In some sort," with which the first sentence begins. This expression antecedently qualifies the doctrine preached in the passage it so modestly introduces. "The man" brings the world into the mind, to be sure; but *in some sort* only, in a metaphoric one. I shall demonstrate, Emerson seems to be saying, the power of the mind and at the same time reveal its intrinsic method and its necessary limits.

For the moment that we ask ourselves how the Soul as mind confronts or takes in Nature, we find ourselves involved with some kind of symbol. We may think we look directly at a real star; yet the minute we inquire how the image comes to us, and is formulated by us as a "star," we become aware of the means, physiological, instrumental, and linguistic, through which what we see is seen. We can then understand that the fact we know is a restatement of a reality that is ultimately inexpressible. We see the star telescoped or radio-waved—or human-eyed. Intellectual "reality" is for us as much as can be mediated by the instruments we use.

Since language is the one constant instrument in all acts of conscious knowledge, language is an essential constituent of all acts of intellectual perception. It is therefore the crucial context in which to demonstrate the instrumentality of all instruments. As a literary man, Emerson was in the best possible position to appreciate the symbolic dimension in each act of knowledge. As Charles Feidelson says, "He who tries to grasp at one moment the mind within and the universe without finds himself . . . regarding both as functions of the forms of speech in which they are rendered."[6]

Here is the functional link between epistemology and literature. Once the world is "put under the mind for verb and noun," once intellectual perception is realized to be in its structure a verbal activity, the poet becomes the representative man to "articulate it" (W.III.20). He who freely "renames" with genius is thereby in the best position to represent the structure of all the other, nonlinguistic "namings," such as the mathematical language of physics.

One has, then, the presence of a language as well as a consciousness of the presence of a language. Finally, one has a further consciousness that by calling the instrument or set of symbols at hand a "language," one is implicitly making the use of ordinary words the central instance of all means of knowing. These steps of consciousness follow in order when we begin to consider the Soul-Nature relation as an intellectual act. "Poetry begins, or all becomes poetry, when we look from the centre outward, and are using all as if the mind made it" (W.VIII.41).

If one's doctrine of the Soul as intellect is—to sum up un-Emersonically—"I name my world," then the most obvious way of naming is going to be the most interesting, the most *literally* true. As a philosopher Emerson takes his place in a line from Plato through Pearson and Freud to Bridgman and Collingwood and Oppenheimer, all of whom have in one way or another rediscovered the fundamentally poetic action of the mind. But Emerson's special value lies a stage deeper. He speaks of the way of the mind not from without, like the philosophers of science or history, but from within. He talks about metaphor, but he also practices it. This is all-important, for the truth in question can be apprehended in its exact and delicate reality only by going through the act one wishes to understand. To enact a truth regarding language *in* language is to make literature. The true sentences about intellectual action will be the sentences that ring true.

This metaphoric tendency ran very deep into the structure of Emerson's mind. It appears, as we have seen, in memories of childhood that antedate his specifically literary ambitions, though retroactively they manifest the same disposition to unite and create that govern his adult life:

When a boy I used to go to the wharves, & pick up shells out of the sand which vessels had brought as ballast, & also plenty of stones, gypsum, which I discovered would be luminous when I rubbed two bits together in a dark closet, to my great wonder—& I do not know why luminous to this day. That, & the magnetizing my penknife, till it would hold a needle; & the fact that blue & gambooge would make green in my pictures of mountains; & the charm of drawing vases by scrawling with ink heavy random lines, & then doubling the paper, so as to make another side symmetrical—what was chaos, becoming symmetrical; then hallooing to an echo at the pond, & getting wonderful replies. (J.X.381)

"What was chaos, becoming symmetrical." How admirable his sensitivity to the structure of this mental act, and how intimately he discovers it in the core of these private memories! Here are models for the metaphoric process that later makes up such deliberate conjunctions as "tilled with light" (J.X.463), or "chlorine and rosemary" (W.I.125), or the famous "The Sky is the daily bread of the eyes" (J.VI.410)—the process that determined the form of the pleasures of the daily walk, the accidental juxtapositions like "green & gold, dry oakleaves & snow," which "enhance each other, & make a delicious mixture to the eye" (J.VII.214). Emerson was all his life exceedingly sensitive to the relations of contrast and similarity. This predisposition, the psychic ground for his metaphoric originality, was for him one more instance of the deep rhythms that guarantee the reality and availability of the world. The structure of every metaphor is an echo of those same organic recurrences that underly the repetitions of literary rhythm. Hence the frequent references in the poetry to the intellectual "rhymes" that echo from one part of nature to another testify to Emerson's belief that tenor and vehicle are naturally united by virtue of the same organic principle. The doubleness of metaphor, like the doubleness of rhythm, is fundamentally justified by the nature of things, of which literature is the verbal representation.

A scrap of popular science illuminates the intellectual action involved. "The diamond and the lampblack it seems are the same substance differently arranged. Let it teach the importance of composition" (J.IV.133). To see the "same substance" one must put diamond and lampblack together in the mind and compare their chemical structures: the word "substance" implies an act of comparison in which one translates both objects into the same molecular language. These metamorphoses, composing knowledge, are the "rhymes and echoes that pole makes with pole," rhythms that strike the mind with "joy whenever genius makes the transfer from one part of nature to a remote part" (J.VII.519). At the same time, as he warns elsewhere, the mind must also preserve a vivid sense of particular differences. "I see the law of Nature equally exemplified in bar-room and saloon" (J.VI.42), but it would be "pedantry" to adopt the manners suitable to one place when in the other. It is not worth seeing the identity of lampblack and diamond unless the separateness is as fully and constantly appreciated.

To *value* metaphor, to experience the comprehension or creation of a particular metaphor as a radical joy, must be to value
the flash of mind we earn as we comprehend that some special
statement within a limited and actual vocabulary is telling us
something about a world. We do not merely use metaphors when
we feel this, but glory in them. This act of knowledge means a
doubling of our own focus. An image that is a way of knowing
about an objective universe may also be an object in itself. A
means recognized for what it efficiently is suspends itself before
the mind as half an end in its own right; yet any means that becomes an entire end, a solid substance before the attention, must
also be felt as provisional, or it will bind and stultify. "Mark
the delight of an audience in an image. When some familiar
truth or fact appears in a new dress, mounted as on a fine horse,
equipped with a grand pair of ballooning wings, we cannot
enough testify our surprise and pleasure" (W.VIII.12-13). The
tongue-in-cheek tone gives precision to the meaning here: the
"dress" metaphor jocularly implies exactly the external theory
of rhetoric Emerson's severer argument silently replaces, and
Pegasus, traditional image of poetic inspiration, is made through
"ballooning" almost a child's toy.

Emerson's displays of conscious metaphor frequently involve
a partial distancing of himself (and his serious addressee) from
the showier qualities of the figure and, at the same time, a quiet
exposure of its epistemic implications. We learn where we are and
with what instruments of science and works of art we are actually surrounded. When a familiar truth appears in a new dress,
it is "like the new virtue shown in some unprized old property,
as when a boy finds that his pocket-knife will attract steel filings
and take up a needle; or when the old horse-block in the yard
is found to be a Torso Hercules of the Phidian age" (W.VIII.
12-13). The intellectual side of the transcendental act, then, the
discovery of meaning in the parts of experience upon which it is
possible to focus, "is like" the elementary act of eloquence, the
giving of a new name to an old thing. Living *is* (metaphorically)
speaking. And contrariwise: the clearer the expression, the
clearer the quality of being, the more vigorous our freedom
within our life. The paragraph from which the two sentences last
quoted are drawn pursues the matter: "A happy symbol is a sort

of evidence that your thought is just. . . . If you agree with me, or if Locke or Montesquieu agree, I may yet be wrong; but if the elm-tree thinks the same thing, if running water, if burning coal, if crystals, if alkalies, in their several fashions say what I say, it must be true" (W.VIII.13). If this means simply that Emerson can find natural images to support his ready-made doctrine, the sentence is relatively weak, though true enough. Elm trees, though, do not think, nor alkalies "say." But if the thought whose justness the elm tree enforces is not an argumentative moral generalization, of a kind Locke and Montesquieu could agree with or argue against, but simply the process of finding a true meaning in images, then something more vital is being said. For the "truth" about metaphor is unsayable except in shape of another metaphor, another use of the world that includes elm trees and alkalies. A "happy symbol" is the only evidence that your thought *about symbols* is just. One understands the meaning of metaphor by seeing one, and then another and another. As Emerson says later in the same essay on "Poetry and Imagination," "Hence the shudder of joy with which in each clear moment we recognize the metamorphosis, because it is always a conquest, a surprise from the heart of things" (W.VIII. 71).

What one wants, throughout one's reading of Emerson, is to develop a sensitivity to situations where the "metamorphosis" is going on in words and life together, where facts *re*-fer. Here is a particularly plain and subtle case from "Literary Ethics":

Truth is such a fly-away, such a slyboots, so untransportable and unbarrelable a commodity, that it is as bad to catch as light. (W.I.171)

For contrast, here is the journal analogue for the sentence:

Knowledge is hard to get & unsatisfying when gained. Knowledge is a pleasing provocation to the mind beforehand & not cumbersome afterwards. (J.III.488-489)

This early version is very flat in comparison. Yet the germ is there: the meanings of the abstractions "provocation" and "cumbersome," turned into metaphor, are the backbone of the living remark that grew from the original voiceless pair of summaries. Voicelessness is their first fault, when juxtaposed with the quizzical, affectionate, humorous control of the finished version.

Emerson found a way to smile at philosophers in general and himself as one of them—how foolish we are to talk solemnly about truth—yet he remains in control all the same, and nothing is yielded to the philistine. This is not an unbuttoned chuckler talking, but an ironist.

The metaphors of the essay version start coyly: truth is, the speaker says, a half-magical child, a "slyboots," and his tone at this point is that of a grown-up shaking his wise old head over the antics of the children. This tone in itself is a joke—a philosopher, a lover of truth, so tolerantly avuncular? Then comes a broader joke still, for it is hard to say the big "unbarrelable" words, words too "cumbersome" to get your tongue around, as recalcitrant as big objects that will not pack easily or even fit in railway cars. The material largeness and clumsiness of things is re-expressed in terms of the muscles you use, not to trundle them about, but simply to roll the names of their exasperating qualities upon the tongue. "Truth" has now become a "commodity" instead of a fey sprite—a commodity that cannot be treated like other commodities, not because it is too hugely substantial but for the opposite reason: it is too light, too spiritual.

The tone again has something to do with the authority of the metaphoric paradox; the voice here becomes more adult, even a little combative, as it becomes conscious of a world which believes in nothing that cannot be put into barrels and transported. The reader is firmly asked to distance himself from such people by the calming effect of the rhythm: "such a fly-away, such a slyboots, so untransportable and unbarrelable a commodity." We are asked to dwell on those multiplied syllables, even to raise the voice a note, stretching the parts of each word ("un-trans-port-able") before we let the second of the two long ones tumble, to catch the mocking tone. The metaphor alone without a rhythm to enforce the presence of such a tone would be less interesting, as we can prove for ourselves by glancing back at another sentence in one of the early lectures: "You might as easily preserve light or electricity in barrels. It must be lived. It cannot be writ" (E-L.I.167-168). Here the image is present, but only as an image; there is no rhythm, and the barrels will not roll.

At the end of the good sentence, the voice turns again, this time into that of an old countryman, as we hear, "as bad to catch as light." This is slang, with a further metaphor embodied in the idiom, for it is colds that are bad to catch. Here is another comparison with a sting: there are those to whom the pursuit of truth is as foolish as trying to catch a cold on purpose. Yet the apparently undignified image is also affectionately appropriate. Like a cold, truth comes out of the air from nowhere, caught perhaps from a relative or a friend, perhaps from a stranger, unmistakable when you have it, uncomfortable but not fatal, quite incurable, a New England custom. And "light," the powerful, dignified image—this too shares the same impalpable, inexplicable inevitability. The spritely child of the first part of the sentence may survive here as a faint echo: it is difficult to catch children too.

We have three major shifts of definition, then, with lesser games of discrimination and conjunction along the way. And since the sentence is so plainly nothing else but the act of defining, repeated once, twice, and a third time to make a musical chord of meaning, and since to hear the whole remark is to hear the parts and then the concord they make together, it is plain that the full pleasure we are able to enjoy includes the pleasure of definition in general, of metaphor as a principle: this is the "text of truth," the evidence of a just thought.

TONE

To sum up: as rhythm is the literary expression of the organic faculty, and metaphor the characteristic literary mode of action of the Soul as intellect, so the moral sentiment, when it moves over into words, becomes tone. The meanings that metaphor embodies exist in the eternity of the impersonal intellect. Tone, though, is always personal; with tone one enters a world where people exist. To speak is to put yourself in a world containing at least you and your listener, a world of moral behavior. By tone Emerson re-enters the world from which the habits of his intellect might tend to exclude him, engaging the moral agency of the Soul for himself and his reader. His letters show how alert he was to the waver and touch of human intercourse, how acutely he cultivated the anxious joys of friendship, how perpetually the interests of his interlocutors, imagined or present, were scrupulously uppermost. The presence of tone is a kind of social test of truth, a sign that one's perceptions ring true emotionally, that they resonate within a self and not in some philosophic void. By tone one shows one's "presence of mind"— a useful phrase, for in one sense it means one's personal note; in another, the amount of impersonal mind, of the Oversoul, that one has at command. In this phrase the two senses are momentarily one, and they manifest one distinct and multiple Soul. One hears in a man's tone the amount of truth that is in him, his capacity for experience, the life he is ready to bring to bear on the human predicament within which you encounter him, the size and range of the Soul in him.

For Emerson it is a characteristic fault of a man like Disraeli that "he makes at last no impression, because the hearer asks Who are you? What is dear to you? What do you stand for? and the speech & the speaker are silent, & silence is confession" (J.VII.503). For the reverse of the same reason Emerson admires the seventeenth-century writers who "jumped into their book bodily themselves" so entirely that "not a pinch of dust" (J.VIII.503) remains behind. "It makes a great difference to the force of any sentence whether there be a man behind it or no. In the learned journal, in the influential newspaper, I discern no form; only some irresponsible shadow; oftener some moneyed corporation, or some dangler who hopes, in the mask and robes of his paragraph, to pass for somebody. But through every clause and part of speech of a right book I meet the eyes of the most determined of men; his force and terror inundate every word; the commas and dashes are alive so that the writing is athletic and humble—can go far and live long" (W.IV.282).

Almost surely Emerson is thinking of Carlyle here, and his words may explain to a twentieth-century reader the otherwise not very comprehensible service Carlyle performed for his fellow Victorian writers. Carlyle could mean a realized if crude success at the task of becoming a man in words, of having power enough to dominate the verbal world, to reduce the school rules to chaos and yet be able to remake a newly relevant individual order. Ruskin and Dickens and Melville learned from Carlyle, in all three cases more imitatively than Emerson. Carlyle's formula for the artist's tone is an aggressive one, and Emerson was not an aggressive man, in or out of language; but he was attracted to power in writing as he was attracted to wealth and bodily strength and even fanatic determination when he saw these qualities in other people. The tendency to derive vicarious satisfaction from the contemplation of such burly identities as Webster, John Brown, or the British nation grew as Emerson himself became more benignly yielding in manner.

There is a certain distance, though, between the true, secret Emerson and the tones he envies and occasionally adopts: it is an experimental rather than an inevitable self that he throws "bodily" into his books. This is more obvious in the poetry than in the prose, for the poems often present speakers who are held at a distance from the mind that composed them. Frequently these semifictionalized identities grow to have a separate name, the better to figure as mock-mythical representatives for the different impulses in their author. So we encounter Uriel, Methuselah, Cupid, Saadi—even a bumblebee and a titmouse. In the verse such projected identities are playful, even capricious. They are not recommended as responsibly as the abstract roles of the prose—the scholar, the preacher, the poet—or as the various representative heroes of intellectual, moral, artistic, or practical action. And the different unnamed voices in the prose are more subtle and responsible still, since they are less obviously detached for separate contemplation, more nearly taken for granted as expressions of his self. The equivalent in prose of the self-mythologizing we find in the poetry is irony; and for Emerson, irony is more serious than myth.

Tone is therefore never entirely straightforward for Emerson. The preacher of self-reliance was also the critic of egotism, and both to an extreme degree. The apparent contradiction may readily be elucidated in general moral terms, but what consistent sense is a *writer* to make of an admonition to "communicate himself, and not his vanity" (W.VIII.229)? In the world of words, how do you tell the difference? Emerson's own answer would appear to be, by adding self-knowledge to self-expression. "A poem, a sentence causes us to see ourselves. I be & I see my being, at the same time" (J.IV.180). The implication is, I see and approve: I calmly am what I clearly see. Here Emerson has gone beyond Carlyle, whose assertions are all blind and from within. Emerson's tone is himself, yet it is also at a distance; he is and he knows who he is. Always he exhibits the Soul as intellect as well as the Soul as self.

Such tonal emphasis plus self-consciousness would apply, of course, only to the interesting moments of tone; one makes a drastic selection to arrive at these. There is no point in elaborately analyzing the dull tones, the preacherly commonplaces, the high-minded vapid identity behind so much of what we cannot, except by force, attend to. Emerson would be the first to encourage us to neglect any presences we cannot respect and be surprised by. The tones that interest are those that genuinely present the Soul impersonated before us, those that involve us in a confrontation with an identity testing itself in words.

One's identity, false or true, blindly committed or self-consciously tentative, is found by distinguishing a self from those who are not oneself. The set of others against whom the early Emerson chiefly defines himself is the world of philistines and traditionalists. His tone is sharpest and most conscious of enemy values in "Self-Reliance." There he swings out unqualifiedly against the world of the wicked dollar and comes forward uncompromisingly as the adviser of rebel youth. There are many quotable sentences that demonstrate the tone that follows from and embodies this stance: "I would write on the lintels of the door-post, *Whim*. I hope it is somewhat better than whim at last, but we cannot spend the day in explanation" (W.II.51-52). There is a tart consciousness in such remarks that "we" are being overheard by a world that will call our ideas "whims," a world whose judgment we are, indeed, in some danger of sharing: to write the word on the door-post defies our own fears as well as the prejudices of the enemy. Tone can be a sign of a war within the self, as well as between the self and the world.

Emerson is as capable of a complementary rigor at the expense of his own, the reformer's, party: "we" as well as "they" come under attack. To be sure, this is more private. It is in the journal that we read of the "exaggerating people" who "talk of

moments when their brains seemed bursting with the multitude
of thoughts" but who had better rest easy: "I believe they were
mistaken; there was no danger" (J.VIII.542). A still better
instance of the tone to be heard here, with its sharpening of the
nostrils and chill set of the upper lip, is a reply he records himself as having made to Ellery Channing. His friend had objected (one can imagine with what willfully capricious cleverness
of his own) to the usurpation of fame by Homer and Shakespeare, which kept out the talented men of the present: "Oh
certainly, I assure him, that oaks & horse-chestnuts are entirely
obsolete, that the horticultural society are about to recommend
the introduction of cabbages as a shade tree, so much more convenient and every way comprehensible; all grown from the seed
upward to its most generous crumpled extremity within one's
own short memory; past contradiction the ornament of the
world, & then so good to eat, as acorns & horsechestnuts are
not. Shade trees for breakfast!" (J. VI.422).

Perhaps this raillery goes on too long, even for a journal
entry; it is possible to pursue such a line of fanciful teasing of
petulantly unappreciated talent only from a conservative position, which Emerson occupies at some spiritual peril to himself.
He cannot afford to identify permanently with the system of
values that would sneer consistently at Ellery Channing. Irony
invariably involves some doubt as to who one is, and, when this
combines with uncertainty about one's standards, it can become
equivocal or spiteful. Emerson by nature is on both sides, and
the ability, or the fate, to be on both sides of an issue is probably
involved with the whole possibility of tone. Single-minded men
need not have any special "presence of mind." But there is bound
to be doubleness in the allegiances of a writer who can express
some single identity sharply enough to be aware that he has
created a self in words, for the awareness places him at a distance from his own self-creation. In irony, a writer invites his
reader to share that distance.

What one prefers to find is a certain hovering evaluation,
a refusal to come down too firmly on either side of the question,
a willingness to let a reader find his own way to the judgment
that ought to be stressed. At Oxford on his second English visit
in 1848, Emerson had a chance to meet "several faithful, high-

minded young men, some of them in the mood of making sacrifices for peace of mind,—a topic, of course, on which I had no
counsel to offer" (W.V.199). The tone of this observation from
English Traits has something in common with the journal entry
on Channing, but it is less simply conservative and morally more
interesting. It is tempting to say that the last sentence is simply
ironic: Emerson had plenty to say on just this topic, had in fact
been saying it all his life. But in all irony the straight meaning
survives as an understatement, and especially so here. Why might
he "of course" have no counsel to offer? For one thing, because
he is not English himself, the issues of religious conformity that
face these young men do not take a form of which he has an
intuitive comprehension. There is an instinctive scrupulosity in
the withdrawal here, very typical of Emerson; there is also
emotional reserve. This may amount to a cool self-detachment
from the spiritual cowardice these Englishmen are ready to
yield to, but it may also express a profounder identification with
exactly this weakness: has he too not made some sacrifices for
peace of mind, now that he is famous, a traveling sage in request
by worshipful foreigners? How then can he speak, except
obliquely, on behalf of courage? He is either too free from the
particulars of these English problems of conscience or too involved in a universal failure of nerve either to blame or to help.
The range of possibilities is implicit in the tone: tart and tender,
reserved, precise, and melancholy. Such doublings of tone enlarge the self that tone presents, and hence give and provoke
more of the Soul.

English Traits is relatively late Emerson; here is a sentence
from *Nature:* "The advantage of the ideal theory over the
popular faith is this, that it presents the world in precisely that
view which is most desirable to the mind" (W.I.59). This is
effrontery, cool and calculated. A voice assumes with casually
innocent authority just the point that his reader would (if this
were not Emerson he was reading) be settling down to hear
argued out. But *this* tone says: you, reader, are not to judge me;
I pass by that illusion with which you are accustomed to flatter
yourself when you read philosophic books; I am possessed by a
perception that need not beg for your acceptance. It is even conceivable that seeing me take my authority for granted will in-

duce in you the shock of surprise that will put you in possession of what I know. What is "desirable to the mind" is, from the ordinary sensible point of view, some illusion, a fantasy that obscures the facts sane men must face. This of course is to misunderstand the point of idealism, a point that Emerson is not putting discursively but leaving to the tone. For "mind" here is not merely the defensive self, which may indeed conceal reality behind a haze of fantasy, but those faculties to which the facts themselves are "presented." If the word "mind" must change its definition, so too must "desire." "Desirable to the mind" is going to mean something like "consistent with the nature of the mind."

Like metaphor, then, tone can be a way to miniaturize doctrine, to preach in words, artfully. I believe the pleasures of the Emersonian tone are at their best when the speaker fronts the enemy and borrows one or another of his idioms to make his point. This is the tonal equivalent of taking over some part of the businessman's or farmer's world to make a metaphor of it; it is a characteristic part of Emerson's most healthy strategy, for it helps to guarantee that the whole world is being assimilated by a man of many parts, a true hero of the Soul. The strategy need not be anything ambitiously or deliberately philosophical. Listen to his description of telegraphy:

We had letters to send; couriers could not go fast enough nor far enough; broke their wagons, foundered their horses; bad roads in spring, snowdrifts in winter, heats in summer; could not get the horses out of a walk. But we found out that the air and earth were full of Electricity, and always going our way,—just the way we wanted to send. *Would he take a message?* Just as lief as not; had nothing else to do; would carry it in no time. Only one doubt occurred, one staggering objection,—he had no carpet-bag, no visible pockets, no hands, not so much as a mouth, to carry a letter. But after much thought and many experiments we managed to meet the conditions, and to fold up the letter in such invisible compact form as he could carry in those invisible pockets of his, never wrought by needle and thread,—and it went like a charm. (W.VII.27-28)

This passage from "Civilization" is as fanciful as the attack on Channing, but nobody is getting hurt. The occasion provides a lazy opportunity for spinning out an agreeable metaphor, a way of keeping the parts of the argument casually together. This tone asks us to sit loose in the world, know as much as we can of it and use what falls handy, like any gossip at the depot. Such a strategy is more regularly transcendental when it hints at a range of meanings beyond those we would consider within such a practical man's field of vision. "By drainage we went down to a subsoil we did not know, and have found there is a Concord under old Concord, which we are now getting the best crops from; a Middlesex under Middlesex; and, in fine, that Massachusetts has a basement story more valuable and that promises to pay better rent than all the superstructure" (W.VII.150). One may hear a moral or imaginative meaning here; the tone leaves it up to the reader, who may if he pleases think of more than drainage. Drainage is still quite definitely the subject and loses none of its dignity in this reference. "We" are farmers of Concord, and the speaker means to go on talking like a farmer, as suits an essay on "Farming," though willing enough to let a reader overhear him saying more than farmers generally intend.

Conservatism as a social judgment is a simplification of self for Emerson; as a grip on facts it is the necessary condition of clear insight. When Emerson has an observation to make about the nature of things, one that has grown out of his relation to life rather than irritability with his liberal acquaintances, this grip on facts, and the plain man's tone that goes with it, can validate the free play of the mind that constitutes his permanent radical base. "There is a crack in everything God has made. It would seem there is always this vindictive circumstance stealing in at unawares even in the wild poesy in which the human fancy attempted to make bold holiday and to shake itself free of the old laws,—this back-stroke, this kick of the gun, certifying that the law is fatal; that in nature nothing can be given, all things are sold" (W.II.107). The sad observation is firmed by the country images, which solidly underlie the philosophic generality, adding a touch of wryness to the tone; what else, the farmer from whose world these images are drawn might say, did you expect. One borrows a tone in such circumstances not to assert or disguise one's real identity as a moral philosopher or as a human being, but to place it among familiar facts, and so confess a fate common to those among whom one actually lives. Tone can unite as well as separate.

"No article so rare in New England as Tone" (J.V.307), he

complains more than once in the journal. To the attentive ear of
that time this tone, the practical man's voice, must have been
common enough in New England, available to a literary man
capable of hearing and isolating the identity and set of attitudes
it expressed. We know from the writers of the Saturday Club
how the plain man's voice could be reproduced accurately enough
as a piece of comic theater. Emerson's use of it is more serious
because it becomes one of his own modes of approaching the
world and himself, and not merely a scarecrow held at a distance
for the amusement and edification of readers who, in social intercourse, would look down on the speaker who used it naturally
without necessarily having an expressible identity of their own
to back up their condescension. The word "article" in Emerson's complaint here itself attests the presence of what neither
he nor New England was really without. In its pure form, without special additions and ironic qualifications, this voice can be
found in such nasal remarks as "He can't make any paint stick
but his own" (W.XII.53), or "We say the cows laid out Boston.
Well, there are worse surveyors" (W.VI.122). Here is the tone
Thoreau based his irony upon, the tone that first identifies Melville's Ishmael. Both of Emerson's literary descendants made far
more of it than he did.

But in complaining of the absence of tone in New England he
more probably had in mind the absence of a civilized presence, a
courteous manner—what the plain man would call "high-toned"
behavior. Here Emerson himself is to my ear unique. There was
no one then in New England who quite caught the tone that is to
be heard here and there in Emerson: "Now then we hear rarely
a true tone, a single strain of the right ode" (J.VII.207-208).
This longed-for superior note can appear on the modest level of
talk where one becomes aware of Emerson's most private voice,
a voice not borrowed half-mockingly from the village but, as far
as we can judge, intrinsic, a manifestation of an uncombative
identity, which speaks from a position nearer silence than the
countryman's voice and infinitely farther from the public habits
of an alien world. We can hear, in the passages where this higher
voice speaks, a virtually unspecifiable distinction, precise, low-
keyed, intimate, unconsciously alert to the weight of words. A
passage from *Representative Men* on the uses of a great man

manifests it well: "He must be related to us, and our life receive from him some promise of explanation. I cannot tell what I would know; but I have observed there are persons who, in their character and actions, answer questions which I have not skill to put. One man answers some question which none of his contemporaries put, and is isolated" (W.IV.6-7). There is something special here, but so undramatic it is hard to catch. In the last sentence, it may finally be noticed that we do not get the ending we surely expect: if a great man answers a question his contemporaries have not asked, the consequence should be something like ". . . and is made a public hero." Instead we get, "and is isolated." The new phrase means both made separate from the mass and made solitary or lonely. The co-presence of the idea of isolation enlarges the idea of heroism. So too the phrase "persons . . . answer questions which I have not skill to *put*" rather than "skill to *answer*." And can "life" receive a "promise of explanation"? In what sense? To read such sentences is to be placed, by slight touches, on the alert. This speaker is not, to be sure, saying anything of the first importance; at present he is not going out of his way, nor does he expect that you should go out of yours, but he does ask that you take notice that his argument is a degree more informative and carefully worked than you had supposed. "The most fugitive deed and word, the mere air of doing a thing, the intimated purpose, expresses character" (W.II.156), he says in another context, and when such a tone occurs prose is character. "Character" is *habitual* moral stance, and its reflection in words marks the habitual respect of a practiced man of letters for his medium.

I hear this tone again in "We do not quite forgive a giver. The hand that feeds us is in some danger of being bitten" (W.III. 162). Is it to be found in the exactness with which "quite" and "some" are placed to do their qualifying work? Or in the imperturbability with which the half-rhyme of "forgive" and "give" is allowed us to do as we wish with? Something is due to the air of disinterestedness with which these literary gestures are made. Nothing is apologized for, and everything that is said is meant, but nothing is explained. Whatever the reader may do to pursue sense while preserving syntax is allowed to be part of the point made. Another remark of the same sort is a character-ization of proverbs as "always the literature of reason, or the statements of an absolute truth without qualification" (W.II. 108-109). There is nobody standing on the sidelines here to react to the gasp of an innocent reader who objects that this assertion, under the guise of casual synonymy, is going a great distance from the first member of the series to the last. Surely it is not good logic to identify proverbs with reason, or reason with absolute affirmations. But the sentence means what it assumes. The canny, or noninnocent, reader is willing to risk the gap and see what the sentence may mean if taken literally. The redefinition of "reason" that is bound to follow will be instructive. "In good society,—say among the angels in heaven,—is not everything spoken by indirection & nothing quite straight as it bifel?" (J.VI.77). Apparently so.

Again, as with the other dimensions of literary action, we are in the presence of some form of doubleness: a doubleness of position and voice, an indication of a willingness to engage a matter on two sides at once. Tone comes in with the evocation of a double judgment upon a situation. A person—the creation of tone—is somebody who doubts the sufficiency of a single statement, who reserves himself, withdrawing as he speaks from his words. You cannot *hear* a man saying something entirely straight, that is, like a telephone book or a street sign. Tone is a way of reminding a reader that he is reading words; like metaphor, like rhythm, this rudimentary rhetorical resource is peculiarly adapted to Emerson's interest in what is radical in the use of language. To notice tone is to notice the independent existence of language, which can bring a phantom person into our imaginative presence. We are necessarily aware that we meet a person, and that we do not meet him—that we are in the act of using language for literary purposes. Tone is to the mind's ear what metaphor is to the mind's eye, but it is more radical than metaphor. We believe what we hear more thoroughly than what we see; the eye is accustomed to be deceived by illusions. A person whom we hear speak, though, exists irreducibly for us, and since the identity of the speaker depends on our own identity as a member of the world in which we and the speaker jointly live, we are deeply involved in the discovery of tone. Persons are more intimately challenging portions of the Soul than the bare mind.

Let me come back to the matter of doubleness. When Emerson asks himself, "shall the young man aim at a leading part in law, in politics, in trade?" he answers: "It will not be pretended that a success in either of these kinds is quite coincident with what is best and inmost in his mind" (W.IV.158). A person speaks here because the sentence splits in two. It voices at one and the same time a deep sympathy with the young man's scorn for the world and a certain awareness, hovering over the word "quite," that the high-mindedness of young men is not necessarily to be taken at their own valuation. This does not mean it is the world's valuation of this quality that should be accepted. The ultimate judge is the person capable of saying, or feeling, the truth expressed in this very sentence; the state of mind here doubly exemplified has the authority to adjudicate the respective claims of youthful impatience and worldly fact. "There is much," he goes on, "to say on both sides." Such tonal puns mark the distinction of many by-remarks like "Such as you are, the gods themselves could not help you" (W.VI.239). One can hear a voice that says this insultingly and another voice, intimate and quiet, that says it encouragingly.

There are many examples of this sort of thing: the more detachable and aphoristic remarks are the easiest to split into their component voices. "I desire not to disgrace the soul" (W. II.163), for instance. One voice, modest and low, makes "not" modify the infinitive "to disgrace"—not to disgrace the soul is all this speaker asks for. Another voice proudly attaches the "not" to the main verb "desire," and pauses oratorically before continuing with the predicate infinitive. The whole sentence then becomes a lofty understatement, flung out magnanimously: I have no intention of disgracing the soul, and you, my audience, know how little likely I am to do so. The proud voice seems a function of the modest one, which the reader hears first with the other just after it, a relation that implies an argument: ask for the least quantity of genuine Soul (or clarity, or insight, or vigor), and you will get enough to be proud of.

This activity of mind is not rare in Emerson—the pleasure of reading the essays is kept up for us by the frequency with which tones redouble and sentences open upon the ear as a chord of voices. As with Swift or any other worthy ironist, nothing extra is said that is not intended as a contribution to the education of the reader, whose power to hear and know is constantly tested: are you alive or not?

Tone selects an inner audience within the whole group apparently addressed. The chosen audience hears two voices, where the larger group hears one only; though finally, as the full sense sinks in, the inner audience will have one sense again. One does not *stay* with doubleness, though one has to go through it to get at a proper view of the straight meaning. Look at "I suppose no man can violate his nature" (W.II.58). The chord of voices here generated about "suppose" creates an affectation of blandness that the chosen ear will detect: an inner voice may be heard to say, "Given my notion of 'nature,' you will surely allow me to presume that no man can violate his nature."

The speaker of a good, noticeable sentence typically pretends to mean less than he does. Is not this the essence of transcendentalism once again? Here too, as with metaphor or rhythm, Emerson can show us the chances all writers who wish to do anything with words are obliged to take, and may as well take joyfully. To mean even one simple thing is extraordinary enough; to mean something besides is literature. But "literature," as we have seen, is only the way we have of doing in special verbal situations something we do anyway in life without noticing it and without pleasure: that is, to create meanings and assume dramatic situations. Literature teaches us to return to ordinary sayings and hear them as what they were all the time, statements standing out with the solidity of voices, the distinctness of a limited meaning, the cadence of an assimilable rhythm. Doubleness is justified because it lets us reappropriate the singleness of "ordinary" experience.

One wants, in order to notice the final admirable note in Emerson's range of tones, a set of terms that are not readily available—terms to describe the key elements of good manners and of pathos. For frequently the best moments of tone seem to involve an underconfession of loss and limitation that complements and makes acceptable radical leaps of spirit. Finally, one wants terms to identify the verbal element in mystical exaltation. It would be worth a struggle to understand the causes of excellence in such a paragraph as the one in which Emerson records his try at explaining the American Idea to some English friends.

They are all on an expedition to Stonehenge. Emerson had been a successful lecturer and man about London society, representing in many ways the American Idea himself, however oppressed he occasionally was by the expectations his audiences and disciples had of him. Just before leaving England, he wrote in his journal a comment incorporated in *English Traits*:

On the way to Winchester, whither our host accompanied us in the afternoon, my friends asked many questions respecting American land-scape, forests, houses,—my house, for example. It is not easy to answer these queries well. There, I thought, in America, lies nature sleeping, overgrowing, almost conscious, too much by half for man in the picture, and so giving a certain *tristesse,* like that rank vegetation of swamps and forests seen at night, steeped in dews and rains, which it loves; and on it man seems not able to make much impression. There, in that great sloven continent, in high Alleghany pastures, in the sea-wide sky-skirted prairie, still sleeps and murmurs and hides the great mother, long since driven away from the trim hedge-rows and over-cultivated gardens of England. And, in England, I am quite too sensible of this. Every one is on his good behavior and must be dressed for dinner at six. So I put off my friends with very inadequate details, as best I could. (W.V.288)

What prevails and governs here is quiet, humorous, inward, able to hold in check occasional man-of-the-world slang ("too much by half . . . a certain *tristesse*") and poetical expansions ("the great mother"); able to shift from the report of an individual afternoon to hints of private reticences and hesitations ("my house, for example"); able, always, to preserve a level-headed communion with an imagined American reader who really understands, a reader, it is worth remembering, whom he could not expect to be reading his journal. The passage ends with a wry acknowledgment that he could not explain, not to these people, not in England. The catalogue heaped up by the commas is, to be sure, imperfect, and he knows it; the rhythm starts ("There, I thought, in America, lies nature sleeping, overgrowing, almost conscious, too much by half for man in the picture"), but it never does come to a climax; the second repetition of the meditative "There, in that great sloven continent" is a sign that he has not yet explained America to himself much more thoroughly than to these clever, not-really-interested gentlemen who have been so kind as to prepare a tour for him. The excellence that remains, the sense of a civilized spirit, lies perhaps in the fine acknowledgment of his own reserve. This reserve he was obliged to maintain by a hundred influences of temperament, situation, audience, and, most intimately, subject: how do you talk briefly about one man's experience of America, especially when you have devoted years to that very question?

There is a parallel note of necessary restraint, though more sharply put and without any implication of a withdrawal for social reasons, in a comment good enough to serve as a kind of master epigram for much—including the literary predicament just exhibited. It appears in "Circles": "But lest I should mislead any when I have my own head and obey my whims, let me remind the reader that I am only an experimenter. Do not set the least value on what I do, or the least discredit on what I do not, as if I pretended to settle anything as true or false. I unsettle all things" (W.II.318). This warning is quite literally true, yet the tone also warns that what is said should itself be taken experimentally. Try, for instance, giving a different weight to the phrase, "have my own head," so as to let it mean something more sober than its rhetorical twin, "obey my whims"—something like, "be in cool possession of my full Soul." Then another voice will be heard that *does* settle something. The same applies to "only," in "I am only an experimenter." Unstressed, it intends modesty; accented, it makes the modesty itself ironic. The whole remark is "unsettling" in its bones.

Let me end this section on literary tone with a sure piece of eloquence from "New England Reformers," which brings together the wit of this last example and the elegiac note struck in the meditation on America. The previous context has established the naturalness and inevitability of each man's relation to an inner "spirit":

This open channel to the highest life is the first and last reality, so subtle, so quiet, yet so tenacious, that although I have never expressed the truth, and although I have never heard the expression of it from any other, I know that the whole truth is here for me. What if I cannot answer your questions? I am not pained that I cannot frame a reply to the question, What is the operation we call Providence? There lies the unspoken thing, present, omnipresent. Every time we converse we seek to translate it into speech, but whether we hit or whether we miss, we have the fact. Every discourse is an approximate answer: but whilst it abides for contemplation forever. (W.III.282)
it is of small consequence that we do not get it into verbs and nouns,

"New England Reformers" is peculiarly rich in examples of tone. This, though, is Emerson at his richest and subtlest. The mystical eloquence is due partly to the calm of assured possession, which is, paradoxically, elegiacally expressed. Can acceptance of "the whole truth" grow only by yielding, in the act, the power of literary expression? The voice is unassertive, on the verge of withdrawal into silence, like an old man so sure he is deaf to questions, and even ready to use conventional terms like "highest life" and "Providence" if these are handy. Yet awareness of the language used is not altogether lost; that degree of self-abandonment would come next, in the stage of pure "contemplation." "So subtle, so quiet, yet so tenacious" is a sequence that moves consciously to an emphasis upon its third word, whose connotations of muscular effort and stubborn retention abruptly oppose the easy image conveyed by the phrase "open channel" established at the beginning of the same sentence. The lofty exaggerations ("I have never expressed," "I have never heard") build authority for *their* rhythmic completion, in the understatedly unemphatic "I know that the whole truth is here for me." The repetition of "I cannot . . . I cannot" firmly removes the talkative ego, the answerer of specific questions, from the reader's presence, for the speaker wishes to make himself entirely empty of pretense before he says, "There lies the unspoken thing, present, omnipresent." One is, I am sure, not meant to hear any theological stress on that "omni-." There is no need of it. "Whoever said it, this is in the right key" (W.VI.248).

AUDIENCE

THE fulfillment of tone is the relation a writer maintains with his readers and listeners, the accommodation they make to his voice. When Emerson wrote of the effect his writings might have or did have upon his readers, he tended to depreciate his own powers of persuasion and to wish for a temperate reaction. He would have liked, he said, to serve as "a friendly & agreeable influence," not as an "explosion & astonishment. . . . I neither wish to be hated & defied by such as I startle, nor to be kissed and hugged by the young whose thoughts I stimulate" (J.VI.86-87). The wish expressed here was presumably true with respect to many readers for whom he was merely an influence, and therefore not an intellectual event they could explain publicly on paper. Besides, the first-rate Americans who were influenced positively—Thoreau, Whitman, William James, even Melville—were "influenced" in ways so indirect or pervasive or complex that it must have been difficult for them to disentangle exactly what they found in Emerson's work from what was in the air (even if their own needs had left them free to be absolutely honest). The spiritual history of these men includes Emerson in ways that inhibited any formal expression of indebtedness. It was in the very nature of Thoreau's relation to the Emersonian initiative, for instance, that the younger man could not account for its total importance to him in any deliberate, once-and-for-all way. And this is still truer of Melville, with his minor acknowledgments and equivocal hostilities. When he mentions Emerson, or parodies his weak side in *The Confidence Man,* or writes comments in the margin of an essay, he is slighting or rancorous, or brief and grudging—although the Emersonian Soul is the very axletree of Melville's active imagination.

There is, to be sure, the famous anecdote about Whitman's reading the *Essays* during his lunch hour and being "brought to the boil" as a result. Whitman prevaricated about this story, though his later comments on his debt are far more generous and full than anything we have from Thoreau and Melville. In any case, the whole character of *Leaves of Grass* is a profound denial of such denials as he is guilty of. One does have John Jay Chapman, whose fine essay I have already referred to. One has Arnold and Clough and, on the continent, Nietzsche, Proust, even Gide. And we have various "minor" people, whose vanities encouraged their exposure of discipleship, for to them an indebtedness to Emerson could seem the most interesting part of their own public character. One had probably better not rely too much on the word of such men as James A. Garfield, who wrote that, although he could not remember more than one sentence from an address Emerson had given at Williams while he was a student, he dated his intellectual life from that moment.[7] The formal occasion on which Garfield was asked to comment is unlikely to have been conducive to full accuracy.

What one picks up from such anecdotes, though, is an idea of how people felt they should express the outlines of the mysterious impact of Emerson's personality years after the period of direct influence. This impact was extraordinarily pervasive, as any reader of the nonfictional literature, the essays and reminiscences, of the late nineteenth century knows. A present-day investigator can find himself turning back with a certain nostalgia to the first generations of commentators on Emerson. These men wrote their books and articles with much less in the way of "material" to work from than we have. Still they were thoroughly conscious of Emerson the man. They knew Emerson's ideas and had a notion of the sources of these ideas, but what chiefly impressed them and justified their critiques was a private response to a certain kind of person—the kind of person we have been trying to derive once more from instances of successful tone—a person who in some uniquely valuable way stood for the Soul in a philistine age with perfect tact, benignity, and grace. Most of the critics in this tradition, from Cabot, say, up to the New Humanists, underestimated the full force of the spiritual originality Emerson stood for. Certainly they had no vocabulary for the kind of semantically oriented appreciation typical of the most recent critical generation. And they lacked the very great knowledge of the literary and philosophic background that scholars have brought to light since. But they were not without a strong sense of Emerson's moral authority.[8]

Today one can best get back to the nature of that authority by consulting the accounts of such Emersonian conversions as those of Moncure Conway and John Albee—both frank and proud members of the discipleship. Stimulated by the report of Emerson's death, Conway wrote a book. In it he recalled

the secret nook near my Virginian home, to whose crystal fount and flowers my eighteenth spring carried a wintry heart. Near that wooded slope the Rappahannock spread silvery in the sunshine, placid after its falls foam-white in the distance, streaming past its margin of meadows to the peaceful homes and spires of Fredericksburg. Fresh from college, now from every career planned by parent or friend I had recoiled: some indefinable impediment barred each usual path: the last shadow settled around me when the law-book was closed to be opened no more. Utterly miserable, self-accused amid sorrowful faces, with no outlook but to be the fettered master of slaves, I was then wont to shun the world, with gun for apology, and pass the hours in this retreat. So came I on a day, and reclined on the grass, reading in a magazine casually brought. The laugh and chatter of negroes pushing their flat-boats loaded with grain, the song of birds, the sound of church-bells across the river, all smote upon a heart discordant with them, at discord with itself. Nature had no meaning, life no promise and no aim. Listlessly turning the printed page, one sentence caught my eye and held it; one sentence quoted from Emerson, which changed my world and me.

A sentence only! I do not repeat it: it might not bear to others what it bore to me: its searching subtle revelation defies any analysis I can make of its words. All I know is that it was the touch of flame I needed. That day my gun was laid aside to be resumed no more.[9]

Albee's first experience was similar. He picked up a copy of *Representative Men* in a bookstore—he could not afford to buy it, at 75 cents—and began to read: "I read a few pages, becoming more and more agitated, until I could read no more. It was as if I had looked in a mirror for the first time. I turned around, fearful lest some one had observed what had happened to me; for a complete revelation was opened in those few pages, and I was no longer the same being that had entered the shop. These were the words for which I had been hungering and waiting."[10] These two young men, one a Southerner and the other a Yankee, shared an experience that must have been common to many others who did not write reminiscences. At the moment of discovering Emerson, both were rather guiltily escaping from the obligations of ordinary life. Their moments of evasion have about them a smouldering, inexplicit, secretive air. Both were half-knowingly in search of an identity that would put them right with themselves. They found it by reading words. In each case there was an absolute, instantaneous, and uncritical absorption of the mind displayed upon the page.

Experiences of this sort seem to have been fairly common in the nineteenth century among solitary, conscientious, and unhappy young people with a fair degree of education, a type the age produced in quantity. Of course Emerson was far from being the only writer whom we know to have been readable in this all-

or-nothing way. We can think of Mark Rutherford reading Wordsworth, finding himself as a result relieved of a very painful attack of anxiety neurosis; or Alton Locke, in Kingsley's novel, reading Carlyle's *French Revolution,* with revolutionary results; or the moony young farmer in Olive Schreiner's *African Farm* coming across Mill's *Political Economy* in an attic trunk. It is interesting to speculate about the necessary conditions of this kind of experience. One seems to need, for one thing, a puritan culture that would predispose its young members to find an extraordinary value in words that can be heard or privately read; words, such a culture would lead them to assume, could be extravagantly and bindingly truthful. Then too one would seem to need a fairly meager or provincial environment, too barren to multiply literary resources and thus diminish the relative claims of any one book. For such an event to happen as a result of reading a secular book, one would also need a situation in which the traditional religious culture as such is in decline, and the original holy book, because it is associated with social forms against which the adolescent feels a need to rebel, is no longer capable of satisfying a surviving instinct to read religiously. It was the ex-Calvinist whose expectations outran the decorous pieties of liberal religion who could find the most in Emerson. A certain lack of specificity is also remarkable. Albee does not remember the words that had such an effect on him, and Conway, though he does apparently remember the words, is unwilling to repeat them. The secret new life they found is not, one gathers, attributable to any specific words, or at least not in any sense another mind could be trusted to recognize. There is something extraliterary about such experiences, something transient generated by the special condition of one person on one occasion.

Though it is easy to associate this kind of reading with the nineteenth century, we can still find analogues in our own day. The use of literature for secret self-discovery is typical of a certain sort of adolescent in any time and place. Teachers occasionally encounter in students claims to a special possessive relation to some book, claims that transcend the normal rules of literary accountability. They tend, perhaps not for any very creditable reason, to be rather harsh with such enthusiasms. Professional readers deprecate responses that cannot readily be made public and arguable, and have little sympathy with the habit of mind that fastens on isolated sentences as supremely meaningful.

Emerson, though, can seem to invite just this kind of reading, which the modern secular teacher has learned to inhibit or disguise in himself and tries to train out of his students. A less nervously sophisticated age would not have excluded responses of this kind. For the Victorians, a passionate private response that engaged the full resources of the Soul was a legitimate goal for reading, and something to be pleased about rather than ashamed of. Responses of this kind still occur, but below the surface of critical respectability; they have become an interruption to the public pursuit of intellectual competency, instead of a part of a process of valued personal change.

Of these two early disciples, Albee is the better witness to the effect a reading of Emerson could have on sensitive minds in his generation. He testifies for all those young men and women who must have read the *Essays* and attended the lectures in the late thirties and forties, few of whom became writers themselves. Many of the best of them must have died in the early years of the war.[11] Albee registers Emerson's special function as mediator of an identity for the youth who "awakens to the fact of his own personality, his ego, his independent being," without knowing more than that this being has claims. "At this critical period it is of momentous consequence in what direction he is drawn; what influences"[12] are brought to bear upon the nascent self, what definition of man is offered to him.

Emerson is exceedingly sensitive to this green-spirited condition and to the quality of such influence as can be received or given. He describes the condition he addresses in several places. "We seldom see anybody who is not uneasy or afraid to live" (W.IV.288), he says, a remark that applies with special force to the young person painfully aware of his own fear of life and therefore suffering the anxieties of an ambiguous identity, with its lack of trust in any native connection between self and Soul. More specifically, he speaks in "Education" of "a young soul with a thought that is not met, looking for something which is not there, but which ought to be there: the thought is dim but it is sure, and he casts about restless for means and masters to verify it; he makes wild attempts to explain himself and invoke the aid and consent of the bystanders" (W.X.144-145). The immediate need of such a young man is to convert his inchoate repugnances and yearnings into a self firm enough to confront the unsatisfactory social world; to establish a positive "independence of spirit" to replace that easy "insulation of place" (W.I. 174) to which, in confusion, he may wish to retire. The role of men of genius is to discover the grounds of psychic confidence for their uncreative fellows; a poet and prophet can thus be "more himself than he is" (W.III.5).

The chief ground of confidence, whether one seeks it from a psychiatrist like a modern youth or from a prophet like the more individualistic Victorian, is the discovery that the power by which one lives in the world, and the power by which one recognizes objective reality, can act within one's own self. One's self can then seem more than merely one of the agencies of the very world, familial, communal, or academic, with which one is incoherently struggling. One wants to discover that the Soul is one's *own,* not a specialized vested interest of society. One wants to see that things are, not because you are told they are by parents and friends whom one loves and hates, but because one can see that they are. This much of the Emersonian contribution to the predicament of the emerging self we could predict from recollecting the core of his doctrine. But the Soul as an influence upon the young was particularly strong in its moral component. The new self which the disciple felt his master's sacred words made available to him was real precisely to the degree that it incorporated, not only the sense of life and the disinterested consciousness, but also the old self's conscience.

This, perhaps, is one of the distinguishing features of nineteenth-century conversions. The conscience, these converts could discover, might be used instead of fought, evaded, or just surrendered to; it could be on one's own side. Thus the self could become aware not only of the freedom proper to it as a natural being, but of the chosen control implicit in that freedom. One became free to follow one's independent sense of right, unoppressed by incomplete rebellions against the conventions of one's social group. Moral responses could thus become interior, an active function of one's proper subjectivity. Albee notices the

presence of this constituent in the response to the Emersonian
word:

At an opportune moment Emerson met the dawning consciousness and
intelligence, and I doubt not continues to do so, of many young men
when it must be confessed they were surcharged with the exaggerations
of self-importance; when their newly discovered powers were seething
in indeterminate and nebulous disorder. He impressed the importance of
a man to himself and the necessity and dignity of self-reliance. Yet he
directed this thought into such lofty meanings and implications as to
effect the cure of egotism and pretension.[13]

"Egotism" and "pretension" make up the disease of those who
must overprotect a false identity they cannot trust to deal with
their own impulses or with the judgments of the world. One
escapes the disease by going through it, baptizing the ego as the
Soul. This is "self-reliance." The new self is at one and the same
time confirmed in its independence of the external forms in which
others repeat the voice of conscience and strengthened in its
allegiance to that same voice heard from within; there, of course,
it speaks in stern accents, only to be heard gratefully by an
identity willing to accept this voice as part of itself. To put the
matter in contemporary terms: "The superego can be on your
side; if you do not know who you are, attend to your conscience;
it may very well turn out to be closer to your real powers than
the affected personality you are so busy defending, the roots of
which are no deeper than your sense of inferiority to the world
you fear." There is nothing silly about such a promise, when it
can be made real.

Thus moral terms were the loaded ones for the sensitive young
man of Emerson's time; they carried the burden of the organic
and emotional facts. Emerson announced, as Albee puts it, that
"the still small voice . . . could be heard in America and today."[14]
The Soul therefore heard the "admonition" (W.II.45) spoken
of in "Self-Reliance," a challenge that revealed its own depths.
Albee became aware of this process by visiting the master, an
experience he generalized like the initial moment of discovery in
the bookstore: "In meeting him the disappointments, if any there
were, one found in himself. For he measured men so that they
became aware of their own stature, not oppressively, but by a
flashing, inward self-illumination, because he placed something

to their credit that would not stand the test of their own audit."[15] This is well said and might hold even truer of the effect of Emerson's written words than of his actual presence, which, as the opening words of the quotation imply, could be a disappointment to a worshipful youth. Insight, or the recovery of self, involved self-judgment, and it could be dangerous. If a man found that he survived exposure to his own accusation and was larger than he thought, as large as Emerson seemed to think a man was, then there could be an immense release of imprisoned energy. If not, he would either be crushed to nothing or remain in a neurotic trap of overscrupulousness. The contemplation of such an alternative is perhaps what set Chapman to criticizing the effect Emerson could have on an overwrought conscience, the kind of conscience that could not be both roused and transcended.

But risks are necessary and can be exhilarating. "I gain my points, I gain all points, if I can reach my companion with any statement which teaches him his own worth" (W.VII.294). The ambiguity is dangerous—one's worth might be all; one fears it is nothing. By challenging one's conscience to do its worst, thereby accepting responsibility for the possession of it, one faces the fear. It may turn out that one's own worth is good enough after all. Emerson could count on reserves of self-confidence behind the apparent shrinking and diffidence in most of the young men who listened. Their very presence before him attested to their wish that he discover for them their own strength—which implied they believed themselves to possess it. His job was to legitimatize and release their own power, to uncover for them an intrinsic sense of being from which the false absolutes of shame could be dropped as affectation.

Such a stress on the new self (or the depths within the old self newly revealed) of the person addressed goes naturally with a modesty in the speaker who arouses these powers. The polarity helps to explain why Emerson's best tone is so often retiring. Emerson recalls how kings can afford to hear "pure truth" spoken to them by humble messengers who are confident of finding in royalty a magnanimity superior to common self-defensiveness (J.VIII.102). More hyperbolically, he imagines in an early journal that, if Jesus were to return to earth, he would say, "you,

You!" (J.IV.277). The dignity of the person addressed is the absolute thing, not because that person is so important in his own personal right, but because he stands for the Soul at that moment, and his is to be the experience of feeling that this is so; it is *his* opportunities for experience that are to be placed before him. No doubt there was in practice a certain relish on both sides of this social paradox, for the young man, whoever he was, had come to the great Mr. Emerson thinking himself very small and green. Yet he came, actually, so that the spiritual balance might be reversed, and Emerson knew this.

Whether such a reader visited Emerson literally, and heard him speak privately, or whether he read the prophet's words in a book, the meaning of whatever was said or read was inevitably within himself. As Chapman puts the matter, in a not very graceful image, Emerson's sentences "get driven into your mind like nails, and on them catch and hang your own experiences, till what was once his thought has become your character."[16] A reader seemed to find "his own secret biography" (W.II.30) in passages written before he was born, to experience the same joy that Emerson himself reports upon encountering in other men's books words that seemed to come from forgotten manuscript of his own. A scholar's job, Emerson thought, is to "replace to" his readers "those private, sincere, divine experiences" of which he is aware they "have been defrauded" by their own inhibitions and cowardice. And sympathetic readers did respond gratefully to the implied invitation. Albee observes with awed admiration that "he is thinking over what you have thought; such is his insinuating, flattering address. He seems to whisper, 'I am merely the organ; the idea is yours.' "[17]

It is then quite literally true with Emerson that his ideal reader "has heard from me what I never spoke" (J.V.569). Emerson's formal justification for this abnegation of his own rights as a mere thinker is his theory that a philosopher is "only a more or less awkward translator of things in your consciousness." If he, or anyone else, fails in "rendering back to you your own consciousness," he should be dismissed in favor of another who may prove more capable of this essential service. Once illumination occurs, "you will find it is no recondite, but a simple, natural, common state which the writer restores to you" (W.II.

345). The job of the oracular writer is simply to make you aware of your own riches. You are restored to the possession of the "simple, natural, common" sense that can see these facts as facts, not distorted by a hundred defenses.

Emerson's ventures, like the positive remarks of any good teacher, are therefore never final; in both cases the putative "Oh, I see . . ." of the attentive listener is the necessary completion. He presupposes the actual (and to him forever unknown) interests of his reader as the context in which the things he says take on their right meaning. What Emerson says is true for him, to be sure, but interesting to others only so far as it is equally true for them. His own life was a kind of laboratory in which to test general principles, which become valid when another finds them true in his own experience. So completely does Emerson work in this fashion that, as Chapman says, "he has probably succeeded in leaving a body of work which cannot be made to operate to any other end than that for which he designed it."[18]

To persons who find within themselves the necessary prompt response, this kind of teaching seems marvelously successful, for the teacher will be invested with the glow of discovery given off by the newly active powers of the student; but to those who fail to respond, for good or bad or simply accidental reasons, it can seem to have no point at all. An attentive person who was flattered by the watchful expectancy with which (according to Albee) visitors to the Emerson household were treated could compliment the master's manner on such visits as like that of the "finest women one has ever seen or heard."[19] But somebody whose hopes had been frustrated could use the same image in a derogatory sense:

I remember well what maidenly letters I used to receive from him, with so many tentative charms of expression in them that if he had been a woman one would have been delighted in complimenting him; but, as it was, you could say nothing about them, but only pocket the disappointment they brought. It is painful to recollect now the silly hope that I had, along the early days of our acquaintance, that if I went on listening something would be sure to drop from him that would show me an infallible way out of this perplexed world. For nothing ever came but epigrams; sometimes clever, sometimes not.

This is Henry James, senior, writing to J. E. Cabot as the latter was preparing his *Memoir,* and Cabot calls the judgment "unjust."[20] But how unjust is it? Thoroughly used to the prophetic mode and milieu, and a fellow Swedenborgian, the elder James could feel himself part of the potential Emersonian audience. He expected just what others got; he was sure that if he went on listening to the voice of the sage, a sentence would strike him that would have a transcendent meaning. It would "show him an infallible way out." He reports that instead he received only epigrams. But the successful listener also received "only" some epigram. Any transcendent sentence would have been, to the literary eye, an epigram—a mere epigram to those for whom it did not happen to supply the awaited imaginative key, those who could not *believe* what they heard.

Both James and Cabot, then, may be understood as missing a chance to understand what the frustrated New Yorker's experience could contribute, as a negative instance, to illuminate the inwardness of a successful reader's response. But while one can put James's irritation to an unintended use, one can also sympathize with the social side of it. It is possible to feel that Emerson does not step forward enough, does not play a proper "masculine" role. The hope that he would show a way out by exerting personal authority can be a fair expectation. For if social reality implies the presence of two persons in complementary roles, the expectations of both sides seem to deserve satisfaction. Someone who has put himself in the position of a follower and finds that his presumed leader refuses to act as a leader, but substitutes a baffling reference to some mysterious action he, the follower, is *not* doing and could only do by abandoning his own role as follower—such a person can be forgiven a sense of anger and frustration.

The statement that Emerson talked too much like a woman was James's image for Emerson's failure to satisfy these social expectations. The failure in his case may be partly accounted for by James's own firm sense of his personality. By the time Emerson arrived on the scene, James was in fact too distinctly himself, too sure of what he knew, to be teachable by the means Emerson employed. Emerson was chiefly a prophet for the young. Yet such a reaction can be paralleled and multiplied by the complaint, registered in the notes to Rusk's edition of the *Letters,* which local newspaper writers made during Emerson's western tours: that the lecturer took an excessively modest tone. Expecting something burlier and more definite, the audiences (if these reporters are to be trusted) were disappointed rather than stimulated.

Having countered the enthusiasm of Albee with the distaste of the elder James, we may return to a positive version of the Emersonian influence. Bronson Alcott was no young man in search of identity in his relations with Emerson. If anything, Alcott was the leader and Emerson the follower. Yet in one famous moment of crisis, Emerson acted for Alcott in precisely the best Emersonian way, doing for him what could not be done for James. In the early months of 1837 Alcott was in a state of despair over losing his experimental school in Boston, and with it the prospect of a solution to his life-long search for an effective relation to the world. He was desolated by unfair criticism of him and his new methods. To one of the newspaper attacks Emerson replied in a letter he wrote Alcott personally. Throughout the tone is admirable, but the closing is particularly impressive: "I hate to have all the little dogs barking at you, for you have something better to do than to attend to them. But every beast must do after its kind, and why not these? And you will hold by yourself and perfectly forget them."[21] It is the final sentence here that is most striking. The voice is entirely quiet and confident, and therefore builds confidence in the person addressed. The attribution of integrity and calm to Alcott obviously made it easier for the unhappy man to possess or renew in himself these same qualities. Alcott gratefully copied the letter, which expressed the "first sympathy that has stolen on my ear from the desolate and doubting present. Only Emerson, of this age, knows me, of all that I have found."

The circumstances here allow us to fill in the necessary prerequisite for such successes as this, a prerequisite that analogous intellectual moments of discovery tend to hide. Alcott finds his solution for himself; but the ambiance of his self-discovery is the love his friend gave him. Because Emerson acted and spoke as a friend, he could be accepted as a prophet of an impulse to which Alcott could rally. In January of the next year, when Alcott's difficulties were by no means yet over, he records in his journal

meeting Emerson on the street and receiving further encouragement. Emerson had said to him, "I know no man of diviner faith
in the soul,"[22] which of course reinforced Alcott's independent
belief in the same entity. Affection was consummated in self-
reliance.

A didactic emphasis on the re-creation of the listener, and on
the positive social and verbal action of the speaker as merely
indispensable means to that end, has a tonal equivalent in the
note of intimacy we have already noticed. Emerson stresses the
advantage a man can take of his own shyness in written words,
which render their author happy and effective to the degree that he
writes "always to the unknown friend" (J.VII.440) or "to God"
(J.V.378), and therefore avoids social inhibitions. His own best
comments on the problems of communication characteristically
start from the side of the addressee. To say that "the hearing
ear is always found close to the speaking tongue" (W.V.47), or
to praise that kind of listening which has "a perfect conviction
that nobody hears but you" (J.III.496), is to keep the emphasis
constantly on the rights of the receiver. " 'Tis the good reader
that makes the good book; a good head cannot read amiss"
(W.VII.296). This good receiver believes himself, as Albee
says, "alone addressed; it is like a personal interview,"[23] though
a "hortatory" one, a "call to me, to you." Emerson once remarked that a proportion exists between the length of a speech
and the distance it assumes between speaker and listener (W.II.
311); if this is so, a speaker of sentences must be the most
intimate speaker of all.

Closeness intensified verges upon incorporation of the two
communicating identities. The perfection of eloquence would be
the abolition of its conditions: Emerson imagines a listener,
amazed by what he hears, who ceases to realize that the words
he absorbed had a source in another person, or were indeed
words at all; he "would have the sense only of high activity &
progress" (J.V.21) in his own Soul.

The annihilation of the speaker's self on behalf of the listener
is a sort of metaphor, false when taken too literally, of the corresponding self-annihilation experienced by the listener when he
genuinely hears something. When this happens, the listener does
transcend the social relation implicit in all uses of words, since

he shares powers which, though authentically his own in the sense that no one could deny they were available to him, do not belong to those parts of his personality that distinguish him from a particular speaker. Reading is not simply the art of discovering and responding to the functional presence of an alien person, though it is at least that. It is also the participation of one's own faculties in the achievement of a common reality. One reads to hear a voice, to know one lives in a world of different voices, and one is not properly reading unless this is happening. But one wants to go on and hear what this voice is saying about something. The act of understanding whatever statement is being made is the consummation of the act of reading, just as the recognition of the person speaking is the necessary preliminary. Emerson's theoretical statements sometimes have a way of hopping over the social means to get at the spiritual end; the end really does exist, even if hopping is not always the way to explain how to get there.

A journal entry says of the act of communication: "All that we care for in a man is the tidings he gives us of our own faculty through the new conditions under which he exhibits the Common Soul" (J.VI.13). Our own faculty feels glorified to us because by its exertion we find ourselves engaged with some reality at the best possible angle. We therefore find ourselves to be at that moment identical with the relevant positive agencies of experience. The exhilarating moral implication is that we *might* know our reality all the time with all of ourselves; we are, potentially, already in the only point of view from which the whole can be understood.

Thus when we read that someone "speaking the most intelligible of propositions is so near as to be already a part of myself" (J.V.70), we should be sure to put the emphasis on the "intelligibility" of the propositions; it is this quality in them that strikes the listener and holds his attention open. "There is for every man a statement possible of that truth which he is most unwilling to receive,—a statement possible, so broad and so pungent that he cannot get away from it, but must either bend to it or die of it" (W.VII.91-92). A true "statement" of this truth would be one that brought on insight, acknowledgment, and self-penetration. Such moments, whoever their mediator may be, are always objective experiences of consciousness. There is for every man a "statement *possible*," says Emerson characteristically; there is no guarantee that it will ever actually be made by anyone. Yet once made, it is bound to be "broad and pungent" in proportion to the emotional ramifications of the truth expressed. Just so far as that truth is vital, just so far does failure to take possession once it has been made available diminish the one it concerns. To neglect such a truth, once it is fairly presented, is indeed to "die" a degree, to kill off those interests that it sums up. Thereby one warps and weakens one's power of response to any truth at all. A true speaker is someone with the immediate authority to prevent such a lapse. "Man, never so often deceived, still watches for the arrival of a brother who can hold him steady to a truth until he has made it his own" (W.III.11).

Naturally this kind of experience of insight is most gratifying where the difficulties are greatest. At the edge of the public light, where expression and agreement dwindle and the inarticulate haze of privacy supervenes; at the beginnings of the realm of ignorance, where authorized versions fail and all conceptions appear equally dubious and equally entertainable: here is the region where truth is constantly to be discovered. This frontier is most sharply present within one's self, where the stir of feeling begins, and the emotional life is therefore the best arena in which to test generalizations that Emerson deliberately kept afloat and unattached from any context. A coward soul is always free to interpret what Emerson says in a way that does not allow it to reach through to the places in him where matters are genuinely in a tangle. "Who listens to eloquence makes discoveries" (J.X.246). One has only to redefine "eloquence" a little to move in the right direction. To *stay* moving is of course harder; it is ultimately a question of tact, of staying in a condition of readiness, the "awe and singleness" referred to in a memory of a conversation with his son Waldo: "The little boy who walks with me in the woods, has no design in his questions, the question which is asked in his mind he articulates to me, over him, over me,—we exist in an element of awe & singleness" (J.VI.35).

The presence of a large audience does not substantially alter the relation between speaker and listener typical of Emerson, but it does sharpen some of the effects we have observed. Emerson speaks of how Shakespeare used theatrical tradition as a spring-board from which his mind could take off. "It holds him to the people, supplies a foundation for his edifice, and in furnishing so much work done to his hand, leaves him at leisure and in full strength for the audacities of his imagination" (W.IV.194). The circumstances of the public lecture, with the sermon tradition behind it, evidently suited Emerson for the same reasons. When Albee read Emerson in solitude, he felt himself "an auditor in a vast temple, with one voice resounding, distant and solemn, and calling upon me to be a God."[24] Something like this might become true in an actual meeting house or lecture hall, even though, as we know, Emerson's voice did not literally resound and the rooms he used were not vast temples. The feeling of "latent omniscience" (W.X.183) evoked in a solitary reader could be sharpened in a situation that raised private hope to public expectation. The mere physical presence of scores or hundreds of others ready for the word would unconsciously heighten any listener's sense that the mind the speaker addressed was a general one—that Man was being spoken to.

In any successful public lecture, the Soul becomes something more than the flash of communication among otherwise isolated minds. It can be felt as a constant presence, in the stirring and stillness of the people, in their willingness to accept the orator's words as a sufficient expression for themselves. In the buzz of its multitudinous existence, an audience constitutes a fund of concern out of which the speaker coins words all may share together, testifying to their unity by laughter, sudden silence, or applause. And if the lecture takes place in a church; if the lecturer was once a minister and still dresses in clerical black; if the topic is spiritual in nature, and the audience has come with expectations half-defined by a religious tradition in which God's possession of the spirit was felt to be a real possibility—then any explicit identification of that shared Soul of the meeting will have a religious meaning.

Such a public situation throws a great emphasis on the immediate relation of speaker and audience. Each listener focuses what Chapman calls his "virgin attention" whenever the attitude of the orator implies authority. The audience pays its speaker the exacting compliment of an "insatiable expectation," longing to be filled, even when it is in fact only allowed to "eat clouds, and drink wind" (W.I.346-347). The speaker, then, stands toward his listeners as nature stood toward him in the moment of inspiration. The "upturned faces" at an Emerson lecture, says Albee, were never disappointed of the sentence that could "cut clean, sound to the depths, soar to the heights."[25] Albee does not mention the other moments when the lecture was no more than an "escapade, a non-committal, an apology, a gag" (W.II.152). But even when he is disappointed, the "good hearer is sure he has been touched sometimes; is sure there is somewhat to be reached, and some word that can reach it. When he listens to these vain words, he comforts himself by their relation to his remembrance of better hours, and so they clatter and echo unchallenged" (W.I.139).

The surviving words of any great lecture can often seem "vain" to the reader who peruses them after the fact. Emerson is no exception. It is difficult, reading the series of lectures as they are now being published or turning over the neat sheets of manuscript, each set stitched into its separate booklet, to feel how the ideal of corporate communication could have become actual with the help of such material as Emerson provided. Much of what he read aloud reappears in the essays, of course; but the cruder context, with its public exigencies of subject matter and organization, seems to lack the close, stringent authority of the essay versions. Throughout the lectures (less so than in the earlier and more diffuse sermons, but still considerably), Emerson seems to be talking down somewhat, as if he supposed that, however little he knew about his big topics, his listeners could be presumed to know even less. Such a presumption of inequality renders eloquence more facile but checks prophetic possibilities, for the Soul acts only in situations where a speaker ventriloquizes the live sense of the meeting. Prophecy is fatally inhibited when the audience feels itself beneath the tepid superiorities of an alien expert. The early lectures are plainer than the essays, more fluent, but consistently less interesting. Everything reads a little flat and obvious, where it is not pretentious. Emerson took more knowledge for his province than his intellectual equals would have granted him the right to claim. How much, a critical reader of these lectures can think, did Emerson know, in any way he would himself have respected, about art or politics or the English worthies? Only enough to display a country-college intelligence well below his proper powers. The lectures are the popular fabrication of an efficient old-fashioned rhetorician. The "we" that tags the sentences is not a real we, not a true group, but a condescension.

So much at least a modern inspector of the remaining evidence may be apt to conclude. What is missing, of course, cannot be restored except by the imagination working upon the memory of occasions when a meager text was no obstacle to wonderful dramatic results. Everyone has such memories of public situations in which the hush of expectancy was gratified. It is by reference to these occasions that one can probably best put oneself into sympathetic relation to past achievements of the same kind. For the modern reader of the lectures, Emerson's success must remain putative, but there is no reason to suppose it could not have been real for those who were unembarrassed by any literary prejudice against public speaking, and were fortified by the special expectations Emerson's presence always raised.

These expectations must be counted in. To generate them, a special audience is needed, prepared not merely by curiosity but by a certain kind of hope. It would seem typically to consist of young men who have received all the education their society can give them, but who feel unwilling to take up the careers society has prepared for them. They find their foot hesitating before the next step they and their elders have assumed they were ready to take. The particular group addressed should also be homogeneous; they must have shared at least the final stages of the education that has brought them to this pass. And they must be aware of their discontent without knowing clearly what to do about it. Any situation that gathers a group fitting this description, under the vague promise that someone may speak to the problem, will create a prophetic opportunity. Whether or not a prophetic voice is actually heard, the mere act of assembly will seem—both to the participants and to those who read about it later—a portent, an omen of undeveloped possibilities, and therefore exciting to the Soul. When the voice *is* heard to articulate the sense of the meeting, we can find the kind of extravagant expressions of conversion and relief that Albee attests to.

PART III

The Soul's Emphasis Is Always Right

THE EMERSONIAN CAREER:
FIRST CRISIS

THROUGH the course of the argument so far, I have been assuming that Emerson's message regarding the Soul is all of a piece. I have tried to trace the ramifications of a single great idea about the act of experiencing and to relate these severally to their reflections in the dimension of words. I have assumed that Emerson's doctrine of the Soul, like the Soul itself, exists in a kind of eternity. This Soul we have seen to consist of a conjunction of the organic faculty, the intellect, and the moral sentiment, and the special work of these distinct agencies has appeared to us through the literary dimensions of rhythm, metaphor, and tone. To arrange an explication in this fashion is to imply that the essence of the Emersonian achievement can be abstracted from the whole body of his work, and reorganized to display its psychic and verbal structure, without regard to the changes Emerson's ideas underwent during his lifetime.

Now to make this assumption is, as perhaps more than one reader has already muttered, an illusion: Emerson's beliefs did change over his lifetime and, with them, his conception of the Soul. I would be inclined to say that the illusion nevertheless contains a preponderance of basic truth. The Soul does act from eternity, as Emerson would have been quick to maintain, and it would not be hard to imagine him defending a method of displaying his ideas about the Soul that he used himself when he dealt as a critic with the work of other thinkers. It is always the Soul that Emerson speaks for—variously at various times in his life, but consistently on its behalf. His major topic, then, may legitimately if artificially be conceived as existing in a certain independence of the personal vicissitudes that influenced his mode of expression.

Still, to talk of the self or personal identity, and of Emerson's didactic commitment to a renewed sense of self for his reader, ought to remind the reader of what my critical point of view, convenient and orderly as it is, has increasingly omitted. What I have been looking at is the doctrine and practice of the Soul in Emerson's best thought and best writing—the ideas and images and tones that ray out from an imaginary point at the height of his spiritual trajectory. It is time to inspect briefly some of the private conditions that create and underlie this trajectory, and the changes in belief and emphasis that express its curve. The life experience of the imaginative artist always bears a meaningful relation to the sense and structure of the works he leaves behind. This relation is never a simple identity, but it is at least an analogy. What a man does in life is *like* what his work preaches for him. To trace a career, then, is to seek out facts and responses to fact that parallel or interestingly contradict the import of the statements we can read. Emerson's life is important, in particular, because we can find within its history and its specific crises illustrations of that alternation between the action and passivity of the Soul which his work transmutes into doctrine and literature. An artist metamorphoses his experience; what remains behind, to be reported and speculated upon by the cooler eye of history, can supply hints to explain what has been lifted up.

The name of the late Stephen Whicher will always be associated among students of Emerson with the rediscovery, for modern readers, of the connection between the phases of Emerson's life and those of his ideas. I owe much in what follows to his work. It will be more obvious still that I take for granted the wealth of biographical information organized by recent scholarship: the operative names here would be those of Rusk and Cameron.

There would be no point for my purposes in reviewing in detail the history of Emerson's early years. The facts of his life begin to be relevant to the reader interested in the development of his ideas when we first encounter Emerson on the verge of an experience of the same character as that undergone by his disciples. The first Emersonian conversion to the Soul was Emerson's own. It started as such experiences often do, during a period of deep unhappiness that seems to have begun to move toward crisis with his entrance into the Harvard Divinity School.[1] Until his graduation from Harvard College, Emerson had been an active, ambitious, virtuous son, student, and budding rhetorician, not as distinguished publicly as some of his competitors, but to all appearances not very different in character and mind from other bright but conventional boys of his class and generation.

Entering advanced study in the spring of 1825, however, Emerson found himself once and for all embarked upon the ministerial career that his family, especially his mother and his redoubtable Aunt Mary, had planned for him. Almost immediately he found that he could not use his eyes for study. This conjunction of events cannot be accidental. It is fair to suspect that the eye trouble was at least partly psychosomatic. It seems to reveal a turning in upon himself of a hostile impulse to resist a social fate he did not want but could not summon the insight and resolution to repudiate openly. If he could not read, he may have unconsciously decided, he could not study to be a minister. By December of 1825, he could use his eyes well enough to write his older brother William in Europe that he was also afflicted with a lame hip, which he could not get the doctors to take seriously (L.I.163-164). He tried to recover his health by the economically logical but psychologically unfortunate means of teaching school—an activity he much disliked and felt he did badly. Meanwhile he became responsible for the support of his brother Bulkeley, by this time a confirmed idiot, a duty that must have increased the pressure of obligation upon him.

Emerson's eyes were operated on, apparently with good results, in December 1825. His first sermon was delivered in October 1826. (In the meantime he had managed to return to theological school.) The story of the origin of this first sermon is well known and instructive. If the traditional account is correct, he must have had the experience on which the sermon was based during the summer of 1825, probably when he was on his uncle's farm in Newton, trying to recover enough health to return to school. He was, the story goes, at work with a Methodist laborer named Tarbox in a hayfield. Tarbox observed, in reply to some remark of the unhappy young graduate student, that men pray all the time and that all their prayers are granted. This redefinition of prayer struck Emerson so strongly that he made his first sermon the following fall a somewhat conventionalized spelling out of the doctrine it implied. A parishioner told him he would never deliver a better. He must have feared this might prove true, for he used the sermon again several times on his southern travels; it was evidently hard to think of a second and a third topic. Always after this, when Emerson reviewed his "natural priests" (J.VIII.554), the men to whom he owed illumination, Tarbox headed the list.

The hayfield experience, whether or not it really occurred as legend has it, falls easily into a pattern of compensatory redefinition that one can detect in Emerson's mature ideas and his mature style. He heard a new and authoritative voice—which came, not from the pulpit, not from a member of the class from which he had been taught to expect the promulgation of religious truth, not in academic circumstances, but in a hayfield, from an agricultural laborer. Yet the essential term remained the same as that implicit in the life he seemed to be resisting: "pray." The word had, however, become reinterpreted. The act of addressing himself publicly to God, as a preacher must, or of speaking articulately of his own wishes—these things were suddenly not merely easy but inevitable. The ministerial career he had just had to give up forcing himself toward was suddenly made possible after all. The essence of that role could be seen within the natural powers of the self. In the light of Tarbox's words, he could have seen that the freedom he had struggled for was already his, his because it was all men's by their very constitution. The discovery is in its structure characteristically "transcendental," but something like such realizations may occur in acts of conversion generally: one finds that the terms by which one thought oneself condemned in fact save, that the test one was nerving oneself to fail has already been passed with honors.

The progress of Emerson's private revolution against his heritage can be read as a repetition of this experience in a series of larger contexts. He was obliged, with great pain, to experience the possibilities of the Soul himself before he could preach it abroad. The immediate results of the Tarbox episode were not conclusive. Throughout 1826 his eyes continued to bother him, and toward the end of October of that year, the month in which the sermon was delivered, symptoms of consumption appeared. These obliged him to give up teaching school.

Through the fall and winter of 1826-27, Emerson was in the

south for his health. Consumption is not merely a psychosomatic disease. But a special association between his symptoms and the profession he was at once fleeing from and preparing for does seem to be made more than once in the letters he wrote to his family from St. Augustine. In January 1827, he observes in a letter to William (who had escaped the family career) that the "stricture" in his lungs came on when he exerted himself preaching,[2] as he did once or twice in borrowed pulpits. The trip south was no real cure, though a vacation in a warm climate was agreeable and interesting. His statements that he was improving seem to have been made to reassure his family and perhaps himself; a lower layer of belief may be revealed by the several references to his lungs in letters to William. Even after his return he complains that his "lungs in their spiteful lobes sing Sexton & Sorrow whenever I only ask them to shout a sermon for me" (L.I.201). This was in June 1827. In the same month, though, he was accepted by the First Church in Boston, where he had preached his first sermon and where his father's career as a minister had ended. He returned to divinity school. He idled and joked as much as he could, to relieve anxiety, and the stratagem partially served. Meanwhile his friend and protector, Ware of the Second Church, had fallen ill, and the older man's fate seemed a portent to his protégé. "You see what lies before your brother," he wrote once more in October 1828 to William—for whom he seems to have reserved this aspect of his worries—"To be a good minister & healthy is not given" (L.I.249).

By Christmas time of 1827 he had met Ellen Tucker, herself already showing signs of the consumption that was to kill her. The searchingly sweet, intense mutuality of their love is plain in her letters.[3] The closeness of sympathy that developed between the lovers in the next three years must have involved the strongest kind of joy and commitment to her presence. Meanwhile Emerson's brother Edward, who had been closest to him in early youth, had become irrevocably insane by June 1828. Marriage with Ellen was settled by December of that year. In January 1829 he was invited to become junior pastor of the Second Church; for Ware, whose sickness had troubled Emerson in the fall of 1827, was obviously dying. Emerson was ordained in March 1829, an event he looked forward to as "execution day"

(L.I.264). The letter of acceptance written to the church was gloomy. In it he makes clear that he did not think he was really strong enough, though he would try to do his duty.

He and Ellen were married in September 1829. Their domestic life, though marred by separation and sickness, was clearly happy. Somewhat over a year later Ellen died, on February 8, 1831. The image of poetry and beauty she left behind never left Emerson. And a year after her death he visited her tomb and opened her coffin.

Emerson's withdrawal from the Second Church over the issue of the Lord's Supper began officially with a letter written in June 1832. The well-known sermon laying out his views followed in September, and the church agreed to accept his resignation in October. The last message to the church was delivered on December 22, 1832. Throughout the course of this year he was ill, first with a sprained knee that prevented him from walking or preaching on his feet, and then with diarrhea—a trouble that may have had a psychic parallel in the cholera that had invaded Boston during the summer, and perhaps also in the issue of the Lord's Supper itself. He remarked to Aunt Mary, apropos of this controversy, that he was "not prepared to eat or drink religiously" (L.I.354). By coincidence the next sentence refers to his stomach ache.[4]

The facts I have been reviewing are established and familiar. To organize them to establish an inner meaning congruous with that of essays not yet written is a dangerous and, at this distance in time, a finally impossible venture. We are all properly sensitive of the limits to which speculation about persons in the past can be carried—perhaps too sensitive. It is easy to inflate the significance of trivial evidence, or evidence that will seem so to anyone but the speculator. Guesses cannot be conclusions. And there is always a certain perversity in reading public statements for a private meaning that cannot, in the nature of the case, ever be tested. At the same time, it would be foolish to let our scruples become automatic or to inhibit, in their name, the sympathetic instincts that carry us toward such tenuous truths as we can reach. One needs to be as tactful as one knows how; but generalizations, though necessarily tentative, even dubious, may still be useful.

The generalization to which the facts of Emerson's early biography seems to me to lead is of this kind. Do not the events of the crisis years suggest the presence of a strong inclination toward death? Many of the people to whom he was close died, and died of a disease that threatened him too. Such deaths could very well have seemed omens of his own dissolution, for when we love, we identify. The more nearly the fate of another is bound up with ourselves, the more vivid an image that fate will supply of what may be in store for us. Moreover, the danger of death seems to have been linked for Emerson with the social identity to which his exterior relations committed him. It cannot be accidental that his illnesses oppressed him most as he prepared and began to practice the duties of the ministry, and left him for good only when he brought himself to abandon it. Nothing but the most total revolution in his way of life could save him from the destruction which loomed ahead. A lesser man could have adjusted to the myriad expectations of others, intellectual as well as social, and never known that adjustment is not life. Emerson was more threatened because he was more sensitive: the absence of life was for him literally death. He had felt life as love for Ellen; but Ellen had died, and he would follow her unless he found a way to rediscover that same life deeper within himself, deeper than the formulas of Boston piety allowed.

The sea voyage to Europe was a much more thoroughgoing repetition of his southern trip, a more effective withdrawal and return. He found himself genuinely free of social constriction and could therefore begin to be healthy. From the earlier escape he had returned to the old way of life; from the second he gained real health and a new identity, which involved, on his return to Concord, a new intellectual and social relation to the world. The abandonment of the old public self was compensated for by the birth of a new one, more effectively public because more profoundly private.

We cannot know for sure why the trip to Europe, of all Emerson's retreats and returns, should have been the one that finally worked and released the energies of the Soul. In part it must have been the decisive break with his professional obligations; whatever he was to be hereafter, it was not a conventional Unitarian minister. In part, it is possible to suspect, the death

of Ellen itself, once it had been fully accepted, could constitute a
relief from the need to maintain certain immaturities of feeling
she had romantically represented. Finally, Emerson's intellectual
progress had reached a stage that justified the social break. The
researches of Kenneth Cameron have shown that the intellectual
side of Emerson's development considerably anticipated his emotional growth, as frequently happens in able young men. His
characteristic ideas begin to emerge in the journals and letters
by the late twenties. An early contact with Berkeley's idealism
had started him in a direction that was confirmed by Coleridge's
idea that God is to be found within. Emerson made the latter
doctrine the major topic of sermons whose texts came directly
from his reading in the *Friend* and in Marsh's edition of *Aids to
Reflection*.[5] A poem, "Gnothi Seaton," which summarizes what
he had learned from these texts, was written in July 1831. As
Cameron puts it, "it is clear . . . that the larger outlines of
Emerson's philosophy were complete in 1831."[6]

This intellectual program had reached a point where the paraphrasable content of the sermons is virtually identical with the
doctrine that may be abstracted from the lectures composed in
the early thirties after his return home, and indeed from *Nature*
itself. The difference is a matter of emotional confidence and
rhetorical firmness. The trip to Europe came at a time when these
new ideas could become true for Emerson, a full expression of a
new-found faith in his own organic life and in the possibility of
a firm social identity that would stand upon it. He was able to
catch up with himself, to see the idea of the inner God he had
read about rendered substantial within him as a trustworthy
enjoyment of life.

The prose style of his journal had been distinctively personal
since the southern trip, but now his ideas also began to take on
the vigor appropriate to someone who has gone back a step to
the ground of his existence and found it secure. By September
8, 1833, he was able to put his new beliefs into a single quick-
moving, half-punctuated paragraph:

But the men of Europe will say, Expound; let us hear what it is that
is to convince the faithful & at the same time the philosopher? Let us
hear this new thing. It is very old. It is the old revelation that perfect
beauty is perfect goodness it is the development of the wonderful con-

gruities of the moral law of human nature. Let me enumerate a few of the remarkable properties of that nature. A man contains all that is needful to his government within himself He is made a law unto himself. All real good and evil that can befal him must be from himself He can only do himself any good or any harm. Nothing can be given to him or taken from him but there is always a Compensation. There is a correspondence between the human soul & everything that exists in the world, more properly, everything that is known to man. Instead of studying things without the principles of them, all may be penetrated unto within him. Every act puts the agent in a new condition. The purpose of life seems to be to acquaint a man with himself. He is not to live to a future as described to him but to live to the real future by living to the real present. The highest revelation is that God is in every man. I (J.III.200-201)

The last "I" after the final period is perhaps the most indirectly appealing quasi-sentence in the whole page of writing. Apparently at first he meant to write something more. In fact the incomplete sentence, however it might have continued, is by itself sufficiently suggestive of the true discovery he had made. The doctrines he summarizes here are themselves summarized in the new first person, whose power to entertain them was an initial proof of Emerson's fresh identity. What was found was a living, unique, independent "I" that could stand at the head of all the sentences that might later be written.

Yet for all that is "new" in these ideas, especially the sense of vital identity that informs them, there is much that is old as well. He has not so much repudiated his past as reaccepted it on his own terms. As in the case of the Tarbox experience, the recovery of powers he could call his own went with a renewed grasp of the inner sense of standards that, in their commonplace form, had been destroying him. As he put it in a journal entry of the following year, "When we have lost our God of tradition & ceased from our God of rhetoric then may God fire the heart with his Presence" (J.III.369). When "God" is lost, God returns; one's revival is expressible in the same terms as one's death; what has been added is a trust that the terms mean a private reality to which they always truly referred.

Stephen Whicher has skillfully marked the equivalences between the old-fashioned repudiated belief and the new doctrine, pointing out how the apparent extremities of transcendental self-assertion were possible because behind them stood the rebaptized verities of New England tradition:

He could proclaim self-reliance because he could also advocate God-reliance; he could seek a natural freedom because he also sought a supernatural perfection; he could challenge society with his heresies because he considered himself closer to the true faith than they; he could assert that the individual is the world because, thanks to the moral law, we know that nothing arbitrary, nothing alien shall take place in the universe; the huge world, which he dared to defy, was really on his side and would not, as it were, spoil his game.[7]

The world was on his side—this is the core of the truth Emerson felt he had discovered. "Fears" had turned to "forces." The new self could be strong because it included the enemies that had terrified the old.

This compensatory shift was considerable enough to found a way of life upon. Emerson returned from Europe able to live once again in his home town with his mother and start serious work on *Nature,* which was to give his new beliefs their first consistent public expression. His first wife's death gave him, he found, $1200 a year[8] (an important compensation for that loss among all his losses). The sum was sufficient to support the psychic independence he had won. "Henceforth," he could say, "I design not to utter any speech poem or book that is not entirely & peculiarly my work" (J.III.361). The immediate result, the early lectures that he delivered in Boston, are a more muffled keeping of this ringing promise to himself than *Nature* or the subsequent essays, but even they express his new freedom of mind. There is a kind of continuous pleasure throughout these lectures in the possession of his own identity, revealed in a delight at contemplating spiritual heroes like Luther and Michelangelo, but also more indirectly in a recital of the pervasive efficacy of "water" in the system of things, or (more abstractly) in the praise of the idea of Man, the principle of heroism in all heroes. It does not seem to be an accident that in the second lecture, "On the Relation of Man to the Globe," much space is devoted to expressing admiration for the skill by which men safely accomplish their purposes in the midst of the natural scene: they can cross the wide ocean, survive storms, evade wild animals. Man, like Emerson himself, is always just escaping extinction by the narrow but sufficient limits his vital and practical resources provide.

The subject matter of the lectures, then, indirectly exhibits a new confidence in the initiating prowess of the subject of action, whether this be impersonal or private, heroic or ordinary. We have further evidence of this confidence in the very choice of the lecture form. Here was a redefinition of the ministry he had been unable to endure, a new platform that compensated for his loss of the traditional authority annexed to the rejected role. Lecturing provided new opportunities to be truthful in his own terms to such topics as would present instances of the Soul at work. He found it was no longer necessary for him to use a fixed traditional language for an experience he had come to know was his own. His new role left the choice of language up to him. Nobody would be present at a lecture on nature or literature or great men equipped with expectations that could inhibit freedom of speech.

He had some further losses to suffer after his return home and the adoption of a new career. George Adams Sampson, a close friend and correspondent, died in July 1834. His brother Edward died in Puerto Rico in October of the same year. This catastrophe had been more or less anticipated; but the death of the other brother who had been close to him, Charles, was more surprising and harrowing. It occurred in May 1835. It is interesting to trace in the letters following this death an interweaving of grief with the conviction that Charles was a kind of alter ego. He wrote to Lydia Jackson, whom he was courting at the time, that she must expect in marrying him to have only a piece of what would have been hers had Charles lived: "How much I saw through his eyes. I feel as if my own were very dim" (L.II. 20). To Carlyle he said that so strong was his dependence on Charles's gifts that "we made but one man together" (C-E.L.I.96) and that Charles was the nobler part of this double entity. But another letter to Carlyle somewhat later could propose, after beginning with a new expression of sorrow at the death, such an uncompromising affirmation of the new and free Emerson as this: "Wake the soul now drunk with a sleep, and we overleap at a bound the obstructions, the griefs, the mistakes, of years, and the air we breathe is so vital that the Past serves to contribute nothing to the result" (C-E.L.I.100). This is not

the voice of a man inclined to interpret the deaths of others as
omens of his own dissolution. The internal shifts occurring before, during, and after the European trip had apparently proved
to him that he did in fact exist in his own right. The habit of
identifying with his brothers persists in the language with which
he mourns Charles. Yet, after all, it was *Charles* who had died,
not himself. He could reinterpret this latest set of losses as
weaker continuations of the earlier ones. He had survived those;
he could survive these.

Whatever unconscious arguments may have accompanied this
phase of Emerson's internal revolution, the drift of events was
by this time clearly in favor of assurance, expansion, and creation. In June 1835 he set down a "statement of the First Philosophy" that summarizes his debt to Coleridge and forms a ground
plan for *Nature*.[9] He married again in September of the same
year. In October of the following year came a son, Waldo. The
child was baptized, as if to mark the compensation his existence
embodied, in the dead Charles's baby robe.[10] It is perhaps significant that the family had wished to name the new child
Charles; Emerson refused, alleging that Charles had disliked his
own name and, besides, Edward had as good a claim to a name-
sake. But the reasons behind the rejection of these other ghostly
identities seem to weigh less than the positive reasons for his
final choice. He gave his son the name by which he was himself
familiarly known. The child's birth can be read as an emblem of
his father's rebirth.

THE LIMITS OF
TEMPERAMENT

To REHEARSE biography literally or speculatively is to stress
the happy outcome of Emerson's period of crisis. Looking back
on the same period from a point in time still further ahead, it
is possible to see a gradual deterioration of the early solution.
We can feel the limits of the successes permitted him. It is pos-

sible to see the new life as a partial conversion, an incomplete cure. The malignant forces, by a dextrous shift of stance, had been eluded; they had even become partly his own to dispose of. How conscious was Emerson of the exact terms on which he enjoyed his adult freedom? One can hear, from a distance, how the tones in which the doctrines are pronounced define these terms. The theory of the Soul can even be seen as "merely" compensation for the inadequacies of the ordinary self. If one's personality is the channel of a loftier identity in which all men of genius participate, one is privileged to assimilate all their powers. Whicher has hinted how the Berkeleyan notion that the "I" creates its world like a fiction might have special attractions to someone who doubted his own reality. The idealist philosophy could rationalize a need to project that doubt outward upon the universe, which would become gratifyingly subordinate to a timid self by owing its existence to inner will and pleasure.[11]

Doubts that the new philosophy had consciously converted into belief continued to appear here and there in Emerson's experience. His pleased astonishment at the discovery that lectures did not exhaust him, that, on the contrary, the more thoughts he gave, the more he had (J.VII.156), suggests an underground worry over the substantiality of his renewed self. This comes out more clearly still in his bitter doubts about the depth of the resources upon which he could draw, doubts that, though finally modulated to the benign resignation of "Terminus," are sharply put in the journal. He gains partial control over his situation, characteristically, by generalizing it, and he speaks often of a certain thinness in the American character. Even the great Webster—always a principal image of a full-blooded, self-confident identity—"cannot do Webster" (J.VI.502) in the American air. And genius seemed to him, on at least one occasion, to be something that once used up could not be restored; he and his generation seemed to be "spending the energies which their father's hardy, silent life accumulated in frosty furrows, in poverty, necessity and darkness" (W.VII.141).

There is an interesting dream, or pair of dreams, that can be read as revealing this double state of mind. It occurred, according to the journal, on September 9, 1861. Emerson dreamed he was lecturing somewhere and caught himself falling asleep; then he was entering a house and found a room one of whose walls had shelves containing valuable vases. The wall itself, however, had a cleft in it and seemed about to fall. In the cleft a man slept; his brother William, who stood by the dreamer, explained that the sleeper was the architect of the house. This figure muttered in his sleep something about a plot to expose him. "When I fairly woke, & considered the picture, & the connection of the two dreams,—what could I think of the purpose of Jove who sends the dream?" (J.IX.339). Certain elements in the dream, even at this distance, seem meaningful enough. We can recall, for one thing, Emerson's good opinion of his strong conventional older brother, who would be a natural authority to point out facts about matters that concerned himself. Then, too, Emerson was proud of his house, to which he had at various times made additions. The room seems to be his own study, and the shelves the bookshelves. If so, the vases would be his own works and papers, as well as the books by other writers that he read as if he had written them. He is himself both the observer and the sleeping architect; the dream in effect exposes him to his own common sense. Sensitive to dreams as he was, respectful as he was of their messages, Emerson could very well have been able to draw a moral, though he does not express any in the journal. The implication of the dream seems to be that his whole life lacked substance to support his rarities and (to change the metaphor as the dream does) that he was not able to stay imaginatively awake all the time.

This is only one dream, and it comes late in Emerson's working life. If it makes a comment, one could argue, it would have to do with his situation in late middle age, when his work was virtually over, rather than with the assumptions behind the creative period. However, there is other evidence for a certain tenuity in the creative self upon which his characteristic work depended. The theme of death continues to run through Emerson's life. I have mentioned already the visit to his wife's tomb. He also took an occasion to look into his son Waldo's coffin, fifteen years after the boy's death. These were the two people other than his brothers with whom he had identified himself most closely. The Mt. Auburn experience we examined when we started occurred in a cemetery. And although the notes in the journal are deliberately limited to moments of life, intellectual or moral, morbid references do creep in from time to time.

To be sure, these may be assigned to the characteristic nineteenth-century sensitivity to death, so much more an imaginative as well as a domestic fact for the middle-class sensibility of that time than for ours. Better, because more indubitably idiosyncratic, evidence of a continuing restriction on the security of Emerson's new self is his sense of isolation. He frequently accuses himself of a failure to love as easily and fully as his belief in the Soul's potential made him wish to do. The remarks in the letters and journal upon friendship show an ambivalent mixture of sympathy and isolation. The man who sourly observes "I cannot go to the houses of nearest relatives, because I do not wish to be alone" (W.VII.14) not surprisingly combined the high romantic value for friendship with a supersensitivity to the inadequacies of actual relationships. Emerson says (perhaps more ambiguously than he is aware) that he could not take entire friendship: he would die of it (J.VI.327). He once calls friends, a little resentfully, "fictions founded on some momentary experience" (J.X.II). At calmer times he can claim to prefer "chronic" (J.VI.427) relations to momentary ones—though perhaps here he was thinking of the less demanding sorts of acquaintanceship, like domestic relations, and not of the intensities that he, like the other transcendentalists, valued so highly. His contempt for "sentiment" occasionally reads as a reaction to the emotional pressure of all possible relations, as well as to the stridencies of some particular friendships. The assertion that "any other affection between men than this geometric one of relation to the same things is a mere mush of materialism" (J.X.189) and his complaint about those who are "devoured by sentiment like premature fruit ripened by the worm" (J.IX.412) have a stridency of their own. They appear in late journal entries, but we can remember that it is precisely at the close of his life that he was publicly at his most benign.

Emerson speaks of his emotional isolation most often with regret, but occasionally the same psychological predicament is something for him to celebrate. "The last revelation of intellect and of sentiment is that in a manner it severs the man from all other men; makes known to him that the spiritual powers are

sufficient to him if no other being existed; that he is to deal
absolutely in the world, as if he alone were a system and a state,
and though all should perish could make all anew" (W.X.83).
The tone here is very positive; but one is tempted to hear beneath it emotional insecurity as well as an intellectual truth. A
more complex statement is sadder, wiser, and genuinely expressive:

Men are best and most by themselves: and always work in society with
great loss of power. They are not timed each to the other: they cannot
keep step, and life requires too much compromise. Men go through the
world each musing on a great fable dramatically pictured and rehearsed
before him. If you speak to the man, he turns his eyes from his own
scene, and, slower or faster, endeavors to comprehend what you say.
When you have done speaking, he returns to his private music. Men
generally attempt, early in life, to make their brothers, afterwards their
wives, acquainted with what is going forward in their private theatre;
but they soon desist from the attempt, in finding that they also have
some farce, or, perhaps, some ear- and heart-rending tragedy forward
on their secret boards, on which they are intent; and all parties acquiesce,
at last, each in a private box, with the whole play performed before
himself *solus*. (W.XII.84-85)

In context this passage continues a paragraph praising genius
in the standard style, saying, as Emerson is always ready to say,
that genius is most itself when it relies on nothing but its own
power. The opening sentences above are consistent with this
assertion, but as the passage continues the tone changes from
perfunctory praise to melancholy recognition. It is not so much
genius as painful isolation that is being described. Men may be
best on their own; but the minute you look at this desirable
solitude, it turns to pain. Men retreat to a "private box"—an
image as funereal as it is theatrical and depressing either way,
for the theater is to Emerson always an emblem of affectation
and falsity. The creations of the self would then become dis-
connected fantasy or hallucination, what he calls "illusion" in
the later essays. The other side of self-reliance, then, can be
deprivation and isolation. It is noteworthy that Emerson himself can make this point as well as can his doubtful neighbor
Hawthorne, or his critical half-disciple Melville, or a score of
later critics who dislike his more positive affirmations.
      Boasts of the advantage of isolation to the "scholar" appear

more frequently, as one might expect, in the published work; the passage above is exceptional. The sense of loss is entrusted more privately to the journal and especially to the letters, where it can appear indirectly through tone even when not rising to the surface as confession or comment. Thus he writes to his brother Charles that it is easier for him to say what he means in letters than to say it in conversation face to face (L.I.191), a remark with some implications of hesitancy and emotional inhibition; but a later letter to Lidian from England is still more explicit and sadder. "Ah you still ask me for that unwritten letter always due, it seems, always unwritten, from year to year, by me to you, dear Lidian,—I fear too more widely true than you mean,— always due and unwritten by me to every sister & brother of the human race. I have only to say that I also bemoan myself daily for the same cause—that I cannot write this letter, that I have not stamina & constitution enough to mind the two functions of seraph & cherub, oh no, let me not use such great words,—rather say that a photometer cannot be a stove" (L.IV.33). There is apology and yearning here, which he could afford, perhaps, to make explicit to his wife. She would, one gathers from the history of their marriage, not really blame him for not being a "stove." There is also acceptance—to my ear, not a complacent acceptance, but a responsible one, which gives him enough freedom to add the minor but genuine touch of wit at the end. A quick change of metaphor is always a sign of self-pleasure in Emerson; isolation, well-expressed, escapes some of the disadvantages of the emotional fact. The ultimate letter to the human race was unwritten and unwritable; but intermediate formulations between that and silence were possible, and he could make them; the wit is a sustaining demonstration of the freedom that his temperament could not hinder him from enjoying.

We can sum up with Chapman's shrewd observation that Emerson knew human feeling chiefly in the form of pain.[12] If the presence of real emotion brought with it a sense of separation from the object of love, whether that object was a star or a friend, we cannot wonder that sentiment, when it appeared or seemed called for, could sometimes hurt or disgust or sadden; or that the lost feeling could become diffused over the actions of isolated intellect.

Of all human feelings, that for women is always a crucial test of the self. The information about Emerson's relation to women that the letters and biographies contain is slight and uninformative. We derive an impression of courteous reticence, of a piercing but inexpressible devotion, a quick emotional undercurrent that could appear in letters but was apparently diverted or chilled by direct contact or by confrontations involving too high a degree of conscious expectation. He remained very close to his mother in a quiet, regular, and apparently unselfconscious way throughout her life, much of which she spent in his household. His second wife he called "Queenie" and "Asia," names that suggest affectionate respect tinged with half-humorous awe, as of a domesticated but instinctively impressive sovereign. His relations with Margaret Fuller and Elizabeth Hoar repeat this preference for authoritative ladies, though the manners appropriate to such an image of the sex proved inappropriate to dealings with the passionate personality of Miss Fuller. With Caroline Sturgis, to judge from the letters, he was still closer to the kind of feelings that, in his domestic relations, he had well under control. The burden of emotion is achingly and hoveringly present in the letters to the last lady, without explicitness and therefore without satisfaction or renunciation. He teases her with an intimacy he can neither yield to nor give up. We have seen how similar feelings are engaged in the relation to Nature herself.

Emerson's first wife Ellen, in contrast, had been far from the queenly type. Young, poetical, sensitive, and sick, she seems to have been a kind of alter ego for him during his period of storm and stress. His love for her appears to have been a romantic projection of his concern with his own identity, like his love for his brothers Edward and Charles. It certainly differed thoroughly from the temperate, sexual, and realistic relation he had with Lydia Jackson. He has little to say about his first marriage. What occurs in the journal is sentimentally inexpressive. It does not pretend to objective accuracy and does not achieve it by accident.

There is also something teasing in Emerson's "sentiment" for his women friends in later life. He protests that he cannot love, but he does not give up the attempt. He tries to provide a simulacrum and steps out of character without really satisfying the

women he addresses. Motives are concealed on both sides, as
often happens when cloudily elevated ladies address prominent
men of letters. The language of these letters is often tantalizingly
and unconsciously erotic. But it does not quite mean what it half
says. Emerson seems to wish to do emotional justice to requirements he cannot naturally accommodate himself to and so cannot
truly name. Instead he talks gently and irrelevantly into the air.
He is more honorable when he can bring himself to ward off
clear demands, as when he writes that very revealing letter to
Lydia after she has accepted his proposal, in which he warns
her quite definitely not to expect the first place in his heart; his
books "divide my day" with "a sunset, a forest, a snow storm,
a certain river-view," which are "more to me than many friends"
(L.I.435). Apparently she accepted the emotional place he thus
prepared for her.

The impressions of a limit to Emerson's emotional freedom
that one derives from the informal papers are confirmed by the
essay on "Love." Ideally, love should be a thoroughly legitimate
act of the Soul. It "seizes on man . . . and works a revolution in
his mind and body; unites him to his race, pledges him to the
domestic and civic relations, carries him with new sympathy into
nature, enhances the power of the senses, opens the imagination,
adds to his character heroic and sacred attributes, establishes
marriage and gives permanence to human society" (W.II.169).
The experience of love unites, in theory, all the faculties of body,
self, and mind. But Emerson could not write a good essay on
love. According to E. M. Berry, "Love" very closely follows the
order of the material contained in Plutarch's corresponding essay
in the *Moralia*, "On Love."[13] Emerson stayed closer to Plutarch
here than anywhere else in his essays, though the classical writer
was a lifelong favorite and Plutarchian anecdotes and references
appear everywhere. One may suspect that the closeness of the
debt is itself a symptom of a lack of imaginative self-confidence.
The resulting essay is a constant embarrassment to the professed
Emersonian, all the more so because it appears in the *First Series*,
otherwise the strongest and most original collection. The rhetoric
is a betrayal: his language is tender, evasive, and indefinite.

Love is more convincingly praised in the poems devoted to or
glancing at it. The strategy of evasion one can feel deflecting the

essay and the corresponding letters takes less effect in a genre wherein Emerson was accustomed to be more cryptic and less inhibited. The aphoristic mode concentrated the impulse to diffuse sentiment. The mythologizing apparatus and the abrupt generalities encouraged by the form preserve the poetry from embarrassments. But, as I have observed in another connection, Emerson the poet seems as a whole less conscious of himself or of an audience than Emerson the prose writer. The prose is more defensive, on sensitive topics, because the more public genre required it.

If the quality of love experienced or expressed is one test of security and freedom of identity, another is the quality of self-assertion. Emerson's new self was brought into public being pre-eminently through verbal affirmations. It is interesting to pick up the scattered comments on the release of aggression such affirmation involves. There are repeated references to the power of language. "Genius delights only in statements which are themselves true, which attack and wound any who opposes them, whether he who brought them here remains here or not;—which are live men, and do daily declare fresh war against all falsehood and custom, and will not let an offender go; which society cannot dispose of or forget, but which abide there and will not down at anybody's bidding, but stand frowning and formidable, and will and must be finally obeyed and done" (W.X.285-286). To be sure, this sort of talk does not sound like "Emerson"—the rhetoric derives from Carlyle, who meant much to Emerson in his period of struggle. But a connection between aggressive statement and the survival of the self expressed, the "live men" who will not be put down, is clear. There is a longer passage in the journal where a still giddier boast of dominion over hostile worldlings is affirmed by the "man who has spoken to them the dread word." "They" try to put the speaker back into the obscurity from which he has emerged and even suppose themselves to have "killed & buried the enemy," but in vain; he reappears, and the "first cry of the Revolution" will prevail (J.V.108-109).

Such explicit violence of language about language seems to reveal a latent connection among aggression, writing, and identity; for the most part this is curiously muted, except where it appears here and there in a tart tone. "Expression is all we want: not knowledge, but vent," he says "we know enough; but have

not leaves & lungs enough for a healthy perspiration & growth"
(J.VII.279). The image is revealing in the work of a man whose
early life had been threatened by consumption. When in this
mood he is prepared to say that "we worship expressors: we
forgive every crime to them" (J.VI.84). But on the other hand
he can feel that a "preacher is a bully" (J.VI.363). Aggression
against the outer world that is checked tends to recoil upon the
self. The achievement of the "direct, solving word" that would
really govern the universe, he says, would "solve us too; we
should die, or be liberated as the gas in the great gas of the
atmosphere!" (J.VII.91). The user of words, it is implied, is
placed in a dangerous position by the rules of the very magic at
his disposal: his power to assert his own identity seems immediately to involve a risk of destruction by the forces released.

To suspect an underground fear and longing to let loose the
aggressive power of language may help to account for Emerson's
unusually inhibited mode of composition. Often, as each *aperçu*
is achieved, the outgoing force instantly lapses and withdraws,
leaving behind a conventionally high-thinking identity, as if a
voice were heard saying: "I didn't mean it—what I'm saying
now is obviously harmless." Emerson's literary strategies—the
journals, the lectures, the essays—can be interpreted as modes
of action adapted to circumvent a capricious fear of his own
powers. His methods allowed him to work as the editor and
paraphraser of his own best moments, keeping him ready, as it
were, to take dictation from his bolder self. "How prompt the
limiting instinct is in our constitution so that the moment the
mind by one bold leap (an impulse from the Universal) has set
itself free from the old church and of a thousand years of dogma
& seen the light of moral nature, say *with Swedenborg,* on the
instant the defining lockjaw shuts down his fetters & cramps all
around us, & we must needs think in the genius & speak in the
phraseology of Swedenborg, & the last slavery is even worse
than the first" (J.IV.434). For "Swedenborg" read "Emerson,"
and you have a suggestive picture of the conditions under which
he found it possible to express his more vigorous self. It was
possible, but only at the ironic expense of being obliged to repeat
an insipid version of his idea ten times for every sentence that
was free and strong.

If a latent preoccupation with death, doubts about his power to communicate emotionally with others, and the presence of some ambivalence toward the aggressive expression of his own genius all indirectly reveal a certain instability in Emerson's creative equilibrium, the progress of his admirations is a more direct instrument from which to make a similar reading. An involvement with the polar virtues of physical force and deliberation (the necessary complements of his own agile insubstantiality) is evident from the beginning of the journal, but seems to strengthen in the public work as Emerson reaches his middle years. He retained all his life a humble appreciation of his powerfully commonsensical neighbors, and the same motive led him to exaggerate the sane practicality of such figures as Carlyle and Napoleon. An alternative to fearing or wishing for the release of aggressive power in his own language was to discover in somebody safely his opposite the strength to assert a self without qualms, as when he admired the eloquence of Richard Owen during his second English trip. Here was one lecturer whose "vinous face" was a "powerful weapon," whose smile was "surgical" (J.VII.421), and who could conduct an argument with enviable consecutiveness. The corresponding American figures in the Emersonian pantheon are powerful speakers like Daniel Webster and the famous Father Taylor. Vital men of the world, they outdid him in their power to organize their thoughts or in vigor of metaphor. To be sure, in soberer moments Emerson appreciated the weaknesses of such men; Webster is a worldly soulless figure, and Taylor ignorant and animal. But the emphasis, when their names appear, is more apt to be upon the positive qualities such men enjoy. His own genius, he was very ready to say, was a poor soil, a "poor sterile Yankeeism" that remained barren unless "tasked" (J.VIII.74). There is something almost automatic in his self-depreciation, the review of the "weak eyes, that will only serve a few hours daily; *no animal spirits,* an immense & fatal negative . . . no Greek, no mathematics, no politics" (L.IV.101).

This particular set of negatives appears in a letter Emerson wrote his brother William reviewing the impression he made on the English, who had just treated him so well on his lecture tour in the late forties. This trip was something of a climax to the growth of Emerson's appreciation of traits opposite to his own.

He saw England, "best of actual nations" (W.V.35), to be full of what both he and American society lacked. Rich, energetic, solidly material, crowded with distinct, well-bred individuals who appreciated him and invited him to fashionable breakfasts, England is the reality that underlies all those secondary essays in the books of Emerson's middle period on "Wealth" and "Manners," essays in which he tries to do justice to the facts and faculties that were not native to him. This sensitivity to the best qualities of his own polar opposites is one of the most appealing sides of Emerson and gives him a special dignity, for geniuses are apt to be obtusely egotistical. Yet there is in his courtesy and modesty a breaking of the very law he reformulated upon seeing the vigorous individualism of England: that "all we ask of any man is that he should thoroughly like his own way of life" (J.VII.354).

SECOND CRISIS

Aʟʟ these considerations taken together can help us to keep in mind the precariousness of Emerson's creative identity. The power to express an authentic response to the world was won by strategies which, though taking some years to work out, had the character of a revolution, not a development. And like political revolutions, his exchange of death for life always had implicit in it the possibility of a reaction. This reaction seems in fact to have occurred over a span of years; the changes were half-concealed by the length of time over which they took place. Emerson continued for a long while to repeat his original insights in diluted concentrations, mixing them with increasing qualifications. But once one's attention is called to the change, it can be traced in a number of vital dimensions at once. The typical Emersonian doctrine alters from transcendental radicalism to acquiescent spiritualism. The prevailing tone becomes milder and less demanding as the audience changes from the wild and solitary young to the well-bred middle-aged who listened to the later lectures: "progress replaces reform; culture, self-reliance; character, greatness."[14] I quote again from Whicher's *Freedom and Fate,* which provides a reading of Emerson's writing career in terms of a shift upward to the creative years and then gradually downward. Whicher attributes this change to doubts about the egotism implicit in the original revolutionary insight, discouragement at the reception of his radical message, his own failure to live a reformed life, disillusionment about his fellow reformers, and, finally, a growing awareness that Nature was too old and too large to be the toy of even the most vigorous spirit. All these factors no doubt played their part. I would be inclined to shift the emphasis to the first of the causes mentioned, the undermining of Emerson's belief in the God-relying self, and to attribute the wearing away of the radical doctrine to interior causes.

Like the period of stress from which it emerged, the creative portion of Emerson's life can be given a rough history. We have seen how the belief that God was in him, that he *was* God when his vital consciousness acted, appears in the journal very early. Its purest public expression is in *Nature,* "The American Scholar," the "Divinity School Address," and the *First Series* generally—the traditional Emerson of the undergraduate anthologies. Emerson himself spoke of the years 1838 to 1842 as especially creative (J.VII.144); the student of his work would perhaps be inclined to move the crown of the trajectory back a little to the early and middle thirties. One clue is the progress of the journal, which begins to sound like Emerson a little before his first visit to Europe, is at its best in the thirties and forties, and then begins to fade out, though entries continue regularly until 1859 and the power to comment succinctly on men, places, and ideas continues strong. As the genius diminishes, the wise man of the world takes up part of the slack.

The original years largely coincide with the life of his first-born son Waldo, as more than one commentator has noticed, and one cannot feel that the coincidence is accidental. The year of Waldo's death is perceptibly a watershed. The boy's birth had represented an affirmation of his father's newfound stability and hope for the future. His death at the age of five seems to have been the end of something essential in Emerson. The true interconnections are, in their concrete and tragic detail, irrecoverable, but a general explanation lies on the surface. Emerson had fallen into identifying too much of what was most precious and precarious in himself with the life of his son. Similar acts of organic projection had occurred in other contexts: he had identified his old self with his brothers, and his new self with God, with the universe, even with the mind of his audiences; but nowhere was he so open to loss as on this side. In the beginning of the essay "Domestic Life," he says that a child enables us "to live over the unconscious history" of ourselves and the race "with a sympathy so tender as to be almost personal experience" (W.VII. 105). The description fits his own case. The death of Waldo brought about the death of the part of himself that sympathy had imaginatively projected into the brilliant child.

The immediate response to Waldo's death in the journal and letters is affecting and illuminating. The position as well as the content of the first journal entry are both revealing. Waldo died, of scarlet fever, on January 27, 1842. The following day Emerson wrote a brief note on an otherwise blank page:

> 28 January 1842
> Yesterday night at 15 minutes after eight my little
> Waldo ended his life. (J.VI.150)

This page of the journal is set off from the filled pages on either side by blank sheets. The entries referring to Waldo in the days that follow are in pencil. The entry of January 30, the first after the note above, is quite long. It lists some remembered details of Waldo's life. Emerson musingly reidentifies with the boy's awakening and innocent mind, so clear a type of that advancing consciousness to whose service the father had devoted his dearest energies: "For everything he had his own name & way of thinking" (J.VI.151). Such grieving praise might describe himself. Waldo had been an artist of the same order as his father, though on the miniature scale of childhood and domesticity. The remembered incidents exemplify the most typically Emersonian moments in the lost life: " 'My music,' he said, 'makes the thunder dance:' for it thundered when he was blowing his willow whistle" (J.VI. 154).

Right after this first long entry, apparently all written on January 30, were two leaves that one can tell were written in ink.

They have been torn out of the volume. Then come two blank leaves. After these is another entry on an impersonal topic, written in ink as usual. But in between two paragraphs of the January 30 entry is a brief interjection in faint pencil, "Dear Waldo."

One of the first letters mentioning Waldo's death, directed to Caroline Sturgis, was written February 4. In it Emerson grieves "that I cannot grieve: that this fact takes no more deep hold than other facts, is as dreamlike as they; a lambent flame that will not burn playing on the surface of my river" (L.III.9). Such loss of affect is a familiar affliction in periods of emotional crisis. Does it not ordinarily mean some fear of the feelings that do in fact accompany an event, but cannot be fully acknowledged? Mourning is at best a difficult state of feeling to express. The rhetoric in this letter is soft and beclouding, like most of the letters he wrote to such correspondents as Caroline Sturgis. Whatever feelings Emerson has dissolve into a haze. "His Image, so gentle, yet so rich in hopes, blends easily with every happy moment, every fair remembrance, every cherished friendship of my life. I delight in the regularity & symmetry of his nature. Calm & wise, calmly & wisely happy, the beautiful Creative power looked out from him & spoke of anything but chaos & interruption; signified strength & unity—& gladdening, all-uniting life. What was the moral of sun & moon, of roses & acorns, that was the moral of the sweet boy's life, softened only & humanized by blue eyes & infant eloquence" (L.III.10). The tone seems to suggest that this diffuse romanticism is what Emerson wished the moral of the boy's death to be. Could it be that Emerson is preaching Emersonianism to himself, by way of an addressee he knows will accept this voice without criticism? The repetition of "calm & wise, calmly & wisely happy" is soothingly inapplicable to the real circumstances. "Chaos & interruption," after all, is what had happened.

Two letters to Carlyle, written somewhat later than the letters to Caroline Sturgis, are more distinct in their expression and, to that degree, more honest. Both contain references to a loss of a portion of his own identity: "you can never know how much of me such a young child can take away" (C-E.L.I.359). Such expressions are the clichés of grief; but the literality of this use of them may be supported by an image in a sentence of the second letter to Carlyle. He says, "the eye of my home was plucked out when that little innocent boy departed in his beauty and perfection from my sight" (C-E.L.I.396). The choice and meaning of this metaphor cannot be merely reminiscent of the Bible to a man whose sense of himself had always been bound so closely to his power of seeing.

The two letters to Carlyle were written on February 28 and March 31 respectively. At about the same time comes an interesting entry in the journal. On March 26 he wrote "I comprehend nothing of this fact but its bitterness. Explanation I have none, consolation none that rises out of the fact itself" (J.VI.166). This is a plain and bitter statement. For it was precisely the power to comprehend, to make something of the charged facts presented to it, that had characterized his own mind at its best. Emerson was an explainer of his experience; he was the *celebrator* of the idea of explanation, a continuous witness to the possibility of understanding. There was manifested in Waldo's death an immense fact, a phenomenon not chosen by its experiencer. Yet, says Emerson in this entry, he saw at first no resource but "only diversion; only oblivion of this, & pursuit of new objects" (J.VI.166). For him, these would be profoundly unsatisfactory alternatives. The death of Waldo tested him at his core, presenting him an image of the death of his creative identity. To the degree that he failed to arrive at a satisfactory interpretation of it, he would be apt to suffer the force of its deeper meaning.

"Threnody" is one such effort at interpretation. The first part of the poem was written during the spring of 1842, at the same time that he was starting the essay "Experience." The signs of natural rebirth served poignantly to remind him of the one life that had just gone forever. Elegaic tradition made an easy connection between spring and the death of the lamented person; so did a long habit of regarding the motions of the outward scene as testimony for life within. Memories of the past, already recorded in the journal, find a new place in moving couplets. Details of the now abandoned scene bring back the day of the death itself and deepen the complaint that nature continues to act in a bereft world:

The eager fate which carried thee
Took the largest part of me:
For this losing is true dying;
This is lordly man's down-lying,
This his slow but sure reclining,
Star by star his world resigning. (W.IX.153)

These first-written lines are the best. Emerson never wrote better. The melancholy facts, the slow, broken couplets, give complete expression to feeling.

Later Emerson took up the poem to complete it with an affirmative interpretation, but the later lines are less successful. He tries to find in the ongoing processes of the natural world confirmation of a faith that the single loss he has suffered is a part of a larger development, a process that required just such a length of life as Waldo enjoyed. To have the whole, and to believe in its beneficent continuations, required acceptance of this loss. His own past gifts, he reminds himself, have depended on just such an acknowledgment of total nature. Of this whole the life and death of Waldo are aspects, like his own genius. This argument is again supported by the elegaic tradition. And Emerson's particular version of the normal generic turn toward affirmation and acceptance of the powers that determine individual life and death is the same as what he recommends in the closing section of "Experience." The poetic ending is better than the prose, but it is still muffled and putative. Emerson was not the first or the last to find grief more real and expressible than consolation.

Other events and shifts of opinion during this time indicate the tendency to see Waldo's death as the death of part of himself. Emerson found himself with a new appreciation of his sturdy elder brother William, who had worked out so satisfactory and solid a position in the world, as he could see when he visited Staten Island between lectures. There seems to have been a complementary shift of feeling with respect to Alcott. The journal of the year contains a long critical portrait of his friend of the past seven years, then about to go to England on what Emerson thought a very impractical scheme. The description seems to sum up and detach for cool inspection the idealist component in Emerson's own character. There also appears in the journal at this period a queer dream, sufficiently exemplifying "chaos & interruption," about an insane person in a crib and an ugly sawing noise. But the principal evidence of Emerson's state of mind at this time is, of course, the essay "Experience."

Emerson began to work on "Experience" within three months of Waldo's death. The editors of the *Works* point out that it owes virtually nothing to the lectures from which he had been accustomed to draw his essay material. The opening in particular is worth noticing in some detail. I quote from the published version—a draft of the first two sentences was written in the journal for April 19, 1842, which helps to date the composition of the essay.

Where do we find ourselves? In a series of which we do not know the extremes, and believe that it has none. We wake and find ourselves on a stair; there are stairs below us, which we seem to have ascended; there are stairs above us, many a one, which go upward and out of sight. But the Genius which according to the old belief stands at the door by which we enter, and gives us the lethe to drink, that we may tell no tales, mixed the cup too strongly, and we cannot shake off the lethargy now at noonday. Sleep lingers all our lifetime about our eyes, as night hovers all day in the boughs of the fir-tree. All things swim and glitter. Our life is not so much threatened as our perception. (W.III.45)

This is well said: the legendary apparatus of lethe and the genius is made real by relating it to the experience of dreams. But, we are surprised to discover, this is waking life that Emerson is calling a lethargy, a half-sleep brought on by drinking the drug that wipes out memory of the past. Where do we find ourselves? Ignorant and dizzy, "we do not know" where we are. We might almost as well be wholly asleep or even dead—as those are who drink lethe.

The essay begins by reviewing the old question, asked repeatedly from *Nature* on: to what end is nature? "Where do we find ourselves?" is a softer, less hopeful, less arrogant version. It means, what can I really do? What actions, given *these* circumstances, are possible for the Soul? To propose new answers it is necessary for Emerson to return once more to the ground from which the Soul has ascended. Where, now that Waldo is dead, can he honestly locate the subject of the primordial act of life?

One might start, ominously, in the midst of sleepy illusion, into which Soul and nature together seem to dissolve. Where is the old confidence in the power of the eye to see clearly, of the body to move freely? We are "ghostlike," he goes on to say, with only enough life to "bring the year about, but not an ounce to impart or to invest. Ah that our Genius were a little more of a genius! We are like millers on the lower levels of a stream, when the factories above them have exhausted the water" (W.III.45-46). The pessimistic use of this old organic image of water is suggestive, and the social content of the metaphor has its own meaningfulness: Emerson thinks of himself as an old-fashioned country miller helpless against the greed of up-river industrialists who have polluted or diverted the stream. A few lines later on the page, the idea of the horizon, another important metaphor in his more optimistic work, has suffered a parallel devaluation: "Men seem to have learned of the horizon the art of perpetual retreating and reference" (W.III.46).

He still believes that "We animate what we can, and we see only what we animate" (W.V.50); but the tone in which this basic truth is now expressed is melancholy. The essay gives a new prominence to "temperament" as a name for the conditions under which the organic faculty operates. This stress is interesting not because it is new, for temperament was always felt to be the way in which one made one's way to the environment, but because the word, seriously used here for the first time, denotes not the subject of experience but the limits set to any particular organism's mode of action. Similarly with the term "illusion," the newly important name for what the organism experiences. Emerson would always have agreed that the senses engage with a universe that the Soul's other faculties see *through,* but this fact of experience was not earlier a cause for sadness. Emerson had been accustomed to take a positive pleasure in the warm surrounding blur, confident of his freedom to transcend and penetrate it (the opening of the "Divinity School Address" is a good instance). Now, though, the metaphysical undependability of the natural scene makes it a kind of inevitable prison for the Soul.

There is evidence too that Emerson's imagination is beginning to be caught in the negative consequence of his old belief in an intrinsic connection between the organic dimension of experiencing and its higher manifestations. Does the vital principle strengthen the intellect and moral sentiment, or does it dominate and despoil these faculties of their independence? If so, mind and conscience cease to be agencies of the Soul. They become effects, mere results of the phenomena they once seemed to master. The whole subject of action is under attack.

Such hints of depression as one can read from the opening pages of "Experience" do not wholly fix one's impression of the essay as a whole. It deservedly stands forth in any reader's memory as one of the best and most interesting of all the essays, whether or not a biographical reference is uppermost in one's mind. "I have set my heart on honesty in this chapter" (W.III. 69), says an often-quoted phrase, and there is much in the firm discriminations of what is possible in life to prove the expression true. Emerson's courageous address to the "mid-world" of fluctuating circumstance is cool and steady as well as sad. There is a chastening authority in the reminders that this mid-world is not all; that the vein of necessity running through the structure of experience occasionally opens to permit freedom of action to higher faculties than those mobilized by a skeptical stoicism. To the possibility of such moments we are more than once directed, but always, I think, from without: the voices of the essay do not include that of the God whose presence is allowed for as exceptional. The norm of presentation is "hardy" and "wise"; Emerson is a worshiper, with due skepticism, of "the life of life" (W.III.72), but he is not, as before, a vatic participant. "Onward and onward!" (W.III.75) is an exclamation made some distance away from the kind of direct experience that would sanction such a tone. The note of resignation, of yielding adroitly before a world that is not apt to alter under a reformer's sanguine eye, prevails sufficiently to trouble the editors of the *Works,* who prefer to see essays end in a permanent rise into affirmation.

What is, elsewhere in the essay, a prevailing tone is most explicit at the beginning. There is therefore reason for the traditional critical concentration upon the opening paragraphs. The section that takes notice of Waldo's death is close to the beginning. (The original draft was written in the journal on February 4, quite soon after the event.) It begins with a generalization that continues the lethe image we noticed earlier: "What opium is instilled into all disaster! It shows formidable as we approach it, but there is at last no rough rasping friction, but the most slippery sliding surface; we fall soft on a thought; *Ate Dea* is gentle" (W.III.48). The tone here is ambiguous. Are we asked to think this state of apathy a good thing? Or is he ironical? Opium dulls pain, but at the cost (in nineteenth-century belief, if not in medical reality) of addiction and fantasy. The implication might be that reality still does have a "rasping friction" but that, drugged as we are, we cannot feel it; we drift aside into sleep, the sleep of the first paragraph. The succoring divine mother of Emerson's optimistic imagery has become Ate Dea, a goddess of strife banished by Zeus to create moral blindness on earth, and her nourishing food is here a debilitating drug. To call this goddess "gentle" would seem to reveal not so much a discovery that disaster is less awful than anticipated as a compulsive need to call a bad thing by a good name. Would not such tactics be a perversion of the old doctrine of compensation? Instead of waiting to see what may come in return for the loss, what good may arrive to compensate for the concrete and overwhelming evil, the mind, in a panic, forestalls the experience of suffering, refuses to go through with it, denies its existence, and asserts that the evil already *is* its own compensation.

After quoting a piece of verse, Emerson goes on, "There are moods in which we court suffering, in the hope that here at least we shall find reality, sharp peaks and edges of truth. But it turns out to be scene-painting and counterfeit. The only thing grief has taught me is to know how shallow it is. That, like all the rest, plays about the surface, and never introduces me into the reality, for contact with which we would even pay the costly price of sons and lovers" (W.III.48). Is it true that grief for the loss of a son has taught only its own shallowness? Apparently, yes, and this can seem the authentically dreadful fact; part of the shallowness referred to is present in his complaint. The poignant try at emotional honesty brings him to a statement that exactly exhibits the *limits* of that honesty. The hint at mountains of reality in the distance suggests what there is in the background that might be felt. A suffering one can "court" is by definition within one's control. It is striking, by the way, how the primitive sense of

touch continues to be, here at a moment of self-testing, a major
vehicle of the act of knowing: "Was it Boscovich who found out
that bodies never come in contact? Well, souls never touch their
objects. An innavigable sea washes with silent waves between us
and the things we aim at and converse with" (W.III.48). The
tone conveyed by that "well" is an immense concession. And the
nourishing fluid has turned to an Arnoldian estranging sea.

Then comes an odd shift of tone: "Grief too will make us
idealists. In the death of my son, now more than two years ago,
I seem to have lost a beautiful estate,—no more" (W.III.48).
No more? We can recall the use of the property image in *Nature*
and wonder whether the loss of an "estate" is not bound to be
important for someone whose property was in the horizon, who
imaged his transcendental insight in the possession of land—and
for whom the literal possession of property was a prime means of
freedom to act as himself. "Idealist" seems in this context to
have its ordinary pejorative meaning alone: grief seems to have
made Emerson a *mere* idealist, a denier of inconvenient realities.

It is worth remembering that grief had had a similar effect,
though a more productive one, at the time of his earlier losses.
The death of Ellen and his brothers did in fact make him a more
convinced believer in the power of the Soul. He had learned then
how the Soul could accept and remake the world. We seem to
encounter here a wish to repeat that earlier triumph over defeat
and loss. But either Waldo meant his own powers too nearly or
the differences of inner and outer circumstance combined made
the later loss less surmountable. In the case of Charles and
Edward, his brothers died, not himself; and Ellen, though an
image of him, proved detachable. But Waldo he had literally
made, and the growth of the infant's mind had apparently
become much too closely interwoven with those faculties in
Emerson of which Waldo was a representative.

He goes on: "I cannot get it nearer to me." Is this said des-
perately or with resignation? "If tomorrow I should be informed
of the bankruptcy of my principal debtors, the loss of my
property would be a great inconvenience to me, perhaps, for
many years; but it would leave me as it found me,—neither
better or worse" (W.III.48-49). The estate image again, and
again it leaves a bad taste. Emerson would have had to lead a

different life if his dead wife had not left him property sufficient to keep him comfortable in Concord, and difficulties over money did trouble his middle and later years. The tone reinforces a continual insistence that the event means nothing: "So is it with this calamity; it does not touch me; something which I fancied was a part of me, which could not be torn away without tearing me or enlarged without enriching me, falls off from me and leaves no scar" (W.III.49). This rings false in two ways: he is claiming, first, that something inward, his love for Waldo, is outward and therefore does not concern him; and, second, that the loss will not "touch" him, a man who has asserted and made good a wish to touch the horizon itself, to import the whole world into his mind. And his image very naturally gives him away. If Waldo is the most precious part of him, to have it "fall off" would leave him an emotional eunuch. "It was caducous. I grieve that grief can teach me nothing, nor carry me one step into real nature" (W.III.49).

We can hear this last sentence as a confession. Grief *could* have carried him a step into real nature, a step farther, indeed, than his philosophy up to that time had gone. Waldo's death could have been a challenge to make good in new emotional terms the belief in active experience he had already found true organically, intellectually, and morally. But apparently this step could not quite be taken; the result (an example of compensation working willy-nilly against him) was a corresponding weakening of the old power to respond in all realms. "The Indian who was laid under a curse that the wind should not blow on him, nor water flow to him, nor fire burn him, is a type of us all. The dearest events are summer-rain, and we the Para coats that shed every drop. Nothing is left us now but death" (W.III.49). There is something dreadful in such candor. "We look to that with a grim satisfaction, saying, there at least is reality that will not dodge us" (W.III.49). But here a truth he had hold of gets away again; it is, precisely, a death that has dodged him. If he could not assimilate and be nourished by the actual end of his son's life, how could he expect to profit by the contemplation of his own?

With these words the paragraph that began with "What opium is instilled into all disaster!" comes to an end. The beginning of the next paragraph, as so often in Emerson, leaps to a general comment on the whole of what has just occurred: "I take this evanescence and lubricity of all objects, which lets them slip through our fingers then when we clutch hardest, to be the most unhandsome part of our constitution" (W.III.49). This conclusion gains in dignity when, as before, one mentally alters the "our" to "my." The next sentences repeat in more general terms some of the melancholy consequences already inferred. "Nature does not like to be observed. . . . Direct strokes she never gave us power to make; all our blows glance, all our hits are accidents. Our relations to each other are oblique and casual" (W.III.49-50). This has always been true for Emerson, especially in matters of style. One could hear these same words said, in another context, in a voice of level-headed warning. But here we hear resignation, retreat, acceptance of limits. The mood of the later "Terminus" is already half expressed.

There are other passages scattered through the remainder of "Experience" where the tone is still more definitely pessimistic:

The persons who compose our company converse, and come and go, and design and execute many things, and somewhat comes of it all, but an unlooked-for result. The individual is always mistaken. He designed many things, and drew in other persons as coadjutors, quarreled with some or all, blundered much, and something is done; all are a little advanced, but the individual is always mistaken. It turns out somewhat new and very unlike what he promised himself. (W.III.69-70)

Is this passage acknowledging the unpredictability of life with joy? Evidently not, though he once could say something much like this, in a different tone, and have it come out as exhilaration. The repetition of "the individual is always mistaken," the vague diction ("something is done"), and the slack rhythms together manifest a mind resigned to endurance. We must draw similar conclusions from the advocacy of the small pleasures of experience, the "potluck" of the day. At one time the mystical equivalent of this advice, a readiness to find absolute joy in brief moments of reality, had been the intended meaning of such expressions. Emerson was able to fall back, without any explicit change of doctrine, on a temperate pursuit of satisfactions, and save himself and a considerable part of his readers from any embarrassing awareness that a decision has been taken to settle for secondary gains, to "mature the unfallen fruit."

From the "transparent eyeball," then, we move to a "prison

of glass which we cannot see" (W.III.52) and which we are shut in by. We look at people, and "we presume there is impulse in them" (W.III.52). But this sympathetic discovery of alien vitality, the primordial organic act of knowledge, is, he now says, an "illusion"; what first seems life is on more careful examination merely a mechanical "uniform tune" (W.III.52). The limits of "activity and of enjoyment" are "fixed" (W.III.52).

This is Emerson's new definition of experience on the "platform of ordinary life" (W.III.52). We hear, before the end of the essay, of the possible escapes; but before we are persuaded by the expected reaffirmation of the spirit, it is worth recollecting that the freedom of the subject in all its ramifications was once asserted as intrinsic to the ordinary life. How far can we trust the balancing assertion that the creative powers of heart and intellect are still free to act? Has not this very doctrine become a conventionalism to which Emerson is bound, as he earlier criticized the preacher for being bound to the dogmas of traditional faith?

 The simplest escape from constriction of being, he says, is an undemanding trust in the immediate motions of daily life. "We live amid surfaces, and the true art of life is to skate well on them" (W.III.59). The man to admire, then, becomes he who is not defeated by the collapse of his larger hopes. The Soul still lives, but modestly. In practice we are moderately free, though in theory everywhere bound. Do not press reforms or be disappointed by their failure. Work, and be content. How much you do will depend simply on your vital force. The latent fire in the universe will emerge more strongly in the indefinite future; its present accidental sparks are only promises. Nowhere in the essays can we find a more tactful respect for the plain principle of life; to this, however diminished and intermittent, Emerson remains faithful. "The great and crescive self, rooted in absolute nature, supplants all relative existence and ruins the kingdoms of mortal friendship and love" (W.III.77). There is a grandeur in the melancholy tone with which this new version of the old truism is stated.

The position with which he emerges has its own subtleties and pleasures, and the wisdom of adopting it should not be hastily despised; Emerson is a distinguished worldly philosopher. In another writer one would not complain about finding such a point of view persuasively argued. But with Emerson one feels that a loss has been sustained. Our regret can readily become general—how many American artists have made or half-made their initial original statements, and then repeated them until energy or illusion ran down? "The star climbs for a time the heaven, but never reaches the zenith; it culminates low, and goes backward whence it came. The human faculty only warrants inceptions" (W.XII.70). As usual, Emerson makes the best comment on his own condition and on that element in his private predicament which foretells the fate of later writers yet unborn. There is, as he says elsewhere, something fatiguing about endless beginnings, or a belief in endless beginnings. Still, the best part of his genius led him to as good an expression of the vital truth concealed in this temperamental and national propensity as any American has made.

The whole story of Emerson's "decline" has been told often enough, and I have no wish to rehearse its details here. At the same time, I have no wish to exaggerate its simplicity or rapidity for the sake of making an easy pattern; the unpublished journals after the death of Waldo have their share of material in the earlier optimistic vein, and Emerson found a use for it in the essays of the middle period. He did not change all at once or change totally. The shift is one of emphasis, and the particulars are necessarily minute. Yet they do accumulate and become decisive by the close of the 1840s. By that time, the moments when some part of the original doctrine is reasserted often (though by no means always) ring false. The all-important journal begins to repeat itself: the same thoughts about Carlyle and the clubs or Tennyson and the Irish host recur more than once. By the end of the fifties, he had ceased to write in the journal at all except under pressure from lecture obligations or the stimulus of a thinking visitor.

A significant earlier clue is the change in the relative literary value of the journals and the essays. In the active years, the journal entries are usually less interesting than the corresponding public versions. But later on, the journal is consistently better reading. Thus a journal remark, "A great deal of God in the Universe but not valuable to us until we can make it up into man" (J.VII.50-51), with its brisk tone and tradesman metaphor, in one of the later essays turns into the flaccidly abstract, "There is a great deal of spiritual energy in the universe, but it is not palpable to us until we can make it up into man. There is plenty of air, but it is worth nothing until by gathering it into sails we can get it into shape and service to carry us and our cargo across the sea" (W.X.276). The younger Emerson would have been able to compress the moral and the technical dimensions into a single sentence.

Paradoxically, Emerson became a successful retailer of his earlier insights at a time when they had lost a good deal of their original authority for him and, hence, their power to attract original expression. The successful lecturer to provincial women was learning through his trips something of the prosperity wordly men could create. Railroad-and-hotel America was more impressive than the failures of the reformers back home, and the leaders of all this practical activity were the men who could offer him interesting hospitality and drum up audiences. This fact was fortified by the experience of English substance and success, as I have already noticed. Indeed, the strongest side of the later Emerson is that part of him which, because it was free to respond to this range of new experience, could express itself distinctly: "We must accept a great deal as Fate. We accept it with protest, merely adjourning our experiment, and not squander our strength in upheaving mountains. Mountain is conquerable also, to be sure; but, whilst you cannot quarry it, let it be a mountain" (J.VII.553-554). The implications for Emerson's general state of mind are clearer when we place this remark against the corresponding use of the same image in the wonderful passage already noticed, where an ideal education is described in terms of uncompromising idealism: "In some sort the end of life is that the man should take up the universe into himself, or out of that quarry leave nothing unrepresented. Yonder mountain must migrate into his mind" (W.X.131).

THE LATER DOCTRINE
OF THE SOUL

Where does this speculative excursion into the familiar facts of the biography leave us? Let us return to a schematic method and try to arrange in order the changes in the doctrine of the Soul that have taken place.

To start with, what has happened to the organic faculty? I have suggested how the discovery that the active principle of being was his personally to enjoy had been the fundamental achievement of the first period of crisis. The strength of nature had become his private strength, a continuous sanction for his thoughts and purposes. In place of this belief we find the later Emerson increasingly conscious of his own weakness.[15] He begins more and more to see himself—and man in general— as passive before energies whose source is external. "I am god in Nature; I am a weed by the wall" (W.II.307), says an illuminating sentence in "Circles," the two halves of which convey respectively the first and the second belief. But if the organic subject of action is outside the circle of his private life, where can it be located now? His answer is, in nature as a whole. The old organic subject, the individual Soul, is increasingly seen as an object, an effect of an exterior cause, a part of a grand exterior whole. Nature acquires life as the Soul loses it.

To replace the old faith in the inward organic activity of individuals, the imagination turns to a larger vision of *natura naturans*. This outward power Emerson finds manifested less in the concrete motions of the visible scene—these are now illusions—than in the secret general force that appears to direct the entire imaginable fabric of the universe. The true energy of nature thus becomes an objective force instead of a subjective experience. Its presence must be inferred from a survey of the epochs of geological, biological, and historical metamorphosis. Of nature's vast process, the races of men, nations, and separate individuals become mere secondary effects. Nature's purposes are not ours; but they are fulfilled, willy-nilly, in the apparently free acts of men—by their indulgences as well as their restraints, by their savagery as well as their virtue. We cannot find in such enormous motions any perceptible link between nature and our private intentions, which seem steadily sacrificed to larger ends of which we must remain unconscious.

There are many passages from Emerson's middle period which are ambiguous, "transitional," susceptible to interpretation in both the old and the new terms. The change could not have taken place as it did if Emerson himself had not been able to preserve a certain unconsciousness about the direction in which his mind was moving. Yet there is always, if we cast our eye over great enough distances, sufficient evidence of a shift of emphasis that becomes in time a change of conception. We begin to hear more about the unconscious tendency of races and climates and institutions, and less about the triumph of individuals; more about history as process and development, and less about history as intellectual construct. The effective subject of organic action is generalized and objectified so that it may become still more deeply primordial, still more profoundly separate from the willfulness of the individual ego; so too that it may become triumphant, as the actions of particular men plainly are not: "How silent, how spacious, what room for all, yet without place to insert an atom;—in graceful succession, in equal fulness, in balanced beauty, the dance of the hours goes forward still. Like an odor of incense, like a strain of music, like a sleep, it is inexact and boundless. It will not be dissected, nor unravelled, nor shown" (W.I.200).

Above all, nature will not cease. The "dance of the hours," the whole system of things, will go on permanently. Its continued operations may be trusted as the individual life cannot. Waldo died; so, in a way, did his father, but nature survives, as it survives all deaths, of nations and species as well as persons. In the first *Nature*, the prevailing question "to what end is nature" had as its presumptive answer, to become part of each individual consciousness. By the time of writing "The Method of Nature," from which the quotation above is also taken, the same question is no longer susceptible to so individualistic an answer:

"Nature can only be conceived as existing to a universal and not to a particular end; to a universe of ends, and not to one,— a work of *ecstacy*, to be represented by a circular movement, as intention might be signified by a straight line of definite length" (W.I.201). This "circular movement," parts of whose curve are perceptible to the humble student of nature's temporal progress, is imagined as spiraling upwards toward an indefinite future consummation, an ecstasy not to be enjoyed by any present self. This final climax will be an experience of the Zeitgeist itself, of an imminent will beyond all actual human sensibilities. The true answer Nature herself now makes to questions respecting her end is a cryptic, "I grow." We are to be "steadied" by considering that "a great deal is doing; that all seems just begun; remote aims are in active accomplishment" (W.I.203).

"Tendency" now becomes a key word. Since the elaborate metamorphosis of the totality is the focus of interest, patience rather than revolt is the appropriate response for individuals. We are in the organic universe preached by *In Memoriam*—and by the close of *Walden*. Emerson the Romantic has become Emerson the Victorian, and his vision of the organic world has become consistent with that of his generation.

This new vision of the action of organic life has a place for aesthetic experience, like the old individualistic organicism. But again there is a shift of emphasis. In the old scheme the focus was on the combination of parts into a unity through the action of an observer. Beauty was a creation of the eye, a function of point of view. Now beauty is still unity in multeity, but the aesthetic experience is not referred to the action of an individual unifier. Nature is already a unity, independent of an observer. Indeed, no actual observer has ever seen this unity, though faith can presume a whole some of whose parts are visible. Beauty is now an ultimate result to be inferred, not a way of seeing available to individuals. We believe in it by generalized expectation, rather than by experiencing it in concrete particulars.

The same is true of practical activity, which had been another important if simple mode of expression for the organic faculty of the Soul. The whole "hitch your wagon" discussion in "Civilization," for example, is an instance of Emerson's newly sharpened sense that nature rather than the Soul is the true agent in the realm of commodity. The woodcutter and delver do their work by allowing gravity, the binding force of the universe, to do it for them. The design of ships and houses is determined by what nature will allow, in the form of the environment and the function the objects are meant to serve. As with the useful, so too for the fine arts. In "Art" we read that the value of a work of art derives from nature, not from the intent of its human author. Even if we do not count the "deductions" stemming from the circumambient factors of material, tradition, audience, and the like, art still owes its successes to the passivity of its creator before "Ideal Nature" (W.VII. 48). Poetry is "free" only when it is "necessary" (W.VII.50)— "every work of art, in proportion to its excellence, partakes of the precision of fate" (W.VII.50).

This new larger vision, among other half-advantages, allows a certain relaxation in the rigor of the moral sentiment. For in a total movement toward an amelioration that can accommodate everything, no kind of active energy need be omitted or even judged. At the cost of losing its moral meaning, its role as somebody's responsible action, any silliness or evil or inadequacy can find a place, if not as something valuable on its own account, then as a lower form of being that in another turn of the spiral may ascend to something superior, an indispensable "worm" waiting its evolutionary turn in the "spires of form." The modulation of the organic faculty outward into a grandly active nature is probably bound up with Emerson's development of a benign tolerance for varieties of social prowess in the economical and political world. "Being," "life," can now be inevitable possessions of all who participate in the total process of nature. It is not by tinkering with private ends that one increases one's share of life; indeed, temperament, race, and circumstance are increasingly felt to measure one's share of vitality, without the influence of the moral will. "There is virtue, there is genius, there is success, or there is not" (W.I.204). This acknowledgment opens the way to a more "realistic" appreciation of the functional power of things as they are.

Thus in *English Traits,* a book in which the new organic vision predominates, the subject of the major sentences is "they." Emerson reports, as a stranger, a guest, and a student of history,

a consummate achievement of race. England is an accomplishment, a great actual system of deeds. The qualities that have
brought it about must be interesting and valuable instances of
nature at work on a broad scale. This inquiry is pleasing to read.
Has England, has any nation, ever been so satisfactorily praised?
The instances of vital strength, with the limiting circumstances
of each, are beautifully identified. Yet one reads rapidly, and
the passages that deserve remark seem rare, especially those
embodying Emerson's criticisms from a higher plane. He says
all that may be said on behalf of stolid, physical, practical force,
over and over. There is insufficient variety of statement, for all
sentences and chapters draw the same conclusion: England is a
material success. The Soul is represented most strongly in this
nation as an anonymous amalgam of the organic and the practical powers of the Saxon race: even the worthies he meets are
less individuals than illustrations of a strong but limited national
spirit.

This national spirit is itself a phase in the larger progress of
the Anglo-Saxon race, which would show itself next, Emerson
thought, in America. To a future guaranteed by the ameliorative
development of natural forces, of which the history of nations
and peoples was only a part, Emerson could look forward with
hope. From that hope personal anxiety, like personal will, was
beneficently excluded. "Modern Science, by the extent of its
generalization, has learned to indemnify the student of man for
the defects of individuals by tracing growth and ascent in races;
and, by the simple expedient of lighting up the vast background,
generates a feeling of complacency and hope" (W.IV.80).

The name for Nature that exhibits her new power most
exactly is "Fate." The change of terminology exposes his new
sense of the roughness, indifference, and terror in the world—
the fixity of its laws, its entire lack of respect for sentimental
preferences. In the early pages of the important essay "Fate,"
Melville might have found Emerson's full acknowledgment of
all the vast alien immutabilities he supposed the New England
sage so guilty of neglecting. The author of *Moby Dick* would
have appreciated that the connotations of "Fate" include "hints
of ferocity in the interiors of nature" (W.VI.8).

Yet the jaws of the shark, however intimidating to Tennyson, are not so distressing to Emerson, not so much of a problem, as other, more theoretical consequences of his acknowledgment that nature is huge, indifferent, and exterior. For once see nature in this way, and one will discover that one is bound within its system. It governs what one pleases to call one's character through the irresistible influences partially knowable as race, climate, temperament, and sex. Our very talents are less our own possession than aspects of the prison that locks up "the vital power" of the subject. What each man thinks he does from himself turns out to be done by nature; the more we know of our deeds, the less they belong to us. The moments of activity of the Soul now appear like transient bubbles on the stream of nature, themselves a part of the flow of circumstance. They are a product of the temporal process, not a participation in an eternity that transcends it. One's escapes from the world are themselves a function of the motions of the world.[16]

If this is so, old hopes of reform must dwindle, for we become aware that even the apparent freedom of the higher faculties is limited to those who, by situation and constitution, can afford to entertain the illusion of liberty. At best, this is a narrow social category. The laborer or the selfish businessman is incapable of becoming poet or prince. And men of superior talent are victims in a complementary way, for their vital power, running through one or two channels, leaves them otherwise weak.

Such a view logically should undermine any belief in the subjectivity of the moral sentiment; for that agency of the Soul would become a kind of epiphenomenon, an illusion of moral freedom accidentally accompanying choices that are in fact determined from without. "Nature is what you may do. There is much you may not. We have two things,—the circumstance, and the life. Once we thought positive power was all. Now we learn that negative power, or circumstance, is half. Nature is the tyrannous circumstance" (W.VI.14-15). But this rendering of the theoretical consequence is not fully accommodated to the new truth. To be consistent, one would have to say that nature is not merely half, but all. Life itself, in this view, should be one of the "circumstances." Besides, the idea of a "negative power" is a contradiction in terms: all power must be positive. The question is, on whose side is the power? Emerson's new answer is, on nature's.

The old vital power, then, the organic capacity, once the foundation of individual action, still exists—exists, indeed, on a far grander scale. It lives as the energy of a system growing multitudinously through all forms of being up to man and perhaps beyond. In the early doctrine nature displayed in its local motions the projected protagonists of an individual's own life. Now it is nature as a whole independent process that is the projected protagonist. Once nature illustrated the Soul; now the Soul appears to illustrate nature.

In "Experience" Emerson says that no "force of intellect" could "attribute to the object the proper deity which sleeps or wakes forever in every subject" (W.III.77). And from without (that is, from the point of view of a reader sympathetic with Emerson's quandary but free of its binding force), it is possible to say that the life thus projected into the System still derives from the projector. Nature, or fate, or race, has the power to bind the Soul only because the Soul has chosen to delegate that power. A historian of ideas can say that the belief in nature as an enormous vital process is a typically Victorian affliction. Emerson was very far from alone in finding that it was necessary to believe in an all-determining Nature, whose terrific effects might in the end be modified for the better by the upward spiral of evolution. It is possible, looking back at the nineteenth century, to see that there was no intellectual necessity compelling thinkers to believe that evolution was progressive. Darwin, it can now seem plain, meant something else. Nature's "determinism" can be seen as a function of the statistical ordering of our knowledge of external events. Far from being a threat to the self, the predictability of nature is no more than a nursery ghost concealing a real development of human knowledge; it is therefore inadvertent testimony to man's continued intellectual freedom, not to his limitations. But clearly such an neoidealist option was not possible in an age in which the increase of knowledge everywhere seemed to point to the invalidation of the old reasons for confidence in the freedom of the Soul. For Emerson, Marx, Tennyson, Spencer, Hardy, the discovery of nature was the discovery of fate, and fate was the denial of liberty, though not of power.

The climactic image in "Fate" is typical of this vein of Victorian thinking and suggestive of Emerson's special quandary.

"I seemed in the height of a tempest to see men overboard struggling in the waves, and driven about here and there. They glanced intelligently at each other, but 'twas little they could do for one another; 'twas much if each could keep afloat alone. Well, they had a right to their eye-beams, and all the rest was Fate" (W.VI.19). The concession is theoretically unjustified, for the eye-beams too should be under the rule of fate, if the ship and ocean are. But, in any case, the images are in interesting contrast with their meaning in earlier contexts. The sea was once for Emerson a prime emblem of the resources of the Soul, frequently compared to a nourishing fluid streaming down to feed the receptive sensibility. But here the "seas of strength," the "liquor of my life" that he had more than once complained was measured out to him in too slight quantities, has turned vast and inimical; once it nourished, now it drowns. And here too sight, the sense especially associated with the intellectual freedom of the Soul, has dwindled until it can provide only a bare proof of impotence.

Emerson does admit almost the whole theoretical result of his new views in one place in "Fate": "In its last and loftiest ascensions, insight itself and the freedom of the will is one of its [nature's] obedient members" (W.VI.21). But immediately comes the familiar turn, by which he seeks to justify a reservation of liberty to the Soul that this statement plainly denies. In doing so he allows himself the inconsistency of supposing that new fate is countered by old freedom; that freedom is itself fated, and the moral sentiment not in prison after all. The effort is gallant but unconvincing: he is obliged to repeat his earlier belief in the same language, as if he could not bear to think through the new problem in new terms. A rather Carlylean "will" is paraded, as a suitably strenuous antagonist to nature. It is not enough.

A slighter, less contradictory, resource is to advise the beleaguered subject to contemplate the eventual ameliorations of the Whole, to accept his private defeat in a contemplation of the grand tendency of things—"he is to rally on his relation to the Universe, which his ruin benefits" (W.VI.47). The unhappiest expression of this half-solution is the closing rhetoric, which proposes that we "build altars to the Beautiful Necessity"

(W.VI.49). Here the language seems to me to go utterly soft; such talk sounds like the cant of a convention as feeble as any Emerson had repudiated earlier.

The best genuine answer to the quandary set by his new conception of nature comes earlier in the essay, and, though Emerson finds his solution and expresses it well, he seems not quite to have appreciated what he had discovered. For if he cannot fairly call the moral sentiment free, given his new premises, he can logically assert that "Intellect annuls Fate. So far as a man thinks, he is free" (W.VI.23). This is so, not because the acts of mind are any less determined by circumstance than the acts of will, but because the idea that nature is the effective agent and man a result of its action is always at least an *idea*. The mind may intellectually conclude that it and all its works are the results of necessity; but the conclusion by which it accepts this belief is itself a free act. The mind cannot get behind itself. It cannot annul its own action; or, rather, the notion that its action is not its own can be true only of other notions than the one it is entertaining at the moment. The *recognition* of necessity cannot be necessitated.

Here is Emerson's real escape—not in fancy rhetoric about building altars to an anthropomorphized figment or in weakly pragmatic remarks about the wholesomeness of acting as though we were free. Here is an escape radically consistent with the old insight with which his intellectual history had commenced. By discovering the necessity of freedom merely to discover necessity, he affirms once more, though now in a much more limited way, the involvement of the subject in its own experience.

God, he had always said, is within. Even though by now large portions of God, metamorphosed in characteristic Victorian fashion into the larger agencies of nature, have migrated without, yet the intellect is one divine function that cannot lapse away from subject to object. It is still true to say that "he who sees through the design, presides over it, and must will that which must be" (W.VI.27). It is even possible to follow this basic and permanent insight with a footnote, calling fate itself a "name for facts not yet passed under the fire of thought; for causes which are unpenetrated" (W.VI.31). Whatever may happen to the other faculties, intellect still represents the Soul.

To be sure, the Soul is thereby left rather naked and scientific. "Just as much intellect as you add, so much organic power" (W.VI.27). So ran the old article of faith: the sum of mind and vitality made reason, as the first by itself made the understanding. What then happens to reason if organic power migrates out toward nature? It becomes something closer to what we would now call pure intellect. Yet, as Emerson encouragingly says, "we never do quite nothing" (W.X.219). When we use our mind, we still do so much that, by a kind of theoretical courtesy, it is possible to talk of our intellectual action as if it implied (as in some cases it may) all we might do if we were wholly free: "What is life but the angle of vision? A man is measured by the angle at which he looks at objects. What is life but what a man is thinking of all day? This is his fate and his employer. Knowing is the measure of the man. By how much we know, so much we are" (W.XII.10). So Emerson puts it, a little sparely, in "The Powers and Laws of Thought," the lead essay in the *Natural History of Intellect*, the final restatement of his philosophy in academic and therefore appropriately intellectual terms.

Finally, we can remember, when we find the latter-day Soul shorn of so much of its earlier glory, that what is lost in theory is recoverable in practice. Even if the will is a whim of chemistry, a mere product when its actions are viewed from without, from within it acts as strongly as the cumulative force of the resources it calls into play. To know what is truly so, the characteristic act of intellect, invariably has practical results. A man will instinctively act according to his knowledge; the clearer that is, the more irresistible the moral and physical consequences of his vision. He will be an agent of nature, to be sure; but just because of this he will be at an immense advantage in any immediate contingency. And his behavior will seem "free" to all onlookers, except philosophic analysts peering down from above. He who knows where the bones are, said Engels, may carve the chicken. A perfected adjustment to nature releases its forces for the service of man, as technical advances prove (not to mention each man's emotional history). It is fear and ignorance that freeze fate into an alien mask.

"Character" had been since the early years Emerson's name

for the involuntary revelation of large-scale organic forces through the moral dimension. "Man, ordinarily a pendant to events, only half attached, and that awkwardly, to the world he lives in, in these examples"—in the heroes of character—"appears to share the life of things, and to be an expression of the same laws which control the tides and the sun, numbers and quantities" (W.III.90-91). The instances he gives of character are apt to be conservative: Napoleon, Chatham, the great merchant, the successful political man. Weight, probity, and firmness are such men's defining traits. They act as agencies of Nature and collaborators with, rather than defiers of, the order of society. To this extent they are effects; but they are also influences on lesser men.[17] From such habitual moral qualities to "the gentleman," as a type of the Soul's action in the actual world, is but a step; hence "Manners" follows "Character" in the *Second Series,* as "Character" itself follows "Experience." Manners occupy the realm of beauty, as character the realm of worth. The gentlemanly ideal of personal action is modest, compared to the revolutionary program preached in "Self-Reliance." It is also general—the mutual agreement of whole generations and societies and not, as the equivalent democratic ideal was earlier, an inference from the careers of a few sages and heroes. Again we become aware of Emerson's new respect for convention, for how else but by convention can a gentleman be defined? Wealth, good nature, and virtue are his constituent traits, all indexes of "natural," that is, customary, power.

A modest, conservative, optimistic version of this new social philosophy is spelled out in various places in the later essays. Its basis in the new view of the natural process is concentrated in such a benign summary as closes "Social Aims": "We have much to regret, much to mend, in our society; but I believe that with all liberal and hopeful men there is a firm faith in the beneficent results which we really enjoy; that intelligence, manly enterprise, good education, virtuous life and elegant manners have been and are found here, and, we hope, in the next generation will still more abound" (W.VIII.107).

The effect of his change of feelings about the position of the moral sentiment may be discovered, by implication at least, as early as *Representative Men.* This book was published in

1850, but the lectures behind it were delivered in the middle forties. These representative men, of course, stand for the Soul. Emerson's different protagonists may be set out in accordance with the old *schema*. Plato is intellect, Swedenborg the moral sentiment, Napoleon the practical faculty, Shakespeare and Goethe the aesthetic and expressive powers. In practice the essays do not do equal justice to all faculties alike. Intellect, as one might expect, is well defended in "Plato," and in much the old style; but Swedenborg is handled gingerly as an unbalanced discoverer of an important ethical method, and his claims to stand for the active moral sentiment are not convincingly followed up. The Swedish thinker is too eccentric and cold-blooded to suit Emerson's conception of a moral hero. In "Shakespeare" much stress is put on the connection between his individual genius and the influences of his age. These do all the creative work for him, supplying sources, interests, and audience, and leaving the poet himself only the last task of finding means of expression for the spirit that mutely informs them. The great man "finds himself in the river of the thoughts and events, forced onward by the ideas and necessities of his contemporaries" (W.IV.190). Genius, far from being original, is defined by its utter receptivity to the "spirit of the hour." So, too, Napoleon is less an actor on his own behalf, or even on behalf of the Soul, than a representative of the world spirit driving the active party of his time. And so with Goethe: the universe strives to be reported, and the writer merely brings this wish about.

"Montaigne," though, stands genuinely for the old initiating subject—but the subject reduced to a modest middle position. The skeptic is he who wishes to do justice to the claims of both the ideal and the practical worlds without committing himself exclusively to either, or endeavoring to incorporate either into himself. The office of skeptic is therefore typical of the Soul in diminished equilibrium: just, clear-headed, unpretentious. A literary expression of the Montaignesque stance may be found in the ironies of "New England Reformers," which concludes and typifies the *Second Series* of essays. There Emerson maintains a careful double attitude toward the pretensions of the reformers he reviews. The tone of detached sympathy constitutes in itself a criticism of their claim to spiritual authority, and indeed of the possibility of any person's representing the moral sentiment. That essay stands in the same relation to the earlier and more absolute "Self-Reliance," "Man the Reformer," and the "Divinity School Address" that the second essay on "Nature" does to *Nature*. From this middle position, established by a tone that dissociates its speaker from particular reformers while maintaining faith in the ultimate triumph of reform, *Representative Men* as a whole is written. The values explicit in "Montaigne" provide the *point d'appui* from which to criticize Swedenborg's grotesque and unfeeling abstractions, or Napoleon's amoral ruthlessness, or Goethe's worldliness. From that position the old enthusiasms of the whole Soul may be placed: admitted, admired, and qualified.

EMERSON AS PROPHET

The new Emerson I have just finished schematizing is an appealing figure. He may seem easier to sympathize with, to "approve of," than the radical transcendentalist. It is easier to believe in the existence of a slight Soul. The lack of pretension, the relative absence of what was incredible in the early vatic stance, is truly admirable. We confront, in the mature ideas and the mature tone, much that effortlessly coincides with the best of a literary and social tradition we can still imaginatively share. The history of American culture since Emerson died would support a high valuation for his later self. When subsequent generations continued to value his first ideas, they understood them as they were diffused through and modified by the image of a gentlemanly and modestly optimistic scholar who remained behind after his radical identity lapsed. And now that "Emerson" exists, if he exists at all, as a certain subtle flavor of intellect, it is to the finished ironies and mature acknowledgments that one can most readily turn to exemplify what remains to be admired by men of the world. His later stance allowed Emerson a more relaxed appreciation of the serial impulses of the mind, a certain freedom to notice what interested him in the world for its own sake, regardless of its ultimate reference to the unused or unusable powers of the Soul. His renderings of the details of experience become more understandable because more casual. The potluck of the day turned out to be easier to put in convincing words than the entirety gestured at in the old phrase of the Mt. Auburn experience, "It was Day." All expression, after all, is of parts, of particles. We would probably find it easier to convince a contemporary skeptic that Emerson deserves attention as a man of letters by bringing forward the passages that show a man of infinite literary tact, a mind capable of sophisticated address, than by holding his unwilling attention to the old expressions of enthusiastic hope. The talent of Emerson is easier to communicate without the labor of explanation than his genius.[18]

In spite of this, it is, I believe, the early doctrine that we should attend to most seriously. We are closest to Emerson when we put ourselves in a position to see the charms of the later thinking and writing as qualifications of a message whose core remains at once simpler and broader, more absolute and more radical. For one thing—a crude but important point—the earlier belief is, at least potentially, *truer* than the later. This is particularly so of the two versions of the all-determining organic faculty. In Emerson's first account, this dimension of the Soul is directly and naturally available to each person. On behalf of this idea, one can always point out that each of us is always in some minimal sense alive; as long as he is capable of enjoying his life consciously, and of seeing it reflected from the particulars into which it is projected, he is free to find himself fundamentally inside the world, originally related to the universe. He can be ready to enlarge his sense of himself as a subject from this starting point. His organic consciousness provides a model for the more sophisticated actions of the self. The other faculties of the Soul, too, are always experienceable in specific moral and intellectual emergencies. Their congruence with each other and with the sense of life can be a possible faith for all who live in the world.

Emerson's latter-day belief in the beneficent forward motion of the total universe, on the other hand, seems less credible as a

description of what is and might be. It is not merely an exterior-
ization of the organic faculty, but an elaboration of its mode of
action into a myth. Like all myths, it bears the marks of its age,
which is not ours. Subjective organicism is at least a permanent
possibility for the human spirit; objective organicism involves a
belief in an ameliorative evolution that cannot help but appear a
Victorian illusion. The Emerson of the later doctrine therefore
separates himself from our condition; he becomes the preacher
of a myth about the Soul, instead of a prophet of the Soul itself.

The earlier Emerson continues, then, as a present witness for
the total subject of action, for the potential interrelevance of all
the faculties that are discoverable within our experiences of reality. Especially he stands for the possible coincidence of reliable
insight and judgment with instinctive organic response. As such,
Emerson's first doctrine of the Soul can still be useful, if not as
a faith, then as a standard against which to evaluate the quality
of experience in an age very different from his. The freedom
to criticize our condition effectively is not the least of the gifts
Emerson can give us. Matched against Emerson's faith in the
subjectivity of significant action, all our tendencies to yield the
theoretical initiative to outward forces can seem suspicious. We
are painfully familiar with the assumption of "common sense"
that enormous areas of our experience cannot be credited to any
subjective agency at all. Theoretically and in practice, we like
to think ourselves victims of exterior gods. The modern consciousness readily defines itself as an effect of irresistible "realities," whether these are psychic needs or political institutions,
neuroses or nations. Rather little is easily felt to be *our own*.
But is such a disposition necessary? Emerson can prompt us to
ask, what makes it so?

Even within the sphere still habitually analyzed in terms of
some formula of subjective action, one can use Emerson's belief
in the unity of the Soul to become more conscious of a prevalent
deterioration and separateness. For the early Emerson, the Soul
is founded on a primitive sense of organic vitality, on our power
to animate what we see. One could scarcely say of modern urban
society that it neglects the organic satisfactions, in actuality
or as fantasy. But few enjoy these satisfactions uncontaminated
by anxiety, and fewer still "believe" in them, that is, connect

the pleasures of life with the special motions of intellect and character. We have an underground culture that makes much of the pursuit of organic sensation, occasionally justifying this desperate endeavor in terms that interestingly echo Emersonian sayings. But sensual acts seem rarely to have moral resonance or intellectual implication. For many they exist and prevail to the degree that moral and intellectual concerns are repudiated, or at least kept safely at a distance. They can seem to stand rather as a kind of animal compensation for a pervasive inhibition of the other faculties, and not as a sacred source of life from which these may be renewed.

While discussing the moral sentiment, I raised some of the theoretical reasons why that portion of the Emersonian message can seem obscure or incredible. An observer of cultural fact may speculate that there are practical as well as historical reasons for finding it hard to believe in the inwardness and relevance of conscience. Moral action seems rare in our world even as something to pretend to. Few seem able to feel themselves moral agents; the self does not comfortably place its behavior in terms of this dimension. The frequently mentioned "crisis of identity" is presumably bound up with this condition. For a disbelief in the substantiality and efficacy of the self can be connected with the progressive weakening of the old belief in one's independent power to arrive at correct moral judgments. Without such a belief, a man subjects himself to ad-hoc systems of expectation generated by whatever group he happens to find himself in. To these expectations all responses are "role playing," not moral action. In such situations, there can be nothing categorical in the demands to which one accedes, and therefore nothing authentic and subjective about the forms of action through which they are fulfilled.

The best answer to such moral anaesthesia is probably implicit in the acts of those who have freed themselves from acquiescent routine and declared war on the evil in the world, like the civil-rights activists and the resisters to nuclear war. It is chastening and inspiring to observe that the rhetoric of these strugglers revives, as if it had never died, the idea that principle is available to individuals, who may find their manhood in obeying it. In such behavior the continuing relevance of the Emer-

sonian belief can be made real again as a lively critique of
habitual passivities and excuses.

Above all, Emerson's first faith can throw a critical light on
the modern fortunes of intellect. The Understanding has tri-
umphed with a completeness that would certainly have appalled
those nineteenth-century prophets who made so much of the
danger experience could suffer from unrestricted rationality.
We live in a world increasingly dominated by separated Mind,
the acts of which present us with problems solvable only by the
application of still more Mind—solutions that will in their
turn constitute still greater problems. And this Mind seems increasingly separated from the thinking of individuals. Yet a
civilization racked by institutionalized technology seems able to
think of no way out of its troubles except the further refinement
of the agencies that caused them.

What would it take to create a new Emerson, who could throw
affirmative light upon the old? It is worth speculating on, if only
to confirm our understanding of our subject. One requirement
would be a convincing idiom. Emerson could reargue the case for
the Soul by using just that term—which, as I mentioned at the
beginning of this book, is not now easily available. He could discover a full vocabulary in which to express his faith in that
branch of the "perennial philosophy" that came to him and his
readers through Coleridge, Cousin, and Swedenborg. The meanings of the master terms in this language happened, for reasons
with which Emerson as an individual had nothing to do, to coincide with a certain stage in the Unitarian idiom, the stage represented, say, by the elder Channing. It was possible, that is, for
Emerson to speak on behalf of the organic subject (my far
clumsier term) by calling it "God" and "Reason" together.
From the point of view of intellectual history, Emerson will
appear a rare coincidence of a set of loaded words, whose inter-
change of energy could explode into vital meaning for himself
and his readers.

In an age of intellectual dispersal like ours, a similar coincidence of major meanings, including among them some sacred
term for vital energy, seems far to seek. "Mind," "imagination,"
"the self," retain their separate shades of useful connotation. It
is hard, though, to anticipate anything but pedantic abstraction

from their use together or apart. The idiom of psychoanalysis is (heavily qualified) available as a mode of description; but we must wait to see if its terms can have charismatic value outside of technical or casually social contexts.[19]

What one wants, then, is not a criticism of Emerson but a continuation—or rather, a continuation that would make the criticism real. Where could one look? To such adolescent impersonators (in Leslie Fiedler's phrase) as Mailer and Salinger? It may embarrass the reader even to place these names before him, much less to instance them as indicators. We are all almost despairingly quick to detect the failure in failures, and in these two cases, one may feel, for good reason.

Perhaps a better register of romantic possibilities in a postmodern age would be such a figure as Paul Goodman. Goodman for years has been vigorously preaching the Soul (though never under that name, which would probably make him wince) from an anarchist-Reichian position. *Growing up Absurd,* the republication of his long comic novel *The Empire City,* and the recent spate of essays, poems, and stories have given his voice far more weight than it had when the conformities of reformist liberalism and post-Stalinist socialism meant more in the experience and opinions of the young. A frequent speaker to college students, he stands in the direct line from Emerson and Carlyle. Anyone who has attended his lectures can testify to the eagerness with which the best of the young listen, hopeful for the true word on sex, politics, and religion. Goodman, like Emerson, has the gift of sentences and comes nearer than any speaker now before the American public to fulfilling the kind of expectations discussed in connection with Emerson's audience. Especially he accepts the chief Emersonian imperative, the romantic necessity to recommence the business of experiencing from the beginning, to expand the native resources of the individual.[20]

It does not matter that I have named Goodman as the best indicator of an Emersonian future; one may substitute others. Restlessness is not culture, and a few good sentences do not make a program. For a developed articulation of anything that would stand comparison with the transcendental impulse and its fine expressions we have, obviously, still to seek. When it comes, if it does, it will probably not be some veteran of older cultural wars who manifests it most convincingly.

For one thing, a new prophet would have to reformulate the basic element in any romantic statement, the appeal to nature. And this would have to be done in a fashion commensurate with the severity of the ecological dislocation that technology widens with every advance. It does not seem quite enough to evoke a merely individual "spontaneity" in imagination, sexual conduct, or thought, necessary as these may be. Such separatist emphases can look too shallow and hysterical, and the random products, like the nonobjective paintings that decorate the grandly conventional living rooms of the rich, will seem the entertainments of an overrationalized world, not its creative opposite. Perhaps something more severe, communal, and intelligent is required to stand as an appropriate ideal of reform for the response of civilized society to the natural universe. We know ourselves to be systematically ruining our ecological base at a rate with which the biologists can scarcely keep up. The effect of such a book as *Silent Spring* suggests that a new prophetic voice might come from among the humane scientists. If so, science will be doing the critical job literature once inherited from religion: to combat death and the devil.

The value of such figures as I have glanced at, then, could be only as bare clues to ways of deriving the fullest benefit from the romantic heroes of the past. Emerson is simply the first and best of these heroes for Americans—the least limited, the most permanently suggestive. The American Adam is mythologically the innocent who was there to start with. It is easy in interpreting him to dwell with a sad complacency on the disillusioned "maturity" that was to follow. But maturity can mean, less attractively, an unanalyzed allegiance to the false norms of groups whose contact with things as they are, especially natural things, has dwindled to the point of insanity. "Adam" is also the innocent eye, the clear mind, the willing heart—the namer of what stands there to be named—and his mythic service is not yet complete.

No work, life, or career from the past can appear deeply interesting to us unless it seems to contain within it an action which upon examination turns out to be something we are doing now, or would like to be doing now. Those elements of our experience that seem valuable but endangered can be strengthened by discovering for them an ancestry of articulate command. An eye that lacks vitality will search for visible evidences of life; a mind that distrusts its own thought will search for examples of thinking that have not lost the touch of life. Emerson's art can echo and sanction our most secret efforts to recover an inside for our multiple worlds.

I cannot leave the reader with a better instance of Emerson's potential serviceableness to this end than by bringing forward, once again, a singular passage. It might have been used earlier as a pendant to the discussion of the individual self and its local opportunities. I have reserved it to end with because its excellencies point the full moral of the Soul's potential in Emersonian language that requires no translation whatsoever for a modern mind. The passage in question is from the insufficiently praised essay, "Spiritual Laws." Emerson is talking about the way the Soul responds to the experience that belongs to it:

He may have his own. A man's genius, the quality that differences him from every other, the susceptibility to one class of influences, the selection of what is fit for him, the rejection of what is unfit, determines for him the character of the universe. A man is a method, a progressive arrangement; a selecting principle, gathering his like to him wherever he goes. He takes only his own out of the multiplicity that sweeps and circles round him. He is like one of those booms which are set out from the shore on rivers to catch drift-wood, or like the loadstone amongst splinters of steel. Those facts, words, persons, which dwell in his memory without his being able to say why, remain because they have a relation to him not less real for being as yet unapprehended. They are symbols of value to him as they can interpret parts of his consciousness which he would vainly seek words for in the conventional images of books and other minds. What attracts my attention shall have it, as I will go to the man who knocks at my door, whilst a thousand persons as worthy go by it, to whom I give no regard. It is enough that these particulars speak to me. A few anecdotes, a few traits of character, manners, face, a few incidents, have an emphasis in your memory out of all proportion to their apparent significance if you measure them by the ordinary standards. They relate to your gift. Let them have their weight, and do not reject them and cast about for illustration and facts more usual in literature. What your heart thinks great, is great. The soul's emphasis is always right. (W.II.143-145)

That this is excellent, I hope need not be asserted—the arguments of this book make the best critical context I can provide for the appreciation I must presume. But the specific manner of the excellence can be brought more fully before the mind by attending to the changes Emerson's expression underwent as his statement shifted from journal to lecture to its final form in the essay.[21] They are minor—that is the point. The work done is of a very simple kind, but it suffices to make art.

The immediate source of this passage can be found in a lecture called "The School." The lecture beginning was a good deal hazier: the second sentence started, "In the next place, this in its primary mysterious combination with the nature of the Individual makes what we call distinctively the genius of the man or the peculiar quality that differences him from every other." This fussy Coleridgizing, itself arrived at through a certain amount of deletion and insertion, has been neatly replaced in the essay by the succinct "A man's genius, the quality that differences him." Rhythm too has been improved throughout the passage, indeed created out of parenthetical clumsiness by a consistent substitution of a march of commas for original interruptive periods. The wordy independence of the lecture version, "and this evidently determines for each Soul the character of the Universe," is reduced to the modest, lower-case, smoothness of the essay's clause, "determines for him the character of the universe." A sermon-like seesaw, "as a man thinketh, so is he; & as a man chooseth, so is he, & so is Nature," proves too smug for effective alteration; it is dropped, and the passage continues directly with what was already good, the fine and simple, "A man is a method, a progressive arrangement."

Farther on much is dropped altogether, apparently because it is repetitious, diffuse, or weakly exemplary. In the lecture there is a sentence beginning, "Hence arises that mysterious emphasis which certain facts, thoughts, characters, faces, have." The single word "emphasis" is extracted to be used in a later sentence in the essay; except for this, the author's eye skips two whole paragraphs and resumes with "Those facts, words, & persons," a series that he rightly preferred to the looser catalogue he first wrote, "facts, thoughts, characters, faces."

In studying such transmutations of the passage from lecture to essay we have the advantage also of possessing a journal version. Emerson's first rendering of his idea took the form of two separate journal entries, one for November 27, 1837, and the other for November 25, 1838. The first is an independent note:

Expressiveness

I magnify instincts. I believe that those facts & words & persons which dwell in a man's memory without his being able to say why, remain because they have a relation to him not less real for being as yet unapprehended. They are symbols of value to him as they can interpret parts of his consciousness which he would vainly seek words for in the conventional images of books & other minds. What therefore attracts my attention shall have it, as I will go to the man who knocks at my door, & a thousand persons as worthy go by it, to whom I give no heed. (J.IV.376)

The second forms part of a longer entry not all of which is relevant. The section Emerson decided to use reads:

This is the reason why you must respect all your private impressions. A few anecdotes a few traits of character manners face a few incidents have an emphasis in your memory out of all proportion to their apparent significance, if you measure them by the ordinary standards of history. Do not for this a moment doubt their value to you. They relate to you to your peculiar gift. Let them have all their weight & do not reject them & cast about for illustration & facts more usual in English literature. (J.V.144-145)

When he first made up his lecture, he brought these passages together, copying directly from the journal entries, but making a few changes, chiefly of omission, as he went. The lecture manuscript shows what happened. Thus he copied "I believe that those facts," but crossed out the first three words to improve emphasis and remove unnecessary egotism, and turned one of the original ampersands to a comma to formalize the series. The rest of the first entry he copied hurriedly, as a misspelling, "knows" for "knocks," proves, but he found time enough to superscribe a "whilst" over the original "and" to bring out a minor logical connection between clauses.

When he turned to the second journal entry, he composed a new transition: "It is sufficient that these particulars speak to me." This is a considerable sharpening of tone over the cozy banality of the old, "This is the reason why you must respect all your private impressions." A new voice is introduced, elevated and proud, consistent with the high sense of the idea it proposes. These "impressions," says the tone, are a man's noblest possession. (When he came to compose his essay later, he found opportunity for further improvement, changing the Latinate "sufficient" to the plainer "enough.") From this point on, he copied again as he wrote his lecture, adding commas to guide his reading emphasis, and dropping the otiose "of history" from the tail of the phrase "by the ordinary standards." This omission came to him as he wrote or rechecked his lecture text, for the prepositional phrase is first copied into the lecture manuscript and then crossed out. Similarly he concentrated "they relate to you to your peculiar gift" into "They relate to your peculiar gift." (Here too his later review for the essay led to a second change for the better. "Peculiar" was dropped, pointing the sentence still more intimately at the reader: "They relate to your gift.")

From this sentence on, the lecture version is an expansion of the second journal entry, apparently composed for the first time as he prepared his text for oral delivery. There are many deletions and interlineations. The pair of sentences that conclude the essay version are written on the lecture sheet in pencil, as if he had used that piece of paper as his rough copy for the essay. In making the final transfer from lecture to essay, he cut "all" and "English" from "let them have all their weight, & do not reject them & cast about for illustration & facts more usual in English Literature." Impatient at the unnecessary illustration from the history of botany he had gone on to use in the lecture, he leaps forward to his conclusion, dismissing some repetitive concluding sentences and replacing them with two phrases from the tangle of interlineations: "What your heart thinks great is great" becomes, with the addition of a comma for emphasis, the penultimate sentence, and "The souls emphasis is the true one," with a new predicate to strengthen the affirmative tone and to create rhythm, becomes the fine ending, "The soul's emphasis is always right."

To attend to the local effect of these small acts of composition is to become engaged in the minute particulars of the Emersonian enterprise, of which the meaning of the passage is simply a rendering in terms of moral adventure. The stringency, the vital demand of this adventure, comes home to us as we follow the leaps of the pen from word to word, from phrase to phrase. Each rhetorical change is an enlargement of the imaginative authority from which the claims regarding the Soul are made.

Literature—here in its most elementary form of rewriting, of changing the good word for the better—enacts the very mind to be advanced. As we compare texts, we move, as Emerson moved, in the direction of that unity of thought and tone which stood in his thinking as the best image for the Soul's proper style of engagement with experience. We are brought closer to the continuous presence of a simple truth, to whose imaginative reality every sentence wonderfully contributes.

And that truth is the one of all the truths respecting the Soul for which the least special argument should today be required. What Emerson is saying in this passage is still his old insight, but that insight put into modestly psychological terms, which should bring it especially close to our private sense of what is true, or ought to be true, about the rewards of consciousness. The paragraph—beautifully supported by the remainder of the essay—is elegant by virtue of its power to concentrate what might otherwise be a matter for trailing peripheral awareness. We all know our experience as progress through a universe of events that is charged with the quality of our minds and repeats the structure of our psychic constitution. But this cloudy motion is too often downgraded to a blur, an ineluctable static interfering with our perception of "objective," that is, conventional, reality. But let us attend to the details of what is inevitable until it becomes meaningful, Emerson answers in rebuke and encouragement. Examine what happens anyway, the stones on which we do in fact stub our toe—to these our line of vision is naturally perpendicular, and we can see, if the spirit wills, exactly what they are. The immediate reward is some small piece of knowledge; the consequent advantage is an insight into our own "method," our special mode of making "progressive arrangements" among our facts, and thence into the tendency of the Soul in us.

The center of the paragraph could even stand as an exact description of the theory of free association familiar from psychoanalysis: "Those facts, words, persons, which dwell in his memory without his being able to say why, remain because they have a relation to him not less real for being as yet unapprehended. They are symbols of value to him . . ." But one does not want to limit the bearing of the statement. Emerson is recommending an awareness that grows continually out of the sense of life, and his description of the knack of it holds because it fits the comprehensiveness, the undemanding alertness, the quick readiness to interpret what calls for interpretation, which should characterize free perception at all times.

A touch that renders the description an act of judgment as well as explanation is the word "value." They are symbols, these facts, words, persons, but symbols of value; they "mean," ultimately, the energies of the Soul whose unimpeded and accurate exertion is the core of life. "They relate to your gift," says another hinge sentence—to what you were given, to what you can give, to what is your particular genius. Let these facts have their "weight," treat them with awe and courtesy: "What attracts my attention shall have it." The ending is formed exactly to finish a passage where tone, the tone of confidence, awareness, tenderness, prevails so soberly and delicately, with a reminder of the transcendent importance of tone: "The soul's emphasis is always right."

Notes

Index

NOTES

INTRODUCTION

1. The history of Emerson criticism has recently been well and conveniently reviewed in the introduction by Stephen Whicher to *Emerson: A Collection of Critical Essays,* ed. Milton R. Konvitz and Stephen E. Whicher (Englewood Cliffs, N. J., 1962).

2. A case in point is an article by Newton Arvin, "The House of Pain: Emerson and the Tragic Sense," first published in *The Hudson Review,* XII (Spring 1959), 37-53, and recently reprinted in *Emerson: A Collection of Critical Essays.* Arvin mobilizes on Emerson's behalf some of the heroes of modern letters—Baudelaire, Gide, and Nietszche—whose testimonials might be expected to impress a sophisticated reader. But the defensive tone, and the time spent on assurances that Emerson was not as silly about evil as some might suppose, are reminders of the strength of the prejudice with which that reader is presumed to start. Criticism of the "moral" Emerson began at least as far back as Santayana and Henry James. Hostile attitudes toward what Emerson was supposed to stand for were encouraged by the climate of opinion created by the modernist revolution of the late teens and early twenties. Emerson's scholarly place is secure—he is one of the Eight American Authors of the literary establishment—but his moral authority continues low. It is still easy for such a commentator as Leslie Fiedler to conclude a survey of recent critical opinion with the complacent observation that Emerson is a "monument to an insufficient way of life." See "American Literature," *Contemporary Literary Scholarship* (New York, 1958), p. 174.

3. Charles Feidelson, Jr., *Symbolism and American Literature* (Chicago, 1953), p. 5.

4. Sherman Paul, *Emerson's Angle of Vision* (Cambridge, Mass., 1952).

5. Robert C. Pollock, "A Reappraisal of Emerson," *Thought,* XXXII (Spring 1957), 86-132. This searching essay has been reprinted in *American Classics Reconsidered: A Christian Appraisal,* ed. Harold C. Gardiner, S.J. (New York, 1958).

6. The literary quality of Emerson has been responded to more or less by almost everybody, but commentators have usually contented themselves with general statements about his style. John Jay Chapman, William James, and H. W. Garrod ("Emerson," *New England Quarterly,* III [1930], 3-24) are notable exceptions among the early twentieth-century critics. The formal studies of Emerson's prose style, on the other hand, are disappointing because they concentrate on his theories of literary expression or categorize his traits of style without relating them to the meaning they form. One valuable article that does hold on to the essential idea

that Emerson's doctrine appears *in* his style is Paul Lauter's "Truth and Nature: Emerson's Use of Two Complex Words," *Journal of English Literary History,* XXVII (March 1960), 66-85. A striking warning against overly intellectual interpretations of Emerson is Roland F. Lee's "Emerson through Kierkegaard: Toward a Definition of Emerson's Theory of Communication," *Journal of English Literary History,* XXIV (September 1957), 229-248. Lee's article also connects spiritual intention with indirection of language.

7. I have in mind especially Vivian Hopkins, *Spires of Form* (Cambridge, Mass., 1951); Philip L. Nicoloff, *Emerson on Race and History* (New York, 1961); Edmund Grindlay Berry, *Emerson's Plutarch* (Cambridge, Mass., 1961); and C. L. Young, *Emerson's Montaigne* (New York, 1941).

8. Stephen E. Whicher, *Freedom and Fate,* Perpetua Edition (New York, 1961).

9. Sherman Paul, *The Shores of America* (Urbana, 1958), pp. 3-16.

10. Warner Berthoff, *American Literature: Traditions and Talents* (Oberlin, 1960). See p. 242, n. 20, below.

11. The group of Humanist scholar-critics that includes Irving Babbitt ("Conclusion," *Masters of Modern French Criticism,* Boston, 1912), G. R. Elliot ("Emerson on the Organic Principle in Art," *PMLA,* XLI, March 1926, 193-208), Paul Elmer More ("The Influence of Emerson," *Shelburne Essays, First Series,* New York, 1904, pp. 71-84), and Stuart Sherman ("Emerson," *Americans,* New York, 1922, pp. 62-121) unites in assuming that Emerson has continuing cultural relevance; that he is, in a word, an artist. They dislike the romantic, antinomian side of him, as one would expect, but admire and try to apply the ideal of a harmonious inner norm, the belief in the subjectivity of moral action, and the notion of impersonality of mind; the hope is to see these qualities rediscovered in Emerson that they may prevail in the world. This impulse is a noble one, and in the right tradition of men of letters. My own view of what is important and applicable is different, but a style of criticism that did not avoid so obvious a part of its duty deserves respect.

12. It is interesting that the portion of the paragraph beginning with the snow-puddle sentence is the first passage quoted by John Jay Chapman in his fine essay, "Emerson" (*The Shock of Recognition,* ed. Edmund Wilson, New York, 1943, p. 607). Chapman must have responded to it, though he does not comment in detail. The sentence is also curiously misquoted in John Tyndall's *Hours of Exercise in the Alps* (New York, 1897), p. 301. We know that Tyndall was one of Emerson's British admirers. He is talking about the beauty of dawn in the mountains, and the contribution of the "inner man" to the effect: "To Switzerland belongs the rock—to the early climber, competent to enjoy them, belong the sublimity and beauty of mass, form, colour, and grouping. And still the outward splendour is by no means all. 'In the midst of a puddly moor,' says Emerson, 'I am afraid to say how glad I am:' which is a strong way of

affirming the influence of the inner man as regards the enjoyment of external nature. And surely the inner man is a high factor in the effect. The magnificence of the world outside suffices not. Like light falling upon the polished plate of the photographer, the glory of Nature, to be felt, must descend upon a soul prepared to receive its image and superscription."

In Gay Wilson Allen's *The Solitary Singer* (New York, 1955), there is a brief reference to Emerson's "mystical experience" on the bare common, which must refer to this passage (see p. 184).

13. Winter and early spring was ordinarily a mean season to Emerson too, as his several references to the sickliness of the time in the letters show. But there is a passage in a letter of February 21, 1840, to Margaret Fuller that shows him sensitive also to the advantages of this time of year: "These spring winds are magical in their operation on our attuned frames. These are the days of passion when the air is full of cupids & devils for eyes that are still young; and every pool of water & every dry leaf & refuse straw seem to flatter, provoke, mock, or pique us. I who am not young have not yet forgot the enchantment, & still occasionally see dead leaves & wizards that peep & mutter. Let us occasionally surrender ourselves for fifteen minutes to the slightest of these nameless influences—these nymphs or imps of wood & flood of pasture & roadside, and we shall quickly find out what an ignorant pretending old Dummy is Literature who has quite omitted all that we care to know—all that we have not said ourselves" (L.II.255).

14. The source for the image, according to Harrison, may be a passage in Plotinus: "There [in the intelligible world], however, everybody is pure, and each inhabitant is, as it were, an eye. Nothing likewise is there concealed, or fictitious, but before one can speak to another, the latter knows what the former intended to say." Quoted in John S. Harrison, *The Teachers of Emerson* (New York, 1910), p. 105.

PART I. THE SOUL

1. For the modern reader most strikingly by Whicher in *Freedom and Fate*. Among the early commentators, William James's anniversary speech stands out for the strictness with which we are held to Emerson's central stress on the manner of experiencing—see "Emerson," *Memories and Studies* (New York, 1911). John Harrison's *The Teachers of Emerson* (1910) is notable among the works of the first-generation commentators for commencing its discussion with a long first chapter on the Soul. His divisions of the topic are not mine, but one of his opening generalizations continues to be a good warning: "In Emerson's conception of Spirit . . . is to be found his final teaching on the meaning of existence; in revealing the nature of Soul all his deepest thinking ends" (p. 78). See also the survey of the doctrine of the Soul in George Edward Woodberry, *Ralph Waldo*

Emerson (New York, 1907), pp. 107-139, a book still frequently and deservedly recommended as a brief general introduction to Emerson.

2. An interesting article on the changes Emerson made while he edited the *First Series* for republication in 1846 points out that Emerson often replaced the term "soul" with a more precise word for the specific faculty in question. A list of the new words thus provides an informal set of some of Emerson's own synonyms for the master term. The examples quoted in the article include mind, reason, thought, heart, profound nature, genius, and the first-person singular. See Paul Lauter, "Emerson's Revisions of *Essays* (First Series)," *American Literature,* XXXIII (May 1961), 152-153.

3. It might be objected that guitar music is not a part of nature. But for me it was at that time and place. Sitting in my room, "nature" was everything I could notice, especially the sounds of the guitar because I noticed them with more of myself: the sounds stirred my heart as well as my ear. The distinctions between what is natural in the scientific sense and what is artificial are made by the intellect and do not appear at the level of experience the event illustrates. I could have drawn an example of the organic faculty at work from an experience of seeing a tree or the surf, but then a part of the point I wanted to make would have been obscured: the Soul works the same way in or out of doors, and it works constantly, for anyone.

4. The Mt. Auburn experience was a valuable moment in the journal for Bliss Perry, one of the last of the Emersonians whose response was conditioned by the afterglow of Emerson's personal authority and a reader who was therefore in a good position to pick out the extraliterary elements of Emerson's appeal. See "Emerson's Savings Bank," *The Praise of Folly and Other Papers* (Boston, 1923), pp. 114-129. The most striking phrase in the passage contributed a title to a novel about undergraduate life familiar to the Harvard community, George Anthony Weller's *Not to Eat, Not for Love* (New York, 1933).

5. One should not let oneself be bothered by the metaphor of "higher" and "lower." Emerson sometimes speaks as if what I have been calling the organic faculty were a first stage in the Soul's action, sometimes the last. The intuition of being can come, for him, either from above or below. The ambiguity is surely one of his proper strategies, which may have been unconscious and certainly was unsystematic, to link the physical and the spiritual, the natural impulse and the supernatural influx. It seems best to call this aspect of the Soul the "lower" constituent of its entire action because this is the position it occupies in intellectual space, once one agrees to treat the religious vocabulary Emerson uses *as* a vocabulary and not as a sufficing name for the reality in question. My assumptions in this book are naturalistic; his could afford to be ambiguously both naturalistic and supernaturalistic.

The term within the Christian tradition that works in a way analogous to the naturalistic term "life" is presumably "grace." From a naturalistic position, one would have to say that grace *means* life. In this matter one is in as limited a predicament as, say, Jonathan Edwards. Edwards would have said, *real* life *is* grace. The poets and thinkers of the nineteenth century had the benefit (such as it was) of standing in a middle position, or muddle, where both the religious and the nonreligious languages were usable, and so experiences involving the sort of action I am talking about had a double valency. One thinks also of Wordsworth and Tennyson—*The Prelude* and *In Memoriam* are both complex paeans to what I here call the organic faculty. By the time one gets to Lawrence, the religious language has become merely rhetoric ("the dark gods"), when it is used at all. By now, to be sure, "lowest" has acquired much of the positive meaning "highest" used to have. This great terminological shift from grace to life stands behind and justifies the ofen repeated comparison of Emerson and Edwards. Of course, a student of romantic writing who worked from Christian assumptions could translate back again from life to grace.

6. A general survey of Emerson's references to the eye appears in Paul, *Emerson's Angle of Vision,* pp. 71-84. Much of the significant imagery is concentrated in Emerson's own words in "Behavior" (W.VI.177-181). Sight has commonly been a crucial sense for those involved in a rediscovery of the powers of the organic faculty. One might think of Wordsworth, Ruskin, and Hopkins, as well as Thoreau and Whitman.

7. There will be more to say about this affliction in Part III, when I review the biography. The facts are obscure. James Elliot Cabot in his *Memoir* quotes an interesting phrase Emerson used about his symptoms: he said that on entering the Divinity School he found his eyes "refusing to read" (*A Memoir of Ralph Waldo Emerson,* Boston, 1895, I. 111). Emerson was obliged to withdraw to his uncle's farm where he did field work in the hope of regaining his health. The verb "refuse" would seem to imply that Emerson was at least in part allowing his sight, the sense with which his identity as a scholar and individual was most closely bound up, to enact the rebellion against the conventional expectations of his world which was later to emerge in distinct social terms, but which at that time in his career was still unconscious. Blindness would be a way of "saying" that, if he could not see in his own way, he would not see at all. The work on the farm could have represented an escape into other modes of physical contact with the world.

8. Henry Nash Smith, "Emerson's Problem of Vocation—A Note on 'The American Scholar,'" *New England Quarterly,* XII (March 1939), 52-67.

9. A scholarly review of Emerson's use of science as a public arena within which to rediscover a part of his own insight into the activity of the Soul may be found in Henry Hayden Clark, "Emerson and Science," *Philological Quarterly,* X (July 1931), 225-260. Pages 231-234 in particular argue that Emerson was attracted to astronomy and the sixteenth- and seventeenth-century heroes of science because they provided him with images of God controlling a universe of vast objects by means of an insub-

stantial law that took effect over vast distances. Astronomy was the grandest conceivable context in which to see a polarity between the Soul and nature. Henry Seidel Canby's *Classic Americans* (New York, 1931) is succinct on Emerson's prophetic insight into the meaning of science, though Canby regrets (properly) his preacherlike propensity to jump to moral applications (see pp. 159-165). There is a survey of Emerson's use of science in Paul, pp. 209-220.

10. Erwin Schrodinger, *Mind and Matter* (Cambridge, Eng., 1958), p. 38.

11. *Ibid.,* pp. 55, 62.

12. John M. Adams, "The Philosophical Historian: Emerson's Theory of History," L. C. Card No. Mic. 61-265 (University of Kansas, 1960). I owe the facts about the connection between Emerson's essay and Cousin to this dissertation.

13. Quoted by Adams, *ibid.,* p. 132.

14. The belief that we liberate ourselves from history by understanding it is crucial to transcendentalism generally. See A. Robert Caponigri, "Brownson and Emerson: Nature and History," *New England Quarterly,* XVIII (September 1945), 368-390.

15. See Whicher, p. 14 and his Appendix, Note A, where the possible sources of Emerson's idea of the "moral sense" or "moral sentiment" are organized. Whicher expresses his own indebtedness to the first scholar to explore the connection between Emerson and Stewart, Merrell R. Davis, in "Emerson's 'Reason' and the Scottish Philosophers," *New England Quarterly,* XVII (June 1944), 209-228.

16. This is roughly where a recent review of the doctrine of compensation comes out: "In our own words we might say that the way a man looks at an experience often determines whether he will find for it a good or evil compensation. If on the one hand the experience was happy, then expecting to have to pay for it may create—psychologically or psychosomatically—the unhappiness which will 'prove' the truth of Compensation. If, on the other hand, the experience was unhappy, then actively looking for a compensatory happiness or insight will often create a good which would otherwise not exist." (In other words still, morality is psychology.) See Henry F. Pommer, "Emerson's Belief in Compensation," *PMLA,* LXXVII (June 1962), 250.

17. The word "culture" somewhat changes its meaning for Emerson later in life. See Whicher, p. 84.

18. Richard P. Adams, "Emerson and the Organic Metaphor," *PMLA,* LXIX (March 1954), 117-130. I owe to Adams some of the ideas summarized in this and the two next paragraphs. He believes that the organic metaphor was more important for Emerson's mature work than what he calls the "formism" Emerson inherited from Plato. By this, Adams seems to mean the classificatory system, which I have presumed derives chiefly from Emerson's readings in popular science. The core of Adams' argument appears on page 124 of his essay: "As I have tried to indicate, their

[the Platonists'] ideas were not really the same as his, and their language, when he borrowed it, was likely to prove inappropriate, though he had some justification in feeling that it offered the nearest practicable equivalent, at the time, for what he wanted to say. The strategy sometimes succeeded; an old term carefully redefined, such as Coleridge's kidnapped 'Reason,' might be used with telling effect. The result was less happy when Emerson, without giving his reader adequate notice, adopted the word 'classification' or the word 'law' from the older tradition and used it to mean the establishment of organic relationships between ideas."

Perhaps the point is that Emerson used classification, or the Platonic idea of reason, when he was directing his attention chiefly to the mind as an independent faculty, and the organic metaphor when he wished to register the connection between the mind and the organic dimension of the Soul's activity. Both are metaphors—the range of the second way of thinking is broader and hence plays a more important part in Emerson's rhetoric as a whole.

19. It is worth keeping in mind in estimating the immediate effect of the "Divinity School Address" that the chapel in which Emerson spoke is small, and so was his audience. The graduating class contained only six men. The address apparently had more effect on those who read it later than on the group of students, relatives, teachers, and friends who first heard it. See D. E. Trueblood, "The Influence of Emerson's 'Divinity School Address,'" *Harvard Theological Review*, XXXII (January 1939), 41-56. (The scandal was of course the result of Andrews Norton's rebuttal and the published controversy that followed.)

PART II. THE SOUL'S EMPHASIS

1. D. H. Lawrence, *Psychoanalysis and the Unconscious*, ed. Philip Rieff (New York, 1960), p. 11.

2. William James is one of the surprisingly few commentators to speak even in generalities about the intimate connection between Emerson's point and the facts of his style. "Truth has to be clad in the right verbal garment," he says in his anniversary address, using a poor metaphor of his own in the process: "The form of the garment was so vital with Emerson that it is impossible to separate it from the matter. They form a chemical combination—thoughts which would be trivial expressed otherwise, are important through the nouns and verbs to which he married them" ("Emerson," *Memories and Studies*, New York, 1911, pp. 21-22). James had reread the works to prepare his speech and arrived at a fresh appreciation of Emerson's central message about the value of the present moment, the authentic individual experience of reality. "This is Emerson's revelation—the point of any pen can be an epitome of reality; the commonest person's act, if genuinely actuated, can lay hold on eternity" (p. 33). Emerson's is "the very voice of this victorious argument" (p. 34).

3. *Correspondence Between Ralph Waldo Emerson and Herman Grimm,* ed. Frederick William Holls (Boston, 1903), p. 58.

4. When Emerson speaks of rhythm he seems to have poetry in mind as often or more often than prose, though what he says is truer of his own prose than of his poetry. I should guess that poetry for Emerson served, among its other functions, as a kind of laboratory in which to experiment upon rhythm in a genre where metrical tradition put into high, even cranky, relief the qualities that reappear more subtly modulated in the prose. Indeed, in the irregularly regular verse Emerson valued for its congruence with the counterpulse of inspiration and rhyme, one sometimes feels in the presence of prose clauses rather than verse lines, each related to the next by equality of imaginative weight rather than by a metrical norm. The well-known lines justifying his bolder practice are an instance. The poet, he says,

> shall not his brain encumber
> With the coil of rhythm and number;
> But, leaving rule and pale forethought,
> He shall aye climb
> For his rhyme. (W.IX.121)

A fine quick remark on the rhythmical quality of the poetry is Morley's, who observed that it seemed to have come from a discontent with prose, rather than from a positive desire to write verse. See John Viscount Morley, "Emerson," *Critical Miscellanies* (London, 1923), pp. 27-29. Emerson frequently calls himself a poet, but there is evidence that he sometimes knew where his sense of rhythm was most sure. "I think now that the very finest & sweetest closes & falls are not in our metres, but in the measures of eloquence, which have greater variety and richness than verse" (J.VI.75). The "now" implies his mind had changed at least once.

5. A belief in the natural connection between walking and verbal expression brought about by the rhythm of the pace is not unique to Emerson or the Concord group. A recent biography of Kenneth Grahame quotes from an essay Grahame wrote for his school magazine rather late in life, which is interesting when juxtaposed with Emerson's language: "Nature's particular gift to the walker, through the semi-mechanical act of walking —a gift no other form of exercise seems to transmit in the same high degree—is to set the mind jogging, to make it garrulous, exalted, a little mad maybe—certainly creative and suprasensitive, until at last it really seems to be outside of you and as it were talking to you, while you are talking back to it. Then everything gradually seems to join in, sun and the wind, the white road and the dusty hedges, the spirit of the season, whichever that may be, the friendly old earth that is pushing forth life of every sort under your feet or spell-bound in death-like winter trance, till you walk in the midst of a blessed company, immersed in a dream-talk far transcending any possible human conversation" (Peter Green, *Kenneth Grahame,* London, 1959, p. 5). This speaker is obviously a very different sort of person from the transcendentalists. He is a crushed late-Victorian

escaping into a sentimental companionship he does not at bottom believe in. The religious overtones are ingratiatingly cozy, and the implied reader is an indulgent materialist. We are a long way from the sharp contact with actual nature that makes for the clarity and consciousness of the American walkers. But the passage confirms the connection between walking and the movement of sentences. The mind, feet, and clauses all "jog," creating a formal pattern that isomorphically relates inner and outer experience.

It would not be hard to find other examples of this connection in the literature of the century. One that could have occurred to Emerson himself is Wordsworth, who had shown his young visitor the gravel walk at Rydal Mount on which hundreds of his more pedestrian verses had been composed.

6. Feidelson, *Symbolism and American Literature,* p. 56. This book continues to be very valuable for any student of Emerson. Feidelson handsomely reviews the development of symbolism as a literary technique and as a body of ideas about language and neatly locates the appropriate instances. His discovery, or rediscovery, of the link through a common interest in symbolic action between Emerson and Melville perhaps has polemic value in an age when prejudice assigns these names to polar traditions. Feidelson's discussion has had a pervasive effect on the course of my own argument.

To acknowledge this is not equivalent to saying that no one has ever noticed the critical position of metaphor in Emerson. A long time ago Chapman observed the essential point in his own sharp and sour way: "If man will once plant himself firmly on the proposition that *he is* the universe, that every emotion or expression of his mind is correlated in some way to phenomena in the external world, and that he shall say how correlated, he is in a position where the power of speech is at a maximum. His figures of speech, his tropes, his witticisms, take rank with the law of gravity and the precession of the equinoxes" (p. 605). This remark is especially valuable because of Chapman's Victorian empirical bias; the description is grudging, if not scornful, but the connections are understood.

7. Ralph Leslie Rusk, *The Life of Ralph Waldo Emerson* (New York, 1949), p. 385.

8. It would be interesting to know more about how late the moral authority of Emerson as a teacher lasted. A well-known article by James Truslow Adams, "Emerson Re-read," *Atlantic Monthly,* CXLVI (October 1930), 484-492, "grants" that "nearly all intelligent, high-minded American youths for nearly a century have, at their most idealistic stage, come under the influence of Emerson's doctrine" (p. 488) of self-reliance. One doubts that this was still true as late as the 1930s; but Adams is one of several who witnessed the currency of Emerson's appeal among young men in the nineties, when Adams first read and underscored the essays, just as he also testifies to the disillusion of many of his generation with Emerson as a guide in maturity.

9. Moncure Daniel Conway, *Emerson at Home and Abroad* (Boston, 1882), pp. 3-4.

10. John Albee, *Remembrances of Emerson* (New York, 1903), pp. 15-16.

11. Margaret Fuller briefly describes the group of New England devotees who looked to Emerson in her review of the *Second Series,* in "Emerson's Essays," *Life Without and Life Within* (New York, 1869), pp. 191-198. A list of some of the young Englishmen who were influenced may be found in Clarence Gohdes, *American Literature in Nineteenth Century England* (New York, 1944), pp. 145-147. Emerson's impact on his lecture tour in England is assessed in William J. Sowder, "Emerson's Early Impact on England," *PMLA,* LXXVII (December 1962), esp. pp. 575-576. Another individual foreign witness to the possibility of selecting random sentences from Emerson that "shot like a beam of light" into the Soul is Herman Grimm, in "Ralph Waldo Emerson," *Literature* (Boston, 1886).

12. Albee, pp. 122-123.

13. *Ibid.,* p. 124.

14. *Ibid.,* p. 136.

15. *Ibid.,* p. 12.

16. John Jay Chapman, "Emerson," in *The Shock of Recognition* (New York, 1943), p. 615.

17. Albee, p. 78.

18. Chapman, p. 601.

19. Albee, p. 21.

20. James Elliot Cabot, *A Memoir of Ralph Waldo Emerson* (Boston, 1895), I, 358. There is an odd story in James's *Literary Remains* (Boston, 1885) of a visit during which, James says, he would lock himself and Emerson in the latter's bedroom, "swearing that before the door was opened I would arrive at the secret of his immense superiority to the common herd of literary men" (p. 296). In a sentence or two James reports his conclusion: Emerson was only an "unsexed woman." The incident, actual or half-fancied, invites speculation. James was looking for a spiritual father with the traditional male attributes of the old Presbyterian God he had repudiated but still could not help believing in. Emerson would not play such a role. In revenge, James denied him the masculine qualities of conscience and intellect.

21. *The Journals of Bronson Alcott,* ed. Odell Shepard (Boston, 1938), pp. 86-87.

22. *Ibid.,* p. 99.

23. Albee, pp. 137-138.

24. *Ibid.,* p. 175.

25. *Ibid.,* p. 137.

PART III. THE SOUL'S EMPHASIS IS ALWAYS RIGHT

1. The facts in this paragraph and those following are drawn from Rusk's *Life of Emerson* (see pp. 111-119). Cabot's *Memoir* has more to say about the experiences behind the first sermon (see I, 111-112).

2. Cabot, I, 120.

3. *One First Love: The Letters of Ellen Louisa Tucker to Ralph Waldo Emerson,* ed. Edith W. Gregg (Cambridge, Mass., 1962).

4. The facts here, as before, are from Rusk, pp. 125-170.

5. Kenneth Walter Cameron, *Emerson the Essayist* (Raleigh, N. C., 1945), I, 169ff.

6. Cameron, I, 180.

7. Whicher, *Freedom and Fate,* p. 57.

8. Rusk, p. 200.

9. Cameron, I, 191.

10. Rusk, pp. 230, 231, 251.

11. Whicher, p. 16.

12. John Jay Chapman, p. 637.

13. Edmund Grindlay Berry, *Emerson's Plutarch* (Cambridge, Mass., 1961).

14. The quoted words are from Whicher, p. 164. A good summary of the argument to which his whole book is devoted may be found on p. 171, of which my paragraph is a paraphrase.

15. This probably had a physiological component. The shift in belief about the locus of the organic faculty paralleled the process of becoming middle-aged. The "weakness" would not have been merely theoretical. His discovery of the Soul was, to start with, a discovery of new sources of vitality in himself; he learned to believe that there was more to man's subjectivity than people realized because he found during his first crisis that he had a great power to live. But after a certain point in life, every man begins to realize that there are no more resources beneath the ones already uncovered. One sees oneself physically on the downward slope, however gentle. Meanwhile one sees that nature continues to give birth to other lives outside one's own. Some such gradual consciousness may have stood behind Emerson's change of belief. Vitality would have been, increasingly, something to perceive outside the circle of his own existence.

16. See Whicher, p. 97.

17. See, for a good paragraph on the new "character," Whicher, p. 83.

18. There has been a growth in the preference for the later Emerson as opposed to the earlier. The drift of Whicher's book, which may indeed almost be said to have discovered the difference between the two figures, is in this direction, with its diagnosis of the transcendentalist and anarchistic phase as a "romance" that Emerson learned to outgrow. It is the view too of Carl F. Strauch, whose article on "Emerson's Sacred Science," *PMLA,* LXXIII (June 1958), 237-250, elaborates the sources of Emerson's belief

in an ameliorative evolution and argues that Emerson reached his maturity when he found means to "reconcile" this doctrine with his older notion of nature as a Platonic emanation. Strauch finds *English Traits* "Emerson's most satisfying book" (p. 249). This same book has been thoroughly studied by another advocate of the "mature" Emerson, Philip L. Nicoloff, in *Emerson on Race and History* (New York, 1961). Nicoloff finds *English Traits* the best place in which to see worked out in detail Emerson's trust in the progressive development of the natural process toward a future of moral elevation through general agencies like nations and races.

19. Norman Brown's *Life Against Death* (Middletown, Conn., 1959) is an attempt to turn the Freudian inheritance to prophetic uses. He thereby makes one of a line going back through such writers as Fromm, Lindner, and Marcuse to Freud himself. The effort to extend the cultural value of the psychoanalytic discoveries and vocabulary is clearly not over.

20. This necessity, or propensity, can seem a severe cultural weakness from a nonromantic point of view: "Almost the commonest observation about American writing is that it has made a specialty of starting all over again. It has done this on principle and with self-satisfaction. It has proceeded as though the past and its models were most useful when disregarded. It has been particularly uncomfortable with precedents. It has been willing to work alone and in the dark, suspicious of other ways of proceeding even when it knows all about them (as nervously and erratically it does usually make a point of doing). Yet the result, technically, is repetition— as if by self-scruple, American writing has been condemned to repeating its own discoveries. Above all else it has been inhibited by fears of some catastrophic loss of personal integrity. As a result its triumphs in art appear as personal triumphs, of principally a personal—and circumstantial—interest. It is out of touch, and prefers to be. It is, in a word, provincial." Warner Berthoff, *American Literature: Traditions and Talents* (Oberlin, 1960), p. 8.

These generalizations can ring very true for Emerson, who is a kind of prototype of the American writer, in this respect as in others. One might wish to reverse or neutralize such a judgment. To quarrel adequately with Berthoff's evaluation of the American writer, one would have to advance and defend an entire theory of what has happened in modern Western literary history. Briefly, I would say that the romantic predicament, of which the conditions mentioned are an American specialization, has been the inevitable one for anybody seeking to express the truth about his experience, since Wordsworth's time at least.

21. The idea as such is an old one with Emerson, unsurprisingly. A very near and early rendering of it occurs in a letter written to his Aunt Mary in 1826: "There are, I take it, in each man's history insignificant passages which he feels to be to him not insignificant; little coincidences in little things, which touch all the springs of wonder, and startle the sleeper conscience in the deepest cell of his repose; the Mind standing forth in alarm with all her faculties, suspicious of a Presence which it behoves her

deeply to respect—touched not more with awe than with curiosity, if perhaps some secret revelation is now about to be vouchsafed or doubtful if some moral epoch is not just now fulfilled in its history, and the tocsin just now struck that severs & tolls out an irreparable Past. These are not the State Reasons by which we can enforce the burdensome doctrine of a Deity on the world, but make often, I apprehend, the body of evidence on which private conviction is built" (L.I.170). But the language here is too conventionally preacherly and high-flown to be interesting for its own sake or to allow any connection to be made between this version and the ones that produced the passage in "Spiritual Laws."

INDEX

Adam, the American, 41, 221

Adams, Henry, 9, 85

Adams, R. P., on the organic image, 82–83

Albee, John: first reading of Emerson, 146; remarks on Emerson, 148, 150, 152, 156, 160

Alcott, Bronson: Emerson's change of attitude toward, 192; encouraged by Emerson, 155–156; mentioned, 9

Argument from design, 53

Arnold, Matthew: definition of criticism, 1, 7; on Emerson's influence, 2

Art: early theory of, 33–35; later theory of, 205, 206, 214. *See also* Beauty

Astronomy, special meaning of, 52–53, 235n9

Beauty: doubts respecting, 87; theory of, 33, 205

Berry, E. M., on "Love," 183

Berthoff, Warner, 6, 242n20

Biography, Emerson's, relation to his thought, 5–6, 165–166. *See also* Emerson, Ralph Waldo; Identity

Blake, William, contrasted with Emerson, 52, 91

Bridgman, Percy, 85, 123

Cabot, James Elliot, 145, 153–154, 235n7, 241n1

Cameron, Kenneth, 166, 172

Carlyle, Thomas: contrasted with Emerson, 8, 46; influence on Emerson, 129–131, 184, 186; letters to, 175, 190–191; mentioned, 106, 147, 201, 210, 220

Channing, Ellery: Emerson's comment on 132; mentioned, 116

Chapman, John Jay: criticism of Emerson, 151, 152, 153, 159; influenced by Emerson, 144; perceptiveness of, 6, 181; mentioned, 2

Character, later theory of, 208, 212–213

Circle, as image, 33–34, 55, 205

"Circles," 142, 203

Classification: illustrated, 82–83; Jardin des Plantes, experience of, 54–55; use of by Emerson, 53–57

Coleridge, Samuel Taylor: influence on Emerson, 21, 50, 172; theory of perception, 26; mentioned, 223

Comic, the, as defense of Soul, 78

"Commodity," 36

Compensation: difficulties of, 72, 74–75; Emerson's theory of, 72–73; in Emerson's life, 168, 198; mentioned, 107

Conversions. *See* Influence, Emerson's

Conway, Moncure, influenced by Emerson, 145–146

Cousin, Victor: Emerson's use of, 60–62; mentioned, 84, 219

Criticism, of Emerson: history, 2–7; future, 220

Croce, Benedetto, 61

Culture, definition of, 80

Darwin, Charles, 53, 209

Death: "nothing is left us now but death," 198; theme of, 178–179; threat of, 176. *See also* Emerson, Ellen; Emerson, Waldo

Dickinson, Emily, 9

"Divinity School Address," language analyzed, 87–91

Doctrine, Emerson's: early, 216–217; changes in, 194, 204; reasons for change in, 188; later, 241n15, n18

Dreams: Emerson's sensitivity to, 96–97; of eating world, 41; of falling asleep, 177–178; of sawing noise, 193

Drinking, as image, 40, 91, 196

Emerson, Charles, death of, 175, 176, 197
Emerson, Edward, 169, 175, 176, 197
Emerson, Ellen Tucker, 169, 170, 174, 178, 182, 197
Emerson, Lidian (Lydia Jackson): letters to, 175; relation to, 181, 182
Emerson, Mary (Aunt), influence of, 167; letter to, 170, 242n21
Emerson, Ralph Waldo: consumption, 169; creative period, 188; decline, 201–208; excursion to Europe, 171–172; first marriage, 169, 170; return to Concord, 174, 175, 176; youthful crisis, 166–176. See also Biography; Identity
Emerson, Waldo: birth of, 176; death of, 188–193, 197–198, 201; importance of, 188; mentioned, 158
Emerson, William: as correspondent, 167, 169, 186; as figure in dream, 178; as representative of success, 192

England, meaning of, 132, 141–142, 187, 202, 206–207
English Traits, 132, 141
Essays, organization of, 79–80
Evil: problem of, 72; privative nature of, 71, 74, 77. See also Compensation
Experience: concrete particulars of, 95, 158, 233n12; "potluck," 199, 215; opportunities for, 222, 226, 242n20
"Experience," 193–201
Eye: Emerson's troubles with, 167–168, 235n7; "eye-beams," 210; references to, 34, 175; pre-eminence of, 37–39, 235n6–7; "transparent eyeball," 15, 199–200, 233n14

Faculties: chart of, 78–79; in "Divinity School Address," 87–91; relation between organic and intellectual, 26, 27, 37, 42–43, 57–58, 59, 64, 80, 81–83; relation between organic and moral, 86–87, 101. See also Mind; Moral sentiment; Organic faculty; Soul
Fate: defined, 37; meaning of, 209–212. See also Nature
Feidelson, Charles, 4
Frost, Robert, 9
Fuller, Margaret, 182, 233n13, 240n11

"Gnothi Seaton," 172
God: defined, 219; in "Experience," 195; justice of, 73; rediscovered, 168, 173; revealed by science, 53; in universe, 34, 201; within, 21, 172, 188, 189, 211
Goodman, Paul, 220
"Grace," ambiguity of, 86
Greenough, Horatio, 106

History, Emerson's theory of, 59–62
Hoar, Elizabeth, 113, 182
Horizon, as image, 34, 35, 194, 197
Humanists, New, as interpreters of Emerson, 2, 145

Identity, problem of, 172–174; ambivalence, 132; aggression and, 184–186; egotism, 130; limits of, 30, 38–39, 48, 176–177, 187; isolated, 179, 180; masks for, 49, 130, 174, 186; relation to tone, 128–129; theory of, 21, 92–95. See also Emerson, Waldo; Tone
Illusion, as prison of self, 180, 194, 200
Influence, Emerson's: as type of conversion, 145–148; change of, 187, 215; Emerson's hopes for, 143–144; future potential in, 9, 217–219; intellectual, 3–4; moral, 2, 145, 148–151, 239n8, 240n11; on John Albee, 146, 148; on Moncure Conway, 145–146; on lecture audiences, 158–161; on other writers, 144; on single readers, 143–158; pervasiveness of, 145

James, Henry (Sr.), disappointed by Emerson, 153–154, 240n20
James, William, 9, 144, 237n2
Journals, use of, 1, 14–15, 88, 201, 224
Joy, defined, 13

Lawrence, D. H.: compared to Emerson, 2, 13, 50; on idealism, 101; mentioned, 31, 91

Lectures: early, 174; generic significance of, 175; public effect of, 158–161; relation to essays, 110–111, 192, 223, 225

Literary quality: as test of truth, 101–103, 125–126, 231n6, 237n18; decline in, 201; evanescence of, 103–104, 107; history of, 188; as sign of control, 181, 184; relation to thought, 5, 8, 36, 65, 83, 123

Love: essay on, 183; inability to, 179; test of self, 182; of women, 182–183

Magnetism, as image, 50–51

Matthiessen, F. O., as interpreter of Emerson, 3

Melville, Herman: influenced by Carlyle, 130; influenced by Emerson, 144, 180; view of nature, 207; mentioned, 3, 4, 9, 136, 180

Metaphor: as system, 55–56; double reference of, 57–58, 59, 60; importance of to Emerson, 119–120, 123, 239n6; in history, 62–64; in science, 51–52, 53, 58, 124; literary, 121–128; necessity of, 43, 65; organic, 83–84

Mind: as faculty of Soul, 21, 23–25, 46–49, 56–57, 119; influence on interpretation of Emerson, 3, 23–24, 66, 119; later view of, 211–212; modern role of, 219; relation to emotions, 179; relation to moral sentiment, 66, 84; singleness of, 58, 65. See also Metaphor; Science; History; Faculties

"Montaigne," position implied by, 80, 214

Moral sentiment: defense of, 69; Emerson's theory of, 23, 66–67, 76; intellectual difficulties with, 68, 218; later view of, 206, 208, 212, 213; relation to intellect, 66, 84; relation to organic faculty, 86–87, 90–92, 110; relation to tone, 128; singleness of, 70–71. See also Compensation; Tone

Mountain, as image, 202

Mt. Auburn experience, 27–29, 178, 216

Nature: changes in view of, 188, 209; elusiveness of, 29–30, 44–45, 85, 193, 199; emotional meaning of, 182, 196; experience of and relation to, 22, 25–29, 34, 37–38, 43–44, 53–54, 56, 86, 121, 174, 188, 196, 203–205, 216–217, 221. See also Fate; Organic faculty

Nature: passage analyzed, 10–15; mentioned, 9, 27, 34, 35, 38, 46, 77, 79, 87, 89, 107, 110, 172, 174, 176, 188, 204

"New England Reformers," tone in, 142–143

Newton, Isaac, meaning of for Emerson, 41, 42, 52

Organic faculty: changes in view of, 194–195, 200; compared to grace, 234n5; earlier view of defended, 216; lapsing with age, 241n15; in romanticism, 91; relation to intellect, 21–22, 27–28, 43, 81–82; relation to Waldo, 189; relation to work, 46; term defined, 28; mentioned, 10–15, 25–33, 33–34, 40, 88. See also Art; Eye; Nature

Organic metaphor, 82–84, 236n18

Oversoul, as term for intellect, 56–57, 129. See also Mind

Parker, Theodore, 49

Paul, Sherman, 4, 6, 15

Plutarch, Emerson's debt to, 183

Poetry, 36, 130, 184; on love, 183; rhythm in, 238n4

Polarity: as inner ambivalence, 86; as means of organization, 80. See also Compensation; Rhythm

Pollock, Robert, 4

Property, as image, 197–198

Puns, use of, 109–112

Reading, Emerson on, 103–105

Representative Men, discussed, 213–215

Rhythm: alternations of in experience, 84, 112, 124; in prose style, 112–114, 223, 238n5; reasons for, 43, 114–116; in series, 118. *See also* Polarity; Walking

Ruskin, John: doctrine of work, 46; influenced by Carlyle, 130

Sampson, George Adams, death of, 175

Schrodinger, Ernst, 57, 58

Science, Emerson's interpretation of, 49–50, 51–52, 235n9. *See also* Classification

Sentence, as unit of style, 106–107

Smith, Henry Nash, 49

"Snow puddle," analyzed, 10–15; noticed by other writers, 232n12

Soul, the: as a whole, 4, 7, 19–25, 77, 165; changes in view of, 187, 193, 194, 199, 200, 201, 203–216; earlier and later views contrasted, 7, 216–217. *See also* Faculties; Moral sentiment; Mind; Organic faculty

"Soul," defined, 19–25, 234n2

"Spiritual Laws," quoted and analyzed, 222–227

Spontaneity: importance of, 84–85; limits of, 221

Stars, as image, 39, 52–53

Sturgis, Caroline, 182, 190

Swedenborg, Emmanuel, 41, 84, 96, 154, 185, 214, 215, 219

"Symbolism," journal entry, 94–95

System, 55. *See also* Metaphor

Tarbox, influence on Emerson, 167–168, 173

"Terminus," 199

"Threnody," 191–192

Thoreau, Henry David: compared to Emerson, 46, 94, 116; influenced by Emerson, 9, 144

Tone, 127–143 *passim*; aggressive, 131; ambiguous, 133, 138–139; borrowed, 134; humble, 151–153, 154–155, 156; mystical, 140–143; "rare in New England," 135–136; relation to moral sentiment, 128–129; tentativeness of, 130; throws light on compensation, 73–74

Touch: contrasted with sight, 39; impossibility of, 197; reliability of, 44

Virtue, defined, 76–77

Walking, relation to writing, 116–117, 119, 238n5

Water, as image, 194, 198, 210

Whicher, Stephen: on change in Emerson, 188; on connection between ideas and life, 6, 166; on idealism, 177; on originality, 173; on Soul, 19

Whitman, Walt: compared to Emerson, 37; influenced by Emerson, 144; mentioned, 9, 31, 32, 94

Words: power of, 184; redefinition of, 73, 76, 109–112; relation to reality, 47, 108. *See also* Metaphor

Wordsworth, William, 13, 31, 91, 147

Work: as expression of Soul, 45–46; place of in later theory, 205

Writing: details of, 223; Emerson's theories of, 105–109; method of, 107, 185; relation to aggression, 184